THE DEVIL'S
ROOMING HOUSE

Also by M. William Phelps

Perfect Poison

Lethal Guardian

Every Move You Make

Sleep in Heavenly Peace

Murder in the Heartland

Because You Loved Me

If Looks Could Kill

I'll Be Watching You

Deadly Secrets

Cruel Death

Death Trap

Failures of the Presidents (co-author)

Nathan Hale: The Life and Death of America's First Spy

THE DEVIL'S ROOMING HOUSE

THE TRUE STORY
OF AMERICA'S DEADLIEST
FEMALE SERIAL KILLER

M. WILLIAM PHELPS

LYONS PRESS
Guilford, Connecticut
An imprint of Globe Pequot Press

Lyons Press is an imprint of Globe Pequot Press

Text designed by Libby Kingsbury

Library of Congress Cataloging-in-Publication Data is available on file.

ISBN 978-1-59921-601-0

Printed in the United States of America

10 9 8 7 6 5 4 3 2 1

For Regina

♣ ♣ ♣

CONTENTS

Part Three
TRIALS & TRIBULATIONS

A Note to the Reader

What you are about to read is a true story. The hit Broadway play, *Arsenic and Old Lace*, which became a Hollywood film in 1944 starring Cary Grant, was based on the life and crimes of Amy Archer-Gilligan, the subject of this narrative.

All of the people, places, and occurrences in this book are real. I used original, primary sources when available: letters, over 1,200 pages of trial transcripts, affidavits, various manuscripts, postcards, newspaper articles, autopsy reports, death certificates, pamphlets, memoirs, books, police reports, diaries, slides, interviews, and other documents and resources I uncovered while researching this project over a period of nearly six years. It is very rewarding and humbling for me to be able to bring to print the stranger-than-fiction truth behind such an internationally recognized story.

—M. William Phelps
January 2010
Vernon, Connecticut

[T]oday we fight an insidious persecutor, an enemy who flat-ters . . . He does not stab us in the back but fills our stomachs. He does not seize our property and thereby give us life. He stuffs our pockets to lead us to death. He does not cast us into dungeons thereby setting us on the path to freedom. He imprisons us in the honors of the palace.

—Saint Hilary of Poitiers

Prologue

SIMMERING DEATH

AT FIRST IT WAS JUST A NAGGING tickle in his throat; later a "pit" in his sour stomach that wouldn't go away. Then something completely profound and material happened, bringing into focus his own mortality. Confined to bed, as his mind raced with thoughts of death, he began to feel he knew how his life would end, and even had an idea when. It was that strange look the matron of the house gave him. She brought him up a glass of lemonade and, without a word, exited the room and walked down the stairs; and he considered that silence, ambiguous as it was, to be the impetus for his demise.

So it was afterward that the local doctor hired by the matron showed up to check in on him. "Whisper," the man said upon greeting the doctor. The last thing he wanted was for the matron to suspect they were talking about her. She was probably listening, anyway, her ear to the wall in the next room.

"You want I should whisper?" the doctor asked with a raised eyebrow. He was puzzled by this bizarre request, but would begin to understand once the inmate started making accusations. The doctor knew the matron was being paid to care for these people. She was a nurse. A custodian of good health. And, maybe most important of all, a Christian, a woman of God—certainly no threat to this man.

"Yes," the man said in a hushed tone.

"What seems to be the problem?" the doctor asked.

In fact, as they talked upstairs, the matron was not snooping around outside the door or listening through the wall in the adjacent room; instead, she stood in the kitchen downstairs. The home she owned on Prospect Street in Windsor had an average of twenty beds filled at any one time. She and her husband had opened for business as a quasi-convalescent/nursing home four years earlier, and had an impeccable reputation within the community for catering to the aged. According to what this inmate was saying, however, she had stood many a night in that kitchen below his bedroom, mixing a deadly elixir of freshly squeezed lemons, warm water, a touch of sugar to liberate the bitterness, and, he claimed, a pinch or two of poison.

Poison?

What type of poison, exactly, the man didn't know. All he could be sure of was that someone had better do something about the woman before she killed him and God knew how many others.

"Mr. Matthewson," the doctor recalled later, "told me that [she] was trying to poison him to get his money, and that she had put poison in some lemonade she had given him."

As the doctor checked him over, Mr. Matthewson pointed to a small sofa chair in the room. "There," he said. "It's over there."

The doctor looked toward the chair. He didn't see anything. What in heaven's name was Matthewson talking about now?

There was a small bottle underneath the cushion, Matthewson explained. He had saved a gulp from the glass of lemonade she had given him the day before, bottled it, and hidden it underneath the cushion.

"I want you to take that," Matthewson explained, "and I want you to test it." Matthewson was sure the test would prove the woman was a murderer.

The doctor walked over to the cushion and found the bottle. Opened it. Put his nose to the lid and took in a deep breath.

A pause.

Then he smiled and, slowly, put the bottle to his lips.

♣ ♣ ♣

On July 10, 1911, just a few miles south of Mrs. Amy Archer's Windsor home for "aged and chronic invalids," something strange was happening in Hartford, Connecticut's capital city. A well-known retired schoolteacher, sixty-eight-year-old Lyman Dudley Smith, was experiencing firsthand what the venerable adage "crazy from the heat" truly meant. For the tenth day in a row now, Smith and his fellow New Englanders had awoken to temperatures in the upper nineties. Over one thousand people—men, women, and children, from infants to the elderly—had died from the heat already. And yes, many more had gone insane. Totally out of their minds. Smith had seen them, standing atop buildings and shouting things no one could understand, threatening to jump. Talking in blathered delusions. Hallucinating. Jumping from bridges into the Connecticut River, only to be carried off by the current to their deaths. It was as if life had turned into some sort of a scripted nightmare, a twilight zone Smith now believed he was spiraling into without a chance of recovering.

On this day, Smith *was* insane. He couldn't take it anymore. The damn heat. Inside. Outside. Didn't make a hoot of a difference. There was no relief. Ice was as scarce as a cool breeze. Finding a fan to stand in front of was a joke. Fresh water was nowhere to be found. The streets of Hartford, same as Boston and New York, were corralled with people too hot to sleep indoors. Mattresses and bassinets and bedsheets were splayed out on the ground all over as if a parade was coming to town. Families crammed the city parks. Businesses closed. Babies moaned as mothers fanned them with old newspapers, scared that dehydration was killing them.

Seeing all of this going on around him, Lyman Dudley Smith was thinking about how it would feel to just end it and leave all the misery behind. He had lived a long, prosperous life. What would it matter?

Smith was no uneducated transient with a brain pickled by alcohol, thinking crazy thoughts of suicide in a slurry of drunken haze. Before the heat wave, the man had been enjoying a congenial retirement. In fact, one of Smith's favorite things to do was wander about the landscape outside his Hartford home, or up north in Maine, where he had a second residence. "He loved . . . everywhere nature beckoned him passionately," a letter to a local newspaper said about Smith. "He was of a frank personality, and readily responded to all things which had a tendency to stimulate the intellect."

Smith had taught penmanship for forty-five years in Hartford public schools. He had written essays and books on the art of putting pen to paper. He was cherished and esteemed by his peers. His great-grandfather had fought for the colonies in the Revolutionary

War, and his grandfather made good as a hero in the War of 1812. As a child, Smith had surely heard stories of great misery and sacrifice told by men who had endured far more dreadful times than he was now experiencing. He had watched his parents suffer through some of the most trying eras, socially and economically, in American history. He had dedicated his life to the noble cause of tutoring. He spoke four languages fluently, and invented the renowned Smith System of Penmanship, which would be taught in schools for decades. "His fine face," said that same letter, "his frank eye always placed him promptly in the professional class."

No doubt about it: Lyman Dudley Smith was of sound mind, but the heat was getting to him on July 10, 1911—the unrelenting monotony, pace, and excess of it. He couldn't take it anymore. Ten days of unbearable humidity and air as stale and warm as hot breath had taken its toll on his psyche. And now this distinguished man stood in the upper room of his home and thought about how he should end it. There had to be an easy way.

⁂ ⁂ ⁂

Meanwhile, the doctor was with Mr. Matthewson back in Windsor inside the Archer Home, wondering what in the name of God the poor man was talking about.

Lemonade? Poison?

The doctor knew the matron, Mrs. Amy Archer, having worked in the Home for well over a year now. She was seen then as the saintly proprietor of a noble cause: tending to the old during a time in their lives when family members, Amy had said herself, would have just as well let them rot and die alone. Her home was a place of refuge and healing for the elderly—a place of convalescence. You paid her, she took care of you. Simple as that.

The woman was no killer; that much the doctor was sure of.

"All right," the doctor said, obliging Matthewson and his little episode of paranoid delusion, "here goes." He put the bottle of alleged lemonade and poison Matthewson had saved up to his lips and took a slug.

"No!" Matthewson cried.

After finishing it off, the doctor said, "If I am alive the next day," wiping his lips on the back of his sleeve, "well, we'll know that there was no poison in the lemonade."

Matthewson couldn't believe it.

They parted ways, agreeing that the doctor would see the patient again the next morning—that is, if he survived the night.

▲ ▲ ▲

Lyman Dudley Smith paced in his bedroom on that excruciatingly hot and humid night—the tenth in as many days. Over the past week and a half, the weathermen in Washington had claimed there was no relief in sight for at least another week. Then they'd put out a report that claimed a cleansing thunderstorm and "cooler temperatures" were going to roll in any hour. After several false reports, no one took comfort in what the weather observers had to say any longer. As far as New Englanders could tell, all you had to do was look around, look into the sky. It seemed the end of the world was approaching. The leaves on the trees were gone, dried up and turned into brittle dust that drifted away with a mild breeze. There was no grass left. It, too, had burned into hay and disappeared. Farmers were counting how many acres of crops they had lost since the start of the heat wave. Heatstroke, exhaustion, dehydration, and drownings had become commonplace.

No one knew what to do.

Smith was a responsible man. He had earned every red cent it had cost him to acquire a college education. He had taken care of himself throughout his life.

Now was no different.

"He was a natural scholar and applied himself to his studies with great diligence," said a relative.

But this heat. It was too much for the guy.

On the night of July 10, 1911, Smith stood in his bedroom by himself and, with one of his favorite pens, decided to take the easy way out. He placed the sharp steel point of a calligrapher's metal quill up to his neck and, with one swift stroke from left to right, slit his throat, falling to the floor moments later, blood pooling around his head.

Within an hour, Lyman Dudley Smith bled to death.

Throughout Hartford, Boston, and New York, others were doing the same thing. Smart, competent, and sane men and women put shotguns in their mouths. Pistols to their heads. Ropes around their necks. Jumped off bridges and into ponds, swam to the bottom, never coming up for air.

Some would say these were the smart ones, because as July 12, 1911, dawned, the worst of what Mother Nature had to offer was yet to come.

⁂

As promised, the doctor showed up at the matron's home to visit with Mr. Matthewson early the next morning.

Upon seeing the doctor enter the room, Matthewson was stunned.

"I'm still alive," the doctor said, adding later, "[W]hen he saw me again that next day he was fully satisfied."

Matthewson was speechless. He could have sworn the woman was trying to poison him. So many had died in the Home under strange circumstances; the clapping of hooves and the snorting of horses' wet noses in the middle of the night often woke Matthewson and the others as they looked out the windows to see yet another body being carried out under the cover of darkness. But here was the doctor of the house—a man of great stature and professionalism, well educated, well liked, and certainly well respected in Windsor, having just recently been named the medical examiner of the town—standing in front of him after having drunk the lemonade.

Matthewson was sold.

"Do you think I would have drunk that lemonade," the doctor said proudly, "if I'd had any suspicions?"

PART ONE

SILENT KILLERS

Chapter 1

THE MATRON AND THE REPORTER

I
T WAS AN EXTRAORDINARY, DREADFUL OCCASION. One of several that Carlan Hollister Goslee would face in the coming years. The brief newspaper article staring back up at Carlan on that frigid morning, December 1, 1909, was both upsetting and confusing, and yet a subtle reminder of how easily we can be fooled. How, in fact, a man can live down the street from a woman for years, tip his fedora to her in town with a gentle "Good day, madam," attend church together on Sunday mornings, but not have the slightest idea of what is written inside the margins of her heart.

Not long after the twenty-two-year-old Goslee had risen from his knees, having first given the day to God, he found himself shocked by the five words before him: ARCHER HOME IN WINDSOR ATTACHED.

Carlan was an illustrious figure in the community, even at a young age. He was a conventional man who dressed conservatively in white pressed shirts, light-brown or black bow ties, dark slacks, and wool suit coats with brass buttons. He had just sat down at the kitchen table inside his Windsor, Connecticut, home on 112 Maple Avenue, when the accusations against his neighbor settled on him. He couldn't believe it. Attached? The Archer Home?

The article accompanying the headline was brief; but, at the same time, direct and critical: Fellow Windsor resident, Amy Archer, along with her husband, James—not only neighbors but also good friends of Carlan's—were in a bloody good spot of legal trouble. They were being sued.

Inside the Archers' redbrick colonial on Prospect Street, a mere rock toss from W. H. Mason's Drugstore, the downtown district, and the trolley depot, and about four city blocks from Carlan's home, Amy and James ran what we might call by today's standards a nursing home. The Archer Home, a private establishment, was one of the first of its kind in New England. Carlan later recalled the unique concept the Archers had developed, along with the initial financial problems their too-good-to-be-true business model faced:

> It was a plan of the Archer Home to take many patients in on the "take care for the remainder of life" plan. Patients were to turn over to Archer . . . their entire wealth in exchange for care for the remainder of their lives.

According to the *Hartford Courant* article, Amy and James were being sued by a former inmate and her family. At first, Carlan had a tough time wrapping his mind around the charges. But as it started to sink in, he surely must have realized there was truth in the allegations. The *Courant* was a newspaper Carlan had himself worked for as a freelance reporter; he was the newspaper's stringer for the town of Windsor, and knew the managing editor's standards. It couldn't be an error. If the *Courant* printed it, Carlan knew the newspaper had solid evidence backing up the story.

As he read, the young newspaperman learned that a complaint had been lodged against Amy and James regarding the maltreatment of an inmate who had paid to reside in what was formally called the Archer Home for Elderly People and Chronic Invalids. Open since 1907, the Home had enjoyed a good standing in town. Now, Amy and James were being accused of abuse.

Even with the story clearly spelling out what had happened, Carlan later downplayed the significance of the charge, recalling, "There was a *minor* lawsuit [emphasis added] brought against Mrs. Archer . . . by the family of one of her patients. At the time, I was with [Mrs. Archer] 100 per cent."

Carlan lived with his wife, Mae, and one child (the Goslees would have five more children in the coming years). He led several lives. He had worked for the Phoenix Insurance Company on Pearl Street in Hartford, south of Windsor, for several years, but he'd also been writing freelance stories for the *Hartford Times* and *Hartford Courant,* mostly about events in Windsor. According to the Goslee family, before Carlan wired his house up to what his daughter later claimed was the first telephone in Windsor—"Number 146"—and called in his stories, he would type out his copy on his trusty Underwood typewriter inside the confines of his federal colonial home, walk the pages down Maple Avenue toward the center of town where the trolley stopped, and hand them off to the trolley driver (greasing his palm with garden vegetables or a few freshly caught shad), knowing the driver would drop the story off at the *Times* or *Courant* that same day.

On top of his many obligations, both domestic and professional, Carlan was also the treasurer for the "Windsor Rogue Detecting Society," a quasi-detective agency in town that investigated robbery, burglary, suspicious fires, and the occasional murder. Like most everything else Carlan did, the ledger he kept for the group was detailed, contemporaneous, and acutely uninteresting. However, crime itself did have an interesting history in Windsor, which was one of the reasons why Carlan was likely drawn to the society. During the eighteenth century, for example, if a man had been caught burglarizing a home or business, he was branded on the forehead with the letter "B." A parent who failed to educate his child was fined ten shillings. Murder, kidnapping, witchcraft, and blasphemy, along with scores of other major crimes, were punishable by death, no questions asked.

Most everyone called him Carl, and knew him as the bifocal-wearing, balding, prudish gent who liked to get involved in Windsor politics, but was quiet about his opinions until he knew what he was talking about. When it came to journalism, he was just good ol' Carl: a reporter's reporter. Mr. Objective. In the ensuing years, Carl would become a town councilman, state representative, fire chief, and judge, among many other important positions in town. At a dinner honoring his eightieth birthday on June 12, 1966, the emcee called Carl "Mr. Windsor," and he certainly lived up to every bit of that name as the years passed.

At twenty-two years of age in 1909, however, Carl was a full-time insurance man and part-time newspaper reporter—the latter position about to come between his friendship with Amy and James Archer.

Windsor townspeople were especially alarmed by the article. Here was one of her patients, arguably an upstanding citizen, pointing an accusatory finger at Amy, who had been seen up until that point as nothing short of a God-fearing, Bible-toting, Christian caretaker of the elderly. The notion that Amy could have mistreated one of her inmates was not only scandalous, but also shameful. Amy and James had opened their business to the welcoming arms of the Windsor townspeople, who, like Carl Goslee, had been behind the couple ever since their arrival.

Looking deeper into the Home's affairs, however, revealed that Amy and James had run into problems before. Back on July 14 of that same year, the Connecticut Humane Society, a group that dealt with the concerns of humans at the time, had been called in to investigate an inmate's claim against the Archer Home. The woman who had lodged the complaint told the Archers' neighbors she was being abused by Amy, and conditions inside the Home were unbearable, even unsanitary. Yet with no laws on the books at the time that mandated any type of accountability for a home such as Amy's, the Humane Society would have to do. Investigators didn't find anything terribly out of place inside the Home; they merely cited Amy and James for not properly ventilating rooms and housing too many patients in one area.

When the Humane Society left, Amy "felt very hard towards [the woman]," an article in the *Courant* reported years later.

Not one to ever let an allegation against her go unchallenged, Amy complained to her accuser's family, then had the woman examined by two of her own doctors (on the Home's payroll), and, finally, by a doctor in the town where the woman had once lived.

The next day, Amy took the woman to the Hospital for the Insane, and no one had seen her since. No one had questioned Amy.

But these new allegations would not go away. They were far more offensive and personal in nature. There was no doctor Amy could call in to back her up. As Carlan Goslee read the article that morning, details of the lawsuit were there in black and white. The allegations couldn't be denied. Amy's business, not to mention her character, was being questioned.

Carl wanted to stand behind his friend. He did not want to judge, even in the face of an article by the very newspaper he worked for. Then again, if he couldn't believe the *Courant*, could he continue reporting for it?

The story in the *Courant* was the first in what would become a series of accusations over the course of the next several years made against Amy and the way she ran her business and treated inmates. The $5,000 lawsuit reported by the *Courant* had been filed by West Hartford resident Narcissa McClintock, a fashionable, well-respected woman who valued public opinion probably more than she should have. Narcissa brought the suit against Amy and James, unable to ignore numerous reports from her mother, Theresa, an Archer Home tenant.

At first, Narcissa felt her mother was being ungrateful and encouraged the old woman to try to get along better with Amy. Theresa McClintock had complained to her daughter in a letter detailing a specific incident inside the Home that had upset her (she had been there all of a week by that point). By the end of the letter, Theresa was begging Narcissa to visit.

Narcissa wrote back at once.

> *Dear Mother,*
> *I cannot possibly go to you now. . . . When I do go I hope I shall hear something pleasant and agreeable and not any more fault finding, as you are in one of the best homes of the state and you are paying the least and have the best room, so I know you cannot fail to appreciate it.*

A few days later, after an even more disturbing letter arrived in West Hartford, Narcissa grew concerned. So, "One afternoon, I went to the Archer Home," she recalled years later, "to see my mother."

It was about a ten-mile journey. Nonetheless, Narcissa needed to find out for herself what was going on with her mother. It was obvious Narcissa considered her mother to be an unvarying worrywart and complainer. Yet something was tugging at her, telling her to visit her mother in person and see for herself.

So she went.

Theresa was confined to bed in an upstairs room. The moment Narcissa entered, Theresa said, "most excitedly," Narcissa recalled, "Oh, Belle [Narcissa's nickname], take me away from here. I had a chill last night, and I called and called for someone to come to me. When Mrs. Archer came, she was ugly and told me to shut up. I asked for some hot water to drink, and for a hot water bottle to be put at my feet. She did nothing for me and I am afraid of her because she is so ugly."

Narcissa was horrified. Was this how a woman who had paid such a generous sum of cash to stay in the Home should be treated? Then again, as she thought about it, perhaps her mother had gone senile. Had Theresa, like the previous woman Amy had dealt with (and gotten rid of), gone crazy?

Narcissa demanded more information.

Theresa went on to describe the horrific conditions under which she had been living.

"My hair is never combed," she explained. Her clothes were never washed. The commode she was forced to use was always filled "with chamber refuse," and often left in her room uncovered, brimming with waste.

And that was just the beginning.

When describing Amy as an "ugly" woman, Theresa McClintock was of course referring to Amy's temperament. Be that as it may, this adjective could have also applied to Amy's physical characteristics. At about five foot three and 110 pounds, Amy appeared frail and grandmotherly, even though she was said to be just thirty-eight years old. Her perpetually glum facial features made her look older; part of this was likely due to the stress of her life's work. Amy had a round face, pudgy cheeks set against brown, beady eyes, and a stubby, hawk nose. In many of the photographs left behind, her gawky, curious stare speaks of repressed inner tension and high anxiety. Lacking anything like a nurse's approachable, caring bedside manner, Amy often presented herself as expressionless, emotionless, and rather stark. One photo, taken around 1911, shows the matron standing beside a grape arbor in the front yard of the Archer Home. Amy's hands are by her side, and she's staring directly into the camera lens, her image melting into the flowers behind her.

Set against her white dress, her face appears pastel and skeletal, almost ghostly. It is a haunting image of a woman obviously hiding something.

The Archer Home for Elderly People and Chronic Invalids was located at the end of a dead-end road, just a few gallops on horseback from downtown Windsor and tucked behind a stone bridge that arched over the Farmington River. Amy and James had maintained the unadorned redbrick home since 1907, the year they had moved into town. Not the most expensive piece of property in town, it was certainly spacious and roomy enough to accommodate about twenty patients at a time.

The home became known as one of the more imposing establishments in Windsor, quite stunning with its dark, eerie facade. The picket fence surrounding the property was in constant need of repair, creaking, leaning, its white paint chipping to the ground like snowflakes. The contrast between the white fence and the red bricks, with the grapevines crawling up the front of the house, made quite a first impression on potential inmates. Many later noted how homey the place felt from afar, even if it might have seemed spooky later, once the accusations started about what was possibly going on. But for many, as they walked through that front gate and climbed the brick steps, toting the last of their earthly possessions, fully prepared to live out the remainder of their lives there, the Archer Home represented a welcome respite from the loneliness of growing old. It was a seemingly pleasant place to live out your golden years and be taken care of when family, friends, and society had, in a sense, put you out to pasture.

The Archers had purchased the colonial for $4,500 shortly before they arrived from Newington, and they started accepting inmates right away. With ads in the *Hartford Courant* and *Hartford Times*, the Archer Home filled up quickly, with a waiting list of replacements. In some respects, the Home was nothing more than a nonthreatening environment, run by a homely "Christian" woman who was the only hope some had left. The aesthetics of the place made it resemble a schoolhouse. Not quite as large as the grand colonials a few miles away on Albany Avenue and Prospect Street in Hartford, where many of Connecticut's wealthy bureaucrats and politicians lived, the Archer Home had a wraparound porch on the first of two levels, a wooden deck protruding out the back face of the second story, a large green out front, and a storage barn out back. It was big enough to accommodate all of Amy and James's needs.

Amy called her patients "inmates," perhaps inciting some to perceive that she considered the Home a prison. Yet *inmate* was a socially acceptable term used at that time to describe residents of psychiatric hospitals, institutions, insane asylums, prisons, or nursing homes similar to Amy's. Rooms were located on the first and second floors, with a half-dozen beds crammed into the attic, which was piping hot in summer and arctic cold in winter. Inside each room, Amy kept a cot, table, and bureau. An early complaint was that Amy refused to keep wash basins in patients' rooms, which forced inmates to share a community bathroom for even their basic hygienic needs.

Entering the house from the front door, a short hallway led to a set of stairs. To the left was a parlor with furniture customary to such a room in any New England home: antique chairs, end tables, elegant silver and pewter candlesticks, photographs and mirrors in hand-carved mahogany frames. Behind the parlor, through a set of French doors, was the dining room where Amy served a menu that rarely ever changed: pressed beef, bread and butter, tea, cake, preserves.

Amy's only child, Mary Archer (thirteen years old in 1911), kept her piano just beyond the dining room, where she entertained inmates on those nights when she felt so inspired.

For the most part, the ebb and flow of the Home was calm and comforting, considering the traffic and number of people inside at any given time. Those inmates who could, helped Amy with chores around the house. When an inmate became ill or needed medical attention, Amy's in-house physician, Dr. Howard Frost King, was called. The handsome Dr. King—always dressed in a suit and tie, with a watch chain hanging off his belt loop—was Amy's personal physician. A married father of two, King had just recently taken the job of medical examiner for the Town of Windsor. With his waxy, walrus mustache, fat cheeks, sunken eyes, and confident—if not cocky—stare, King bore a striking resemblance to a young

Teddy Roosevelt. It's clear that King and Amy had a close personal relationship. Rumors of a love affair would surface later, but would be proven false.

King grew up on a farm in Suffield, ten miles north of Windsor. After graduating in 1891 from the prestigious Connecticut Literary Institution, a private school, King spent two years figuring out his prospects before deciding on Brown University for three years, finally completing his medical degree at Albany Medical College in New York. From there, he went to work at Hartford Hospital for six months, and then started his own practice near his new home in Windsor, located just down the road from the Archer Home.

Amy and King's professional relationship began after he took over from Dr. Newton Bell, who died in 1910. Bell had served as medical examiner in Windsor, and, since its inception, had been the Archer Home physician. Dr. King stopped by the Home periodically to check in on Amy's ailing patients, or to answer Amy's midnight requests to retrieve the body of an inmate who had expired and take him or her to be embalmed.

Amy demanded that the bodies be taken out of the Home immediately after death. The inmates, Amy claimed, did not want to wake up to a rotting corpse. It was not only bad for business, but brought down the spirits of the healthy inmates.

While working for Amy, Dr. King was a dedicated soldier to the cause—and even for a short time afterward, as well. He had little to say about his boss, good, bad, or indifferent. Later, however, perhaps succumbing to public pressure, when it became obvious that Dr. King could have been covering for his boss, King called Amy's house "a rather queer sort of place." In retrospect, he said, he believed the establishment could have been run far better. "The inmates were not getting the attention and the consideration they deserved in view of the money many of them paid."

What worried King more than anything, he explained, was that Amy had "herded" patients "together rather closely," which was, in theory, the same complaint made by Theresa McClintock. Some rooms had three beds. And many of the inmates, King added, "were allowed to take care of themselves to a considerable extent."

Surely not what they were paying for.

▲ ▲ ▲

By February of 1910, Carlan Goslee's uncertainties about Amy Archer, not to mention what might possibly be taking place inside her home, began to gnaw at the young reporter. He wasn't telling anyone, but Carl was slowly beginning to think that maybe he had misjudged Amy. The story Theresa McClintock told was quite eye-opening. The more the woman talked about it, the more it seemed that perhaps Amy wasn't the practicing Christian she had made herself out to be.

"I thought she was a wonderful person," Carl said of Amy years later, "but as the investigation continued, I began to have my doubts."

That investigation started shortly after James Archer died suddenly one day, without warning, on February 2, 1910, and Carl began to consider that there might be more to the death than what at first seemed to be just an unexplained, untimely tragedy.

Nonetheless, Carl had to be careful. His public status around Windsor made him "one of the town's best known citizens." His multiple identities—reporter, insurance man, military band major, friend of Amy Archer—would begin to affect his daily life. As Carl began to ask questions around town after James Archer's mysterious death, word got back to Amy. She was determined to do everything in her power to stop Carlan from besmirching her name and tarnishing her reputation, planning a campaign against him over the next few years to prove he was no more than a scorned friend seeking revenge. Someone looking to make a name for himself as a reporter at the expense of Amy and her Home.

"Few people realize," a reporter once said about Carl, "that his active role in public life almost cost him a chance to work on the biggest news story of his entire career."

Chapter 2

QUIET MENACE

As new englanders eased themselves into bed on the unusually hot summer night of Friday, June 30, 1911, most were undoubtedly thinking about the upcoming weekend and Fourth of July celebration. The family picnics and parties. Fireworks and flag waving. Beer and wine and music and dance.

What no one knew was that the upper atmosphere around the Northeast and Midwest on that night was making several remarkable (and soon-to-be deadly) adjustments, a meteorological event, it would turn out, surpassed by none. There was a swirling blend of high- and low-pressure systems heading toward each other, the highs racing faster than the lows (because hot air is lighter than cold), both on the move, like an invisible tidal wave, heading west to east. While that uncharacteristic phenomenon began to shape itself, a band of extremely hot, tropical air formed over the Great Lakes region and moved slowly east. Fundamentally speaking, a blanket of fire was kindling, preparing to drop itself over some 464,536 square miles of Yankee land and 6.6 million people.

Carl Goslee was now focused on what he believed was the biggest story of his career—but it had nothing whatsoever to do with the weather. That McClintock lawsuit had got Carl thinking, so he started to ask questions around Windsor—this, after he had searched through Town Hall records and uncovered an Archer Home tax bill that had gone unpaid.

As more information became available to him, a picture began to emerge. Carl would explain his growing concerns in his reporting, writing simply, "The death rate is too high." Carl had seen firsthand information regarding the number of deaths at the Archer Home as compared to the rest of the town, and it nagged at him.

Indeed, Amy's patients were dying at unprecedented rates. Since she'd opened, Amy had lost nearly two dozen inmates in four years. "Death certificates," Carl reported years later, "received by the Windsor Town Clerk show that there were 60 of them since the place opened," a number that far exceeded a normal death rate among similar homes in the immediate Hartford area.

Carl began to think that Amy was not only possibly abusing inmates, but also murdering them. Perhaps his experiences in the Windsor Rogue Detecting Society fueled a bit of his suspicion. Yet whatever the case, Carl was now driven to find the truth, in spite of the opposition he faced.

"Many people in town thought that Amy was a wonderful person," wrote Carl's daughter, Barbara Goslee Sargent, "and Dad got many threatening telephone calls. They thought she was a very caring and philanthropic woman because she did so many nice things for Windsor."

The McClintock family lawsuit (which Amy made certain was settled out of court) turned out to be only the beginning of Amy's problems. Carl soon found out that the latest in a series of suspicious deaths had occurred just weeks ago, on May 25, 1911. Eighty-one-year-old Hilton Griffin had died of "general debility [and] old age," Dr. King wrote on Griffin's death certificate. What the doctor had failed to do was indicate any type of an extended illness.

Carl Goslee realized that few would share his suspicions at this point. He needed positive proof and hard evidence before he could wage a formal public campaign against Amy. And even then, he was sure to run into those in town who simply would not believe him. "Because of this investigation," Carl recalled before his death, ". . . [t]here was much sentiment against me because [Amy] was perceived to be a very saintly and generous woman."

If there was one characteristic about him that would help Carl now, it was his patient resoluteness. Carl took his time with whatever he did. He decided to study the obituaries written for Windsor over the past several years—especially the past few months—and see where it led. The problem was, Amy didn't simply have a few supporters; she worked *hard* to maintain her flawless image, especially as she began to hear that Carl was snooping around.

"She sent flowers to [the families of] her victims," Carl wrote, "and donated money to the [local] Catholic Church..." One woman later claimed that Amy had even bought the church an organ.

In short, people in Windsor loved Amy. They believed she was providing a service to the town, the state, and, of course, to all those elderly residents who had no family or friends to care for them, along with those whose families had no room or energy to do so. Windsor socialites rallied to Amy's side. There was no way, many were quick to say, that Sister Amy—given that nickname because she was rarely seen around town without her trusty Bible in the crook of her arm—was killing people. Poor woman; she had just lost her husband. Her only child had no father. She spent her days and nights catering to elderly men and women, some of whom did nothing but nag and bother her while she tried to keep up her business without the help of a man around the house. Why not just leave her be?

"Miss [Archer]," Carl said later, "moved in the best circles, and it was hard for some to believe that she could be guilty of such crimes."

Carl's editor at the *Hartford Courant*, Clifton Sherman, was intrigued with the information one of his "star" stringer-freelance reporters had been providing. But he was still not sold on the idea that proof-positive murder was happening in what many viewed as a house of hope. Carl was on to something, no doubt about it. Sherman could sense it. Carl was not one to bark up the wrong tree or continue running with a story that would fizzle. He had evidence—circumstantial, yes, but a case was building.

Sherman, a middle-aged man with a full career in the newspaper business ahead of him, was a respected, conservative editor. He was now in a position to either act on his newspaper's reporting or to let it fall by the wayside. Sherman had been with the *Courant* as managing editor from 1893 to 1900, when he left for a job at the *New York Sun*. He returned to the *Courant* in 1904. He had a home in Dover, Vermont, where he saw himself reading and fishing and living out his retirement years once he had left the newspaper business. A graduate of Amherst College, before heading off to school Sherman had wanted to become a lawyer or doctor; instead, he decided to follow in the footsteps of his father, a Brattleboro, Vermont, correspondent for the Springfield (Massachusetts) *Union* newspaper. After two weeks' training in headline writing at the *Union*, Sherman began his editing career in 1888 at a rate of seven dollars per week.

Sherman explained to Carl that he'd get back to him regarding where to take the story next, but he encouraged the reporter to keep digging. There was an answer in there somewhere. Carl just needed to find it.

▲ ▲ ▲

Saturday, July 1, 1911, dawned as a rather inconsequential day, save for being one of the warmest mornings the Weather Bureau had ever recorded in New England history. Further inland, near Hartford and Windsor, without the breeze from the Atlantic cooling things down some, it was much warmer. In fact, normally cooler states throughout the country, such as Michigan, Minnesota, Iowa, Nebraska—and even Ontario, Canada—were going to register temperatures well over 100 degrees by day's end, inciting many to recognize that the summer of 1911 had arrived on one hell of a memorable note.

Out of its Washington, D.C., office, where forecasts were generated, the Weather Bureau predicted that New England would experience "moderately high" temperatures for the week beginning July 1. A hot wave* bearing down on the "Middle West" will "moderate" in the coming days, the report noted. New Englanders and Midwesterners could expect "moderately warm, light, variable winds," with "fair [temperatures] to-night and also on Sunday." No sign of an extended period of hot weather was mentioned. As far as Bureau analysts could establish, the worst the summer would produce was just then bearing down on the Midwest and New England. June temperatures generally ranged from 60 to 90 degrees, depending on

---

* Near the turn of the century, *hot wave* was the more common term newspapers and meteorologists used to describe an extended period of heat. Today's more popular term, *heat wave*, was also used, but far less universally.

the jet stream. But now July was here—and she was blazing. Enjoy the brief spell of heat. Jump in a swimming hole. Fan yourself with a folded-up newspaper. But don't fret: The heat will come and the heat will go.

For Connecticut residents it was just another July getting off to a steamy start. New Englanders were used to the hot weather, and with the summer social season officially getting under way, there'd be plenty of distractions. Coastline and river beaches, resorts, and community pools were packed. Schools were closed for summer vacation. What was all the fuss about? After all, what would summer be without the heat?

Hot or cool, for those in the Constitution State who didn't enjoy a wealth of leisure time, summer was all about work, which often meant hard labor—in the fields, city buildings, factories, or on the water. New England had a long history of using its natural resources to remain competitive in regional, national, and global marketplaces. Summer was one of the busiest times of the year. In his popular 1897 novel, *Captains Courageous*, Rudyard Kipling wrote about the lives of the Northeastern "salt bankers," detailing their often-turbulent trips on schooners from Gloucester, Massachusetts, out to the Grand Banks of Newfoundland, in search of the almighty codfish. Along the boomerang-shaped coastline of Manhattan, one hundred or so miles south of Hartford, and the Connecticut coastline, July brought with it the search for the elusive bluefish, especially in places like Annadale, Staten Island, Sheepshead Bay, Long Island Sound, and the Race, just off Block Island. Fishing was a primary source of income for those New Englanders who had been handed the trade from past generations and lived along the hundreds of miles of zigzagged, fishable coastline.

As the Industrial Revolution seemed to explode around her, business wasn't going so well for Amy Archer. In a way, Amy was a pioneer in privatized elderly care. By and large, New York and Boston were superior cities to Hartford and Windsor because they already had privatized elderly care systems in place. But the Insurance Capital was teeming with manufacturing and clerical jobs, and people to fill them. Part of the reason Amy and James had relocated from Newington to Windsor was because Amy believed Hartford was the perfect backdrop against which to set their new business, which would be the first of its kind in the state.

Positioned in the center of the state, midway between New York City and Boston, Hartford was called the *Huys de Hoop* (House of Hope) by the Dutch when they settled the city in the early 1600s. Hartford offered a wealth of opportunities for the automobile and insurance industries, which is what the city became known for throughout the country. At the turn of the twentieth century, much like Boston, Hartford was one of the foremost places in the United States to live, work, and visit. Abraham Lincoln had made the trip in the mid-1800s, giving a powerful speech downtown that underlined the importance of New England's role in the abolitionist movement. The Beecher family (including Harriet, who would write the masterpiece *Uncle Tom's Cabin* in her downtown Hartford home) had grown up west of Hartford, in Litchfield—in fact, directly next door to Amy Archer and her family, the Duggans. The Beecher family eventually moved to a more stately manor across the way from Mark Twain's immense estate on Farmington Avenue, after gaining a nationwide reputation for its staunch opposition to slavery and support of the temperance and woman's suffrage movements.

After Lincoln's visit, Hartford went through a gradual social revolution. By 1900, immigrants were flooding into the region, as if a map at Ellis Island had listed Hartford as one of the top locales in the country to settle. The population grew nearly twofold between 1900 and 1910, from 80,000 to 150,000. The growth was welcome. The Underwood Typewriter Company, like the Pope (automobile) Manufacturing Company and Colt Firearms, needed workers desperately, as did the Electric Boat Company in New London, which had built the first U.S. Navy submarine, the *Holland*, in 1900. And so, by the tens of thousands, swarms of foreigners made the steamboat journey north from Manhattan—Germans, Russians, Poles, Irish, Italians, Lithuanians. In Amy's view, all of these people would one day become feeble and old, in need of a place to live out their golden years. Starting the business south of Hartford was a smart move. Business would boom. In fact, in just the four short years since she and James had opened their doors, several similar homes run by the city had followed suit downtown.

Like certain sections of Manhattan, Hartford developed a reputation for being a bit on the rough side, despite some parts of the city that reflected a Victorian charm. The towering image of the city's staggered skyline from the perch of a steamboat heading up the Connecticut River from Long Island Sound must have filled eager immigrants with awe upon arrival, striking them with the same rush they likely felt as they made their way into New York from Europe. Hartford was a city of boundless infrastructure and construction, seemingly made more aesthetically pronounced by the thousands of acres of flatland crops—tobacco, mostly—surrounding it. Mark Twain had written several of his classic novels in his downtown estate, and praised the city for its uncanny similarity to the larger port cities he had visited and written about along the Mississippi. To live and work in any part of New England—especially Hartford and Boston—spoke of prestige, prominence, affluence; it meant respect and admiration from those out West, down South, in the Great Plains, and, particularly, back home in Europe.

▲ ▲ ▲

Hartford bustled on July 1. It was a Saturday, and despite temperatures in the 90s, women walked through Bushnell Park and along Main and State streets near the Old State House, wearing their usual attire: petticoats, corsets, full-length dresses. Men wore top hats and suits, while children rode Pope bicycles, played tag, and otherwise enjoyed the steamy summer day. Horse-drawn carriages galloped over dirt roads, the stench of their steeds' feces mingling with the exhaust from the newest Pope automobiles, while trolleys drove residents and visitors from Springfield, Massachusetts, through downtown, south, and on to New Haven and Manhattan. As the temperature continued to rise, the humidity soared, coming in near 72 percent by mid-afternoon.

A true "scorcher" was going to be recorded in the books.

Carlan Goslee was consumed by the story he had been chasing for the past two years. That lawsuit back in 1909 had lit a fire in the cub reporter. Despite the bizarre nature of many of the deaths inside the Archer Home, and the fact that there had been dozens of them since the Home opened, no one in town was speaking out about it. This sent Carl into the community to ask why. Someone needed to step forward and say something. Too many bizarre things had been reported by prior and current inmates. It was this reporter's edge—the gut instinct reporters have for a story they believe in—that pushed Carl to not give up.

Carl was an uncomplicated man who adored his wife, Mae, and the family they were building. He knew this was a remarkable story; the death toll alone had the potential to be unprecedented. This was quite a departure from the simple way of life Carl had come to know in Windsor, as he described in a personal essay he later wrote:

> *Saturday nights in Windsor homes were spent getting ready for Sunday. After an evening meal, the wooden washtub was made ready for the baths in the kitchen. While everyone waited their turn for the bath, Dad would get out the hair clippers and barber's shears and cut the hair of those who needed it. Most of the boys in those days had very close cuts.*

While Dad played the part of barber, Carl's mother would sew buttons on clothes or fumble with "a stitch to be taken in or out for the growing children." When Sunday came, it was all about God.

> *Sundays, most families were on hand for the church services, and Sunday schools were attended by young and old. During the long winter nights, it was the practice in many homes to pop corn and make popcorn balls. As the atmosphere began to clear, social activities became more numerous. The old folks' concerts and square dances were popular at Town Hall.*

This solemn yet idyllic small-town life was shattered for Carl as he began to think about a town resident who could be responsible for dozens of deaths. As much as he wanted to ignore the inevitable, Carl could not get over the marked increase in deaths of Archer Home inmates. Granted, old people died. But Carl had already been down to Town Hall to dig through the death notices signed off on by Dr. Howard King. In doing so, he had latched on to another source, which told him right away that something was terribly off.

"After I brought the many obituary notices to the attention of Mr. Sherman," Carl later wrote, "I told him that I had investigated the Black Book which contained records of the poisons purchased at the W. H. Mason Drugstore. I told him that [Miss Archer] had bought large amounts of arsenic."

Arsenic?

Carl had made a stunning discovery at W. H. Mason's Drugstore downtown. He and a fellow reporter had noticed that Amy (or an inmate from the Home) had been purchasing large quantities of arsenic for years. Now, either she had a tremendous rodent problem, with rats the size of full-grown men, or she was using the poison for other purposes.

Numbers don't lie. As an insurance man, Carl knew this perhaps better than most. One purchase made by Amy herself, a rather large dose of two ounces, had been picked up two days before one man at the Home had suddenly dropped to the floor, vomited profusely, and died.

Despite these discoveries, Carlan didn't want to stand on a soapbox and accuse his old friend of murder. He would unearth the facts carefully.

Carl's brother, H. L. Goslee, who worked for the town, wrote to Amy that May to ask about an unpaid tax bill at Town Hall. Although James Archer was dead, there were bills in his name that Amy needed to make good on. Carl figured this would be a good distraction. He wanted to keep Amy's mind on her finances while he kept looking into the purchases she was making at the drugstore.

Amy felt threatened by what she saw as an unwarranted attack. She believed it to be a ruse Carl and his brother had cooked up to make her look bad in front of her fellow townspeople, which would eventually add credence to Carl's drummed-up suspicions and accusations.

In other words, a witch hunt.

As she often did whenever her character was attacked, Amy fired back, this time in her own letter. Amy felt the Goslee family had gone too far this time, with this allegation that she'd ducked out on unpaid tax bills. Amy felt Carl was behind it all.

"I find the [bill] you spoke of . . . does not belong to us," Amy wrote back to H. L. Goslee, Carl's brother. "Since dear Mr. Archer died I have only received the bill for the taxes; that is all I have ever been notified of." Amy was incensed. She said she had never "heard of a world [that would] think of taxing a Home of this kind . . ."

Amy Archer was the victim. What business was it of a reporter and his family to accuse her of not paying her bills? This was surely not the *true* focus of Carl's concern; he was clearly after something else.

Carl was not one to let things go. When he got involved with something, he saw it through until the end. It disturbed him that so many people had died at the Archer Home; he knew there was more to it than mere "old age," as many of the death certificates had claimed. And now, with the mysterious passing of James, Amy was obviously ignoring his debt by not making an effort to pay the bills he had left behind, the young reporter decided a different approach was necessary.

Chapter 3

SILENT KILLERS

As a young boy during the early 1850s, Franklin Andrews awoke one morning to a throbbing pain in his hip. It was excruciating, like an electric shock beginning in his lower back, creeping into his hip socket, and zapping the back of his leg. Within days, little Franklin's hip swelled. He could barely walk.

Franklin Andrews likely suffered from a condition known as congenital dislocation of the hip, which in the ensuing months and years caused one of Franklin's legs to shorten. Thus, from his earliest days, as he hobbled along and struggled to walk normally, Franklin earned the moniker of "lame." It would define him. Asked later about Franklin, friends would say that except for his "lameness," Franklin had always been in great health.

Growing up on a farm, Franklin Andrews took pride in being able to fend for himself at a young age. By the scorching weekend of July 1–2, 1911, the fifty-seven-year-old farmer and factory worker had begun to feel the pangs of old age creep into his shaky bones, which had stiffened over the years. He hadn't been able to work on the farm his parents had left to him in years. In early 1910, Franklin had spent thirteen weeks in Hartford Hospital, where he was treated for rheumatism in his shoulders and legs. After the stay, however, Franklin "improved constantly in health down to the day of his death," according to a report prepared by the Hartford County Supreme Court of Errors.

On the morning of July 2, 1911, Franklin Andrews, along with his fellow Connecticut Yankees, opened his door to another hot and humid day. By this time Franklin had sold his parents' farm and moved in with his elder sister, Emily Francis. He shuffled back and forth between Wallingford and Yalesville to board with another sister. It seemed that no one wanted old Franklin around anymore;

both sisters were battling the rigors of old age themselves. However, according to his half-brother, Warren Andrews, up until the day he started looking for an alternative place to live, Franklin "was perfectly healthy and well, with the exception of his lameness."

Moreover, Warren Andrews added, Franklin Andrews "never" complained about stomach problems; he didn't have any stomach issues whatsoever, or "boils or abscesses"—all ailments Franklin Andrews would be accused of suffering from in the coming years.

As the sun burned off the morning haze, Franklin Andrews took his routine "five- to six-mile" walk around the Yalesville neighborhood where he was staying during this period. Franklin had taken walks like this one just about every day of his adult life, lame leg or not.

The conditions over the past forty-eight hours in the state had gone from reasonably bearable—considering a heat wave was in the works—to downright intolerable. By 2:00 p.m. on July 2, Hartford broke a century-old record, logging a 100-degree temperature. STARTED AT 75 DEGREES, read one headline the following morning, and [REACHED] 100 BEFORE 2 O'CLOCK. The official Weather Bureau observer, stationed atop Hartford's Mutual Building, recorded that "to-day [is] one of the hottest days for many years."

And then bodies began piling up—those agonizingly painful, heat-related fatalities—as Mother Nature started claiming victims. Yet as the torturous heat also came down on the town of Windsor, Amy Archer saw a great opportunity to begin planning her malicious crimes.

Two young women drowned in Hartford's Riverside Park just off the banks of the Connecticut River when their boat capsized. In addition to those lost lives, four more drowning deaths were reported around the state on the same afternoon, on top of nine deaths in the Hartford area alone from various heat-related injuries. It had turned so hot that several men had to be talked down from fire escapes and the tops of buildings after becoming "crazed by the heat," one reporter wrote. In one such incident, a man named Frank Tirka had to be manhandled down "with considerable difficulty" from a fire escape in back of the Sterling Theatre in Derby, Connecticut. Tirka had climbed the escape ladder in a demented frenzy while complaining of being chased by some unknown, invisible person.

It was just the beginning.

Boston and New York reported much of the same. Scores of dead already, only three days into a heat wave that had, by this point, cast a blanket of hot air over much of the Midwest and even parts of the South.

Weather Bureau officials remained confident, however. Everyone stay calm. Relief was on the way. Its forecast for July 3, published in newspapers across the country, predicted FAIR TO-NIGHT AND TUESDAY; COOLER BY TUESDAY NIGHT.

This was great news for municipal workers and city planners. At New York's Coney Island, an estimated 400,000 people converged on the "beach resort" with hopes of beating the heat. Throngs of citizens, bunched together like parade goers, dressed in boxer shorts and the skimpiest bathing suits of the day, flowed into the resort by boat, trolley, train, car, and on foot.

Surprisingly, the Coney Island police had little trouble keeping things under control that afternoon. "They were all too hot to make trouble," police captain Thomas Murphy reported. There were lines to get into the ocean. Shifts of swimmers alternated. Police and park employees used megaphones to control the crowds as they swelled around bathhouses and the shoreline.

With so many people sweating, dehydrating, searching for cool water, packed full into one of the only places near Manhattan to swim (without fear of drowning in the strong Hudson and Harlem currents), the only serious issue of the day turned out to be skinny-dippers and nude sunbathers. By late afternoon, it became so hot that people were shedding their clothing, seeking some sort of respite from the blazing temperatures.

"I admire Greek statuary in its place," Murphy said mockingly, "but its place is in a museum."

Additional excitement that day came in the form of a "crazy blonde woman" who was likely drunk. With two men hanging off her arms, the woman "invaded the island in the afternoon," the *New York Times* reported, "dressed in a combination pantaloon and harem skirt, which even hardened Coney [Island policemen] said was the most remarkable costume [they] had ever seen." She wore a kind of belly dancer's outfit, the only exception being that hers was cut up the legs and she wasn't shy about showing as much skin as possible. Dancing with one of her male companions, the woman's performance shut down the attractions at Coney Island—that is, until she was kicked out of the park to the roar of the crowd.

The heat didn't let up even as darkness fell. More than 100,000 bathers decided to sleep on the beach and in and around the park. As everyone settled in for the night, the pickpockets and thieves came out like vampires.

In Philadelphia, a dozen people were reported dead, ranging in age from nine months old to fifty-five years. The heat did not discriminate. Downtown Philly, like Boston and Hartford, was packed with city dwellers who were camping in the parks and on the streets. Mattresses were tossed out of apartment-building windows and lined up along Main Street in Hartford, where women held their children and the men fanned them as best they could.

As the crowds grew and the heat and humidity continued to climb, authorities worried about what would happen the following day, when the Fourth of July arrived. On July 3, the situation could be called orderly chaos. Reports were filed from Hartford, Boston, and New York, noting that with so many people inundating city streets and parks to seek refuge from the heat, ice and water would soon become commodities to fight over. And then what?

Another problem was that most major cities were not equipped to handle large swells of human beings all at once. Standing in the streets, some were struck and killed by trains and trolleys because there was nowhere left to stand. Others were trampled by horses.

Then body heat became an issue. With so many people packed together so closely, the heat index rose. Heat exhaustion became the new enemy.

If the heat and humidity didn't let up soon, New England officials faced one of the biggest emergencies they had ever seen—a natural disaster, in effect, so silent and invisible, there was little anyone could do but ride it out, hoping and praying for the best.

Chapter 4

HUMBLE BEGINNINGS

WHEN THE ARCHER HOME OPENED IN 1907, Amy and James operated under the motto that helping people endure the rigors of old age was their calling. In James's case, the idea that convalescing the elderly could be both a noble proposition as well as potentially profitable was appealing; however, Amy's goals were far more financially oriented and motivated. Make no mistake about it: The woman was in it for the money.

Amy and James had developed a simple payment plan. You could either pay between "$7–$25 per week," one advertisement read (that was for shelter, food, and medical care), or pay a one-time flat fee of $1,000, which Amy called her contract for "life care." If you didn't have the $1,000 and you still wanted the all-inclusive plan, Amy was willing to work with you. She offered some inmates the opportunity to sign over any property or assets they had, or to pay the fee in installments.

"I have a splendid home for my lifetime," one inmate wrote to a friend not long after entering the Home. "If I choose I put in 1,000 dollars [and] am taken care of with Board and Clothes and all Bills Paid and a decent Burial, so I think I am well off."

The concept Amy and James created was a somewhat innovative idea, and townspeople valued and respected Amy's resolve and dedication to her business, especially after James died. Four years into the life of the business, however, with James now dead and buried, things were starting to go wrong for Amy. None of what she had planned was taking shape.

Meanwhile, elderly—or convalescent—homes were popping up everywhere. By the end of 1911, there would be similar homes up and running in Connecticut, New York, and Massachusetts, while across the country plans were being made to construct homes as fast as stone, brick, and mortar could be set.

One of the largest nursing homes in the country, that of the Franciscan Sisters of Chicago, would ultimately provide nursing care services for 150 residents by 1960. Founded in the mid-1890s by Mother Mary Theresa Dudzik as a home for "poor women and children and the older population of northwest Chicago," Mother Mary "saw that the Franciscan tradition could be the model for the creation of hospitals, schools and communities that would improve people's lives."

By the year 2009, approximately 16,000 nursing homes would serve aging Americans across the country. There is no way to prove that Amy and James Archer were the first to open an official nursing/convalescent home (as a privatized business), but it's clear that they developed a pioneering model that would sweep across the nation and turn elderly care—at least in the private sector—into a potentially profitable business.

▲ ▲ ▲

Franklin Andrews was trying to figure out his next move in life. His two sisters who lived nearby could not take him in; they were too old and frail themselves. So Franklin called on a friend from Wallingford, who lived east of his parents' farm in Meriden. He explained that he wouldn't need to stay long. He was thinking about making a trip to Hartford to see his other sister, Nellie—she had room—but Franklin didn't want to burden her, either.

While Franklin considered his options, his friend obliged him with a place to stay.

▲ ▲ ▲

The Archer Home was located outside downtown Windsor on Prospect Street. From the second floor, facing east, one could look out and see a reflective glare—a mirror image, essentially—of the ten-story-tall pine and maple trees protruding off the banks of the

Connecticut River. An impressive body of water Native Americans called the *Quenticut*, this magnificent river was a major means of transportation for New Englanders in the late 1800s and early 1900s. It provided a direct route to the Atlantic Ocean about sixty-five miles away, and to the towns along its shores, from Vermont to Long Island Sound, boasting "uninterrupted access to the channels of commerce along" the way.

During a stretch of hot weather such as the one blanketing New England as the 1911 Fourth of July dawned, the water gave off a putrid, skunky odor. When the rains came, the dirt roads along the river's shore turned into flooded, impassable mud baths, while acres of saturated crops wilted and drowned. During the winter, the river generally froze solid from side to side, yet remained too fragile to cross.

The town of Windsor was established in 1633 as the first settlement in Connecticut, and saw the first New World execution of a witch in 1647, years before the witch hunt in Salem, Massachusetts. Windsor became home to workers in the wool and paper mills located along the Farmington River, which intersected with the Connecticut not too far away from the Archer Home. By far, though, tobacco farming and brick making were the town's strongest economic assets, the first crop of tobacco said to be planted in 1640 with seeds brought to the region from Virginia plantations.

For Amy Archer, whose business had recently been drained of funds because of the McClintock lawsuit, the thriving town of Windsor might have seemed like the ideal location to continue trying to make it work. The people, save for a small group of Carlan Goslee's band of supporters, still embraced Amy and her business, and believed it was good for the town. And no matter what Carl said, or was in the process of supposedly proving, as the July Fourth holiday approached, the fact of the matter remained: Amy started to fill beds once again.

"She has applications quite often for more . . . ," wrote one inmate near this period. "It's a nice Place, not over 5 minutes walk from the Post Office."

Despite what Narcissa McClintock and her mother had charged, there was nary an open bed at the Archer Home that Amy couldn't fill. Moreover, Amy was now bullhorning the notion that perhaps many of the problems associated with the lawsuit were born out of James Archer's treatment of the inmates.

"The defendants," said the lawsuit complaint, "in every way endeavored to prevent and hinder the plaintiff from making her wants known . . . or caring for her when she needed care, and she has suffered in body and mind by reason of . . . neglect. . . ."

Although the suit charged both Amy and James, it was James, Amy began to insist, who had caused the McClintocks' concerns. Amy said over and over that she'd had nothing whatsoever to do with the maltreatment of an inmate. She had loved James Archer, sure, but at times, he could be lazy and careless. According to Amy, he was not always the nicest man.

Chapter 5

DEVOUT CHRISTIAN

ON THE FOURTH OF JULY, 1911, THE SUN rose in Connecticut as an out-of-focus yellow and orange fireball. Temperatures just after sunup were already in the low 80s. No one knew just how historic this Independence Day would be; deaths related to the excessive heat began to occur within that hour of dawn in cities and towns throughout the state.

Amy would have been dressed on this morning the same as any other—in a black or white ankle-cut skirt over a corset. Dark or light stockings. Maybe buckled leather shoes, as in the American steel-beaded black kid pump with the Louis heel. Or a traditional boot (the female version of the men's Splat Shoe), laced up her shins, that looked a lot like a roller-skate shoe without the wheels. She was often spotted sweeping the front porch in the morning. Her black hair was routinely pulled back into a bun. She wore a large white bow tie on some days, with a checkered men's dress shirt, and resembled legendary Public Enemy Era crook Ma Barker during her younger years.

The Fourth started like any other day at the Home. Breakfast was on the table by 8:00 a.m., bedpans emptied (if she felt like it) by 9:00, lunch served by noon. By 2:00 p.m. Amy was at W. H. Mason's near the trolley depot ordering supplies, undoubtedly talking to Mr. Mason about her day. Amy Archer was living the American dream: business owner, custodian, and proprietress to the old. She provided room and board, daily care, meals. And while her inmates paid a sum, they were her family, Amy suggested.

"I have had hundreds of aged, helpless and infirm and have ministered to their wants and given them such comforts as the Home could afford, and I think they were all satisfied with the treatment received," Amy said.

Furthermore, she felt that the idea she was deliberately and callously harming patients was preposterous. "I have been in this work for many years," she said, "and there are very few young people who give up their life to this cause."

Amy challenged the public to seek an alternative to her "service," to see if, in other words, the elderly would have a better chance anywhere else.

"I am willing you should canvass the State of Connecticut," she wrote to one potential inmate who was having second thoughts after hearing rumors that the Home was not all that Amy had built it up to be, "for the same terms for what you receive in return and I only too well know the same as others, you will not be able to find another offer this I know . . . I know it is hard for you to pack up . . . and I assure you I do [not] hold the slightest ill feeling for any unkindness shown me, and would advise you not to come here if you are not perfectly satisfied with the lovely room and your nice home . . ."

In that same letter, Amy made the point that if the man didn't want to stay at the Home because of the rumors, well, that was of no bother to her; after all, she had a list of people waiting to get in. Amy wrote: "I have a number on my list, but I would not disappoint you nor be guilty of causing you a moment's worry. . . . If you decide to go elsewhere, please come to see us when you can, and remember—I wish always to be your friend in your joys and sorrows. [I]t makes no difference whether you come or not as far as friendship goes; if I can ever be of assistance to you in any way, I will be very glad to."

⚜ ⚜ ⚜

What Carl found as he began to delve more deeply into Amy's business was that even among those in town who had initially embraced Amy's arrival years before, some were now beginning to consider the accusations against her. Part of them centered around reports that the local undertaker was showing up more and more frequently in the middle of the night with his horse and buggy.

Amy pretended to seek a better understanding between her and the townsfolk, especially Carl Goslee, who she now viewed as an enemy. Being a "devout Christian," as she had told people, one might assume Amy prayed for those who denounced her and believed any opposition to her ideas was some sort of test of her faith and commitment. Truth was, Amy had no interest in God. Anxious to prove her business was legitimate, or perhaps protecting her source of revenue and what little respect she had left, Amy went after Carl and the newspaper he worked for, writing a letter to the state's attorney in Hartford, Hugh Alcorn, warning him that there was a witch hunt going on and she was tired of it.

Dated May 22, 1911, the letter read: "I presume it is unnecessary for me to tell you of the *Courant* reporters' conduct toward my home. They never saw best to write of my caring for people for nothing—as I have in a number of cases. After he [Louis Robert Thayer, one of Carl's colleagues] went to Middletown, Derby and hounded me all these years—all he could find against me that he dare print . . . was I let that bill . . . run over."

Amy insisted that in addition to Thayer's deeds, Carl had "[written] up a book of falsehoods" about her and passed it around to townspeople who, in turn, "dared him to print them," which he never did, incidentally. Carl was trying to rally public opinion to the side of those who had died, while Amy initiated a campaign to keep her good standing in the community. Carl's fellow *Courant* reporter Robert Thayer stepped into the fold around this time, and started asking questions.

Amy was adamant: The deaths inside the Home were mere coincidences that were being misinterpreted, especially by those who didn't know the details behind each death. These were old and ill people, she said. They couldn't be expected to live forever. Amy cited a story to Hugh Alcorn she thought would best clarify the predicament she found herself in—something that no doubt stirred Carl to want to dig ever deeper.

"This man inhales chloroform for Asthma of the Heart," Amy wrote to Alcorn. "He felt badly and had a little Gin in a bottle about the same size"—a common way to treat such an ailment back then. "By mistake," Amy said, "he drank the chloroform." Praising herself, Amy said she was "by his room at the time and called the doctor at once. No one ever had a closer call, although we never had a sudden death—that is, where the person was not ailing for months."

When a relative or neighbor of an inmate heard of Amy's rather bizarre behavior of denying inmates care, herding inmates in small rooms, and strange happenings going on inside the Home in the middle of the night she always gave the same type of reply. "I have always done everything possible for me to comfort those who came into my home," she wrote to one man whose brother had lived there for a time and claimed she had bilked him out of $500. "I would not be low enough to take advantage of anyone . . . and you and all the demons living cannot destroy good work. May God punish you and yours as you so richly deserve."

Even as Carl was now openly accusing his former friend of, if nothing else, egregious acts of malice and unprofessional conduct, the town socialites were reluctant to go after Amy just yet. Many saw her as an example, someone who could light the spark of entrepreneurial spirit in the hearts of women throughout New England. A woman like Amy, working alone after the unexpected death of her husband, was proving that women could carve out a niche for themselves in what was a society dominated by male entrepreneurs, like Rockefeller, Morgan, and Carnegie.

On paper, Amy's business model showed vision. She preached hard work (though she hardly lived it). "A life of this kind is trying," Amy wrote to a potential inmate who had inquired about a room, "and severe, one which few follow, but if you do feel that you have any regret about coming or that you can do better, try it—I know what I am talking about. Since we came here," she added, "19 different families went into this same work—there is not one here now, and they, not one, continued to work one year."

Chapter 6

LEFT BEHIND

IN AND AROUND THE HARTFORD AND WINDSOR areas of the Connecticut River, several events were planned for the Fourth of July holiday. Golf tournaments. Horse races at Riverside Park. Military parades. Tennis and baseball games in Pope Park. Concerts. Motorcycle races. Carnivals. And, of course, fireworks.

Plenty of pop and sizzle.

With the Weather Bureau predicting an end to the heat wave, many of the events went on as scheduled, which only added to what was fast becoming a plethora of growing problems.

The Weather Bureau had promised relief—but it kept getting hotter. "Great suffering and many prostrations in the large cities," read one report from Hartford that night.

Earlier that morning, at 10:00 a.m., it had been 99 degrees, with reports of 104-degree temps coming in from Boston and New York. Records were dropping like people. Outside Boston, in Beverly, the mercury hit 108. Another problem: There was no breeze. The hot air seemed to hover like a fog and just sit there, stagnant and stale. This only added to an already asthmatic atmosphere that caused breathing problems for infants, the elderly, and the sick.

That evening, Hartford resident Hannah Cavanaugh, an otherwise healthy forty-four-year-old mother, headed off with three friends to the fireworks display scheduled along Connecticut Boulevard, just across the Connecticut River from downtown. Hannah lived on Albany Avenue, a main thoroughfare, about a twenty-minute walk from the Boulevard. She had no idea that by this point in the day, the festivities had been canceled because of the heat.

As Hannah and her friends approached Morgan Street, preparing to cross the Connecticut River, Hannah fainted. Just like that.

No warning. No dramatic prelude. The woman had simply dropped to the ground, unconscious, as if her legs had given out.

A friend called an ambulance. "But no doctor was asked for and so no one responded." Panic-stricken, Hannah's friends flagged down a man who happened to be driving by. His name was John Dorsey.

"What's wrong?" Dorsey asked as he stopped, his arm hanging out the window of his Pope automobile.

They explained.

Dorsey acted quickly. He got Hannah into his car and "stopped at the Office of the Police Surgeon F. A. Emmett," who also hopped into Dorsey's car and "administered a hypodermic injection" as Hannah was quickly driven to St. Francis Hospital, on Collins Street, a few miles away. Along the way, Hannah went into convulsive shock, her body shaking and trembling as if she had epilepsy.

In the parking lot of the hospital, F. A. Emmett worked on Hannah, but she turned white, and then blue, and her heart stopped. Amid the chaos, Dorsey and Emmett carried Hannah into the hospital as fast as they could, where she was pronounced dead a few moments later.

A widow, Hannah left behind two sons, a daughter, and a brother.

♣ ♣ ♣

What happened to Hannah Cavanaugh on that blazingly hot July Fourth evening would be repeated over much of New England and parts of the Midwest. An element of what led to Hannah's death was the era in which she and her fellow female heat-wave victims lived. In the 1900s and up through the late 1930s, women weren't expected to leave their homes—summer or winter—without dressing in proper Victorian-era garb: corsets, petticoats, and dresses that covered their bodies from neck to ankle. On that day, Hannah wore a weighty dress, made of a thick fabric, likely cotton or wool, which insulated her body, keeping the body heat contained. As Hannah began to sweat, the excessive heat had nowhere to go. Essentially, Hannah overheated the same way a car without fluids might.

In New York the ambulances were "busy all day," transporting people to the hospitals as twenty-eight reported heat-related deaths occurred. There were certainly dozens more that went unreported.

In one instance, the famed actress Julie Marlowe, performing in the first act of *Macbeth* on Broadway, was overcome by the heat and rushed to the emergency room. Marlowe's doctors told her she could not continue with her performances until the heat moved out of the region.

"While Miss Marlowe's condition is not alarming," a statement from the theater read, "it was said her temporary retirement was deemed necessary by her medical adviser in order to prevent a more serious breakdown of her health."

This was one of the reasons so many flocked to the outdoors and slept in the streets: There was no relief indoors, where temperatures were said to be 15 to 20 degrees warmer. Over 500 deaths could be directly attributed to the heat wave in New England alone since it began. Throughout the nation, such big cities as Pittsburgh (fifteen fatalities), Chicago (nine), and Kansas City (eight) reported deaths. There is no way to determine how many more deaths in the small towns surrounding the larger cities were due to the heat, but the number could have been in the thousands.

Then, as this fourth day of the heat wave merged into day number five, and officials thought it could not get any worse, a new problem emerged: lack of clean drinking water and ice.

Chapter 7

THE BIBLE THUMPER

DURING THOSE YEARS WHEN AMY WAS VIEWED as nothing more than a harmless caretaker and nurse, she had been told by many who showed up at the Home for the first time that she reminded them of their grandmother. At times, Amy had a pleasant, homey way about her. Many felt comfortable being around her, imagining Amy standing over a wood-fired stove, stirring a pot of homemade soup, wiping her hands on her apron. A striking image, actually, rather quintessential New England—a woman on a lazy Sunday afternoon, her boisterous family around her, the house filled with the sweet smell of dinner and the soothing sounds of life.

The life of Sister Amy Archer up until the point she arrived in Windsor—she could have been in her late thirties or older (there is an account of Amy's birth in 1873, another "years earlier," and yet another in 1877)—was far from that Norman Rockwellian picture. When they arrived in Windsor, Amy and James had been married for a decade. But then James died "unexpectedly" on February 10, 1910, shortly after the Archer Home began experiencing financial problems, a situation brought on exclusively by the McClintock lawsuit. What had sparked the interest of Carl Goslee and Robert Thayer was the cause of death listed on James's death certificate: Bright's disease, a turn-of-the-century name doctors used to describe acute or chronic nephritis—kidney disease. It was rare that a person, even someone getting on in years, would die in this manner without any pre-existing health conditions. Bright's disease didn't just come on overnight; it was an ailment patients dealt with for years and died from slowly.

Amy and James had one child, Mary, who was thirteen in 1911. She had plans to see the world after attending the Campbell School, a private prep school in Windsor. Part of Mary's academic focus was her passion for the piano. Mary loved to gather the elderly around during the evenings in the downstairs parlor and play. They would sit and knit, read, or just marvel at the way the young beauty effortlessly belted out one standard after the other—Schubert, Mendelssohn, Chopin, Schumann.

At the time Amy and James opened the Archer Home, quality health care was either an act of charity, or readily accessible only to those with enough money to pay for it. "Life care for $1,000," as Amy advertised in the local papers, seemed to show Amy's marketing genius. To the outside observer, life inside the Home was what the end of life should have been like for anyone getting on in years. Amy liked to say she was their mother, custodian, and friend. She had said a number of times that she believed she was doing "God's work." She was getting paid, yes—but she was also giving something back to the elderly that no one else in their lives could, and it hardened her soul when people like Carl Goslee and his salivating colleagues at the *Hartford Courant* questioned her nobility and character.

"It seems as if all the world has turned against me," Amy said in a defeated tone as news about the investigation got back to her, "and at times I feel a forlorn and defenseless woman, but I try to have faith in God, and my love for [Mary] will give me strength to live . . ."

Although dozens of her inmates had died throughout those early years, the sentiment Amy broadcast publicly was that she was greatly saddened by each passing. At times she set up funeral arrangements and sent bouquets of flowers to grieving family members, which town residents didn't realize, until years later, that she was contractually obligated to do. She'd even said publicly that she had taken it upon herself to pay for funerals when family couldn't be located and/or could not afford it—a patent falsehood, as that service had also been written into many of the contracts Amy signed.

On occasion, stories of mistreatment of patients, like the McClintock case, trickled into town, especially as Carl began talking to residents. At one time admired for her courage and ability to support herself and her obvious capitalist spirit, Amy's reputation was slipping with each new day, and some were thinking that maybe they had misjudged her. Scores of inmates had died at the Home since she'd opened, leading many to start believing that there was more to the deaths than natural causes.

So as usual, Amy fought back. "I am told it is claimed that I took persons under a life contract and tried to make a profit by poisoning them," she released in a public statement near July 4, 1911. "An examination of the records [in my home] . . . will show the absurdity of such a statement."

By this point, Amy was taking in about $500 profit each month. Still, what had started out as a prospect with great potential had turned into a failure. After all, in order for a bed to open up and new revenue to come in, a patient had to either die or leave. With beds always filled, Amy had to maintain the Home for months with no new income; hence, the suspicion that she was creating the turnover herself.

When asked, however, Amy insisted that it wasn't the lawsuit or the business model that had drained her bank account. No. In fact, Amy was making a new claim. "It has taken nearly every cent of my money to provide for my father and mother in their last illnesses," she said, ". . . and my invalid sister, who has not walked in thirty years. I am a poor, hardworking woman . . . This is Christian work, and one that is very trying, as we have to put up with lots of things on account of the peculiarities of the old people."

This was the first time Amy gave an explanation as to why the business was sinking. Her parents and sister were ill and needed her help.

Carl Goslee and Robert Thayer set out to interview Amy's family and friends to see if this was just another story.

Chapter 8

THOUSANDS OVERCOME

DESPITE A STRONG PUBLIC SENTIMENT THAT THE COUNTRY WAS heading in the wrong direction, both socially and industrially, since the turn of the century the America surrounding Amy Archer had become a hotbed of opportunity. The spirit of the nation, at its industrialized core, was focused on the great demand for natural resources—mainly coal—and the manual labor needed to unearth it. The great transcontinental railroad had been running for nearly fifty years. Medical and scientific ingenuity led to research and advances at universities across the nation. A postage stamp cost two cents. Beef was twelve and a half cents per pound. There had been a recent explosion of births, and the national population rose to somewhere near ninety-three million, with a little over one million settling in Connecticut. There were no suburbs as we know them today; instead, rural farming communities, or, as they were called, "hubs," were scattered around larger cities.

By July 6, 1911, the Weather Bureau was still promising relief from the heat. A "break in [the] hot wave [was] at hand," said one dispatch, adding that "breezes" had brought "relief in many sections" of the country. The people of Hartford, Windsor, New York, and Boston would not have agreed. The temperature in Hartford, with that imaginary *breeze*, dropped all of 1 degree on July 5, and still managed to hover in the mid- to upper 90s. Most states affected by the heat wave reported that "thousands [were] overcome." Cities posted bulletins warning of behavior that would contribute to heat stroke and other illnesses related to heat exhaustion. These caveats seemed almost silly in their simplicity, but had the obvious not been pointed out, officials feared, some would not use common sense.

On hot days wear thin clothing and avoid the sun rays. . . .
Take baths often . . . drink considerable amounts of cold water
(not ice water) for the purpose of inducing perspiration. . . .
If prostrated by exhaustion and excessive heat, the patient
will be pale and faint. Remove to shade, place on back with
head on level with body, loosen all tight clothing, and rub
hands and feet until circulation is restored. Bathe face and
body with warm water, and apply warm cloths to the latter.
Give hot drinks, tea, coffee, milk or water.

With death and suffering on the rise, ambulances roamed city streets like police cars, cruising for victims. Then the subways in New York closed. Reports of horses dropping dead poured in. City buildings closed. And hundreds of thousands of people flocked to city parks once again to battle the heat. This, mind you, as the Weather Bureau once again promised cool weather the following day, July 7.

♣ ♣ ♣

The town manager of Windsor once called Carl Goslee a "symbol of good." Indeed, Carl was a dedicated man who "demonstrated wholehearted enthusiasm for doing good in the community." More humorously, well into his later years, Carl was called the "Bicycling Great-Grandfather." He had never gotten his driver's license or owned a motor vehicle. "I didn't have the money when I was raising a family of six children," he said. Thus, everywhere he went, Carl generally got there on two wheels. Beyond the many positions Carl held in town or the many nicknames bestowed upon him, Carl was most proud of his fifty-plus years as Sunday School superintendent for the Grace Episcopal Church. Yet it was Carl's reporting standards and reputation as a persistent investigative journalist that gave him the most celebrity in the years after his death.

"Though most of his newspaper work was part-time," Carl's obituary stated in the *Hartford Times*, "he was thoroughly professional . . . His colleagues used to say that if there was a dogfight in Windsor, Carl Goslee knew all about it before it broke up and could tell the pedigrees of both dogs and the genealogies of their owners."

That reputation, along with his keen news sense, were going to help Carl's cause as he flagged the attention of his *Courant* editor, Clifton Sherman, and explained his suspicions of Amy perhaps killings inmates at the Archer Home in order to free up beds to make more money. In turn, Sherman alerted the state prosecutor, Hugh Alcorn, that there was definitely something sinister going on inside the Archer Home. Sherman and Alcorn were friends. They often talked about what was happening around town. Although there's no record of it, Alcorn must have told Sherman that he needed more evidence before he could open an investigation, because Alcorn would not get "officially" involved for a number of years. Still, if Carl was convinced, well, that was enough for Sherman.

After discussing it, Alcorn and Sherman agreed that the investigation in this early stage should be conducted in secret.

The more Carl found out as he started to ask questions of former inmates and their families, the more it became obvious to him that the one-time payment of $1,000 Amy was asking inmates to fork over was only the beginning of what could be considered a motive for murder. In fact, Amy was having some of her patients sign over their life savings, holdings, and land shares, tricking them into it or forging signatures. Then there were reports of Amy pillaging inmates' bank accounts on her own.

Despite his trust in Carl, Clifton Sherman needed to be certain that his newspaper's assumptions were backed up by hard evidence. It was one thing to accuse the woman of stealing her patients' life savings, and another to call her a murderer. There were inmates inside the Home, after all, who'd had nothing but good things to say about Amy. One of them was George Scott, a Hartford resident who had spent some time inside the Archer Home, but had since moved out. Interviewed in 1911, Scott explained to the *New York Times* that the authorities and those "others" accusing Amy "were not giving [her] a fair chance."

Soon after, Amy's daughter, Mary, now without a father, started talking to townspeople, calling on those who knew her mother best to step forward and defend her against such scurrilous allegations. A gifted piano player/prodigy, Mary threatened to quit her job as organist for St. Gabriel's Church if the rumor mill and "talk" about town continued, saying her focus would have to be on defending her mother—especially if no one else had the backbone to stand up and fight for her.

Dr. Howard King, still on the Archer payroll, also continued to defend Amy, saying, "I believe that [Amy] has been a victim of persecution, as any number of people in town dislike her personally and have caused suspicion to be directed against her. [Amy] is in some respects a little queer, but I do not think it is possible that she committed the crimes . . ."

As people took sides, Carl Goslee went to work behind the scenes, undoubtedly worried that perhaps the recent heat wave would serve as the perfect veil to commit murder. If the elderly population across the country was most susceptible to death by heat exhaustion, would Amy amp up her spree of murders and attribute their deaths to the heat?

Carl was now certain that where Amy Archer was concerned, anything was possible.

Chapter 9

FORECASTING THE WEATHER IS NO SCIENCE

GUGLIELMO MARCONI WAS VACATIONING in the Swiss Alps with his brother, Alphonso, when the thought, as if it were a cheerful holiday memory, struck him: *wireless telegraphy*. While lying in his hotel suite bed one night in 1894, it occurred to the Italian-born inventor that messages could be sent through electromagnetic waves instead of wires. By July 1911, a mere seventeen years later, Marconi had patented the first wireless telegraphy. His new technology could broadcast weather forecasts for the Weather Bureau to steamers trudging along the coast of Cape Cod. The transmission of changes in temperature, atmosphere, and weather patterns to ship captains proved vitally important. Now it was possible for weather observers to alert ships of impending weather-related doom, and, potentially, save lives.

While methods of communication had improved, the technology behind weather forecasting made the endeavor at best a gamble, or a scientific guessing game. A good example was the report coming out of Washington on July 6, which stated that relief from what was now an unbearable heat wave in its sixth day was in the cards for New Englanders. Unfortunately, over the next three days, it would only get hotter. Sure, it rained in Manhattan, but only for five minutes—as onlookers stood dumbfounded, watching the droplets of water evaporate on sidewalks as though hitting a frying pan.

In addition to the heat, there was now the problem of dangerous heat lightning. In one instance, three people participating in a funeral party, in the midst of burying a victim of the heat wave in Philadelphia, were struck and killed. This, as evening temperatures hovered in the high 80s and close to 90 in most eastern states.

By 1900 weather forecasting still suffered from the bad reputation it had carried for the past hundred years. Most people had a hard time seeing science and weather together under the same light, branding meteorologists and forecasters "weather prophets" and "observers." It was said that the first "chief weatherman" in Europe was so humiliated for his wholehearted belief in meteorology as a science that he slit his throat in shame when he was taken to task.

In the region of Hartford and Windsor, perhaps the most difficult aspect of forecasting the weather was the sheer speed of atmospheric change. The substratosphere over Connecticut, Massachusetts, and Rhode Island, mainly because of the jet stream, was in constant motion, changing and forming different weather conditions. Mark Twain, during a speech in 1887 titled "The Weather," summed up the trickery involved in foretelling New England's often varying weather patterns: "I reverently believe that the Maker who made us all makes everything in New England but the weather. I don't know who makes that, but I think it must be raw apprentices in the weather-clerk's factory who experiment and learn how, in New England, for board and clothes, and then are promoted to make weather for countries that require a good article . . ." Later, Twain would take it one humorous step further, making a statement in jest that would become a Twain notable: "If you don't like the weather in New England, just wait a few minutes."*

A year after he died, Twain's words didn't seem so funny anymore. New Englanders were battling what had turned into a killer of immense proportions, and they wondered if a thunderstorm *could* snap the heat wave—and if not, what was it going to take to cool things down?

♣ ♣ ♣

The concept of opening an elderly nursing home as a business came to Amy in 1901 while living in Newington, Connecticut, about ten miles south of Windsor. She and James had moved into the home of a prominent Newington businessman, John D. Seymour, whose wife had recently passed away. Seymour was aging and ailing at the

---

* This quote has been published two different ways. "New England" is, at times, part of the quote, while at others it is not. I chose to use the most commonly reported version.

time. With no family to speak of, the old man needed someone to care for him as he grew older and sicker. In exchange for room and board, Amy and James agreed to tend to Seymour's fundamental needs: cleaning and cooking, the chores around the house, health care. Amy explained to Seymour that she was a nurse and knew basic medicine, in addition to all the latest "remedies" of the day.

Seymour was thrilled; it was exactly what he needed.

Even Carl Goslee, in his earliest reporting, made the claim that Amy was a trained nurse, writing, "Amy was born in Litchfield [Milton] to James Duggan and Mary Kennedy Duggan; she trained as a nurse at Bellevue Hospital in Manhattan.... She married James Archer in 1901. She and her husband moved into the home of John D. Seymour to take care of him—Seymour died in 1904 and the Archers stayed on, caring for elderly boarders."

The problem with Amy's training at Bellevue is that there is no record anywhere to document that she had even set foot in the hospital, as patient or nurse trainee.

If there were problems for Amy and James in Newington, they were not reported. By the time Seymour died, shortly before Amy and James relocated to Windsor, the Seymour estate had become a rooming house for elderly patients under Amy and James's direction and care. As they made their way from Newington to Windsor, telling friends and acquaintances in Newington that they were going to make a go of opening a "home" of their own, a public show of warmth and support followed.

"Mrs. Gilligan was a church-going woman who donated stained-glass windows to [the] town church," one woman from Windsor noted after the rumors began to swirl. "I had heard her story for years and never doubted it ..."

Soon after the Archers moved into Windsor, townsfolk started referring to the outwardly religious matron as "Sister Amy." The self-proclaimed nurse told people upon her arrival in town that before her training at Bellevue, she had attended a private school in New Milford, Connecticut. She knew medicines, Amy insisted, but would "never give any unless ordered by the physician. Not even in the case of sudden illness. No. I always call [the doctor]."

Windsor residents bought it. But as trustworthy and motherly as Amy first appeared, here it was, four years since she'd opened the doors of the Archer Home, and nobody had bothered to check to see if the woman could prove she had the credentials to run such a place—that is, until Carl Goslee began knocking on doors and tracking down people from Amy's past.

Amy had no trouble filling beds and placating the neighbors if reports of minor problems made their way into town. "We have been fairly successful financially . . . our capacity is fourteen and we're always full," Amy told a reporter during her early years in town. "We are," she added, "entirely self-supporting. I sometimes take in guests at a monthly rate, though I don't like to because relatives so often neglect their aged. Their payments stop coming and I have to bear the expense myself. Usually I get a lump sum upon admission for life care."

The idea that the Home was set up for just fourteen inmates was an outright fabrication. Amy had no fewer than seventeen to twenty inmates in her home at any given time. But had she given an accurate account, Amy would have corroborated the accusation that she often "herded" inmates into the same room, just as she had been accused of by the McClintock lawsuit.

▲ ▲ ▲

During that first week of July, when the heat wave began to devastate New England, Amy was at home tending to her inmates as best she could with Carl Goslee breathing down her back. She opened all the windows in the house on July 8, in preparation for another scorcher of a night.

Meanwhile, Franklin Andrews, who had been forced from his parents' farm after their deaths, asked his good friend, Howard Francis, if he could stay with him in Wallingford for a time—at least until Franklin figured out what he was going to do and where he was going to live for the rest of his life. Franklin knew of Amy's home, having seen the ad in the newspaper. The seed had been planted some time ago; maybe that was the answer.

Howard Francis said his friend could stay as long as he liked, so Franklin Andrews, toting his one trunk of belongings, moved in. During the period Franklin stayed with Francis, he never showed any signs of sickness other than his normal lameness. In fact, Franklin, who was fairly strict on himself when it came to exercise and eating right, slept well, Francis later said, ate well, and *never* complained. Not once. About anything.

At a certain point, Franklin decided that his stay with Francis had come to an end. Francis accompanied Franklin to the Meriden station the day Franklin boarded the train for "Miss Archer's Home in Windsor." Franklin had expressed an interest in going to the Archer Home and Francis assumed that's where his good buddy was heading. But Francis was wrong. Franklin was actually headed to Hartford, to room with his sister, Nellie Pierce, who lived at 213 Garden Street with her husband of twenty years, William, a cashier for the Hartford Steam Boiler Insurance Company downtown. William had sent word to Franklin that there was a job opening for him at Hartford Steam if he wanted it.

Franklin liked that idea. Work was good for the soul. Kept you young and active.

So he packed and headed to Hartford in search of a new life.

Chapter 10

THE BIGGEST BOARDINGHOUSE
IN NEW ENGLAND

THE FEDERAL EXPRESS WAS RUNNING AN HOUR behind schedule. A finely built machine, she was plugging along at about sixty miles per hour on Tuesday afternoon, July 11, trying to make up time cruising swiftly through Fairfield, Milford, and other southern Connecticut coastal communities. Suddenly, something went terribly wrong. Three weeks prior, just beyond the depot in Bridgeport, a new track crossover had been installed. Most trains running behind schedule took the crossover route, hoping to make up valuable lost time along the Hartford, Springfield, New York City line.

As the engineer, who had never driven the southern Connecticut route before, took a corner much too fast in Bridgeport, he did not see the cautionary signals warning him of the dangerous turn and twenty-foot embankment on the left that seemed to swallow up the land mass in front of him.

"The engineer was told to slow to 15 miles [per hour]," a train representative later said. But he didn't.

It was near 3:00 p.m. when, a few miles away from this treacherous corner, a Fairfield police officer, patrolling his normal beat on Fairfield Avenue, heard a tremendous crash. Steel against steel. Crumbling and twisting.

He ran.

Coming up on the crash site a few moments later, the police officer heard screams of agony. He stopped and looked over the small hill in front of him to see the electrical wires near the train tracks sparking, smoke billowing from the wreckage below—and several Pullman train cars demolished into a mere pile of scrap metal.

Men, women, and children, the cop could hear, were moaning for help, many of them trapped inside a burning section of the wreckage, unable to get out. The officer ran for the nearest firebox, pulled the handle, and then did the same on the police box next to it.

Six Pullman cars were "hurled down the embankment" at great speed. Some of the passengers, corralled in the last three cars (which did not leave the tracks), included the St. Louis Cardinals National League Baseball team, many of whom darted from their quarters without a second thought and ran down the hill to help.

The engineer, who likely could have explained what happened, was killed, along with eleven others. By the end of the day, forty-four were reported as injured. It was the worst train accident in the history of that Federal Express route.

Still, even with the wreckage, the disagreement over who was at fault, and all the dead, the Federal Express accident wasn't the top story consuming New Englanders. It was the damn heat—it just wouldn't let up. Ten days into the heat wave and temperatures were still climbing. Some wondered if it would *ever* end. Weather Bureau predictions, with their continued promise of relief, had turned into a joke.

It had become a daily ritual for many to wake up and look at the front page of the newspaper to see how many more had died from the heat the previous day. Men fell dead while digging holes, financially unable to stop work on the farm even though the heat was excessive. There were reports of women picking blueberries one minute and then lying on the ground and struggling to breathe the next. One man riding through Hartford had fainted, only to fall off his wagon and be trampled to death by the team of horses that pulled it. Another woman was sitting in bed talking to friends when she fell back and died of heat stroke. The numbers were alarming. From Washington, D.C., to Maine, no fewer than 1,000 lives had been lost in some capacity due to heat-related illness. There were more deaths, certainly, that went unreported. Every morning, the newspapers listed the dead, their ages, their occupations, and, in many cases, where they were when they perished. So a fatal train accident was not so much news as it was a diversion from a disaster of major proportions that had been carrying on for nearly two weeks already—and was still getting worse.

In typical political fashion, Washington public officials released a statement which, in all of its insincerity and shallowness, did its best to downplay how much the rest of the country was suffering—by trying, incidentally, to shoulder the brunt of the disaster.

WASHINGTON HAS HEAT MONOPOLY, one headline proclaimed. The article went on to explain that while the entire country was supposedly enjoying "relief from the hot wave," Washington was still on fire. This was simply not true, as the East Coast, from Maine to Georgia, had reported no dip in the mercury. In most states, temperatures had gone up.

Another problem became the great demand for the electric fan, which manufacturers could not keep up with. This, as the city of Hartford reported forty-six more deaths on July 7.

In certain cities the price of ice ranged from $3 to $10 a ton, as demand became impossible to meet. In Buffalo, for example, one of the coldest cities in the East at any other time of the year, there had been an additional 40,000 tons of ice produced since the start of the heat wave. But it still wasn't enough. Refrigerator cars had all but given up trying to keep products cool. It was impossible. If necessary, officials said, ice would be sold only to families. Those companies that depended on ice for their daily needs would have to shut down until the heat wave ended.

"We are way short," said the owner of the Webster Citizens Ice Company in Buffalo. "With manufactured ice we may pull through if there is only a letup in the weather."

In what can only be described as a scene of apocalyptic proportions, trees began to shed their leaves as if it was the end of autumn—this because of so little rain and such extreme heat. Grass turned a hay-like brown and pulverized into dust. Crops, millions of acres of corn and flax and wheat and beans and everything in between, wilted and died, rotting on the ground. Tobacco, the chief product for families in Connecticut and Massachusetts along the Connecticut River Valley, not to mention New England's top crop, had all but disappeared. With the exception of those farms directly on the banks of the Connecticut River, where water could be diverted into channels, the tobacco crop of 1911 would be the worst in recorded history.

Then milk cows stopped producing.

On Monday, July 10, in Hartford and Windsor, more records were broken. The official temp in the city at two o'clock that afternoon came in at a scorching 100.5 degrees. However, "Showers are on the way," claimed one prediction by the Weather Bureau, apparently undeterred by the criticisms of the past week, "and there is promise of cooler temperatures [soon]."

Weather Bureau forecasters did not back down. A thunderstorm was predicted to move into the region and cool things off any day. One weatherman, stationed in Hartford, explained how rare an event the recent heat wave was, noting that the "country will witness another Halley's Comet before it again experiences as hot and dry a summer as this."

Boston reported temps in the mid-80s—in the middle of the night. Boston Common was given the strange name of the "Biggest Boardinghouse in New England." A reported 3,000 people had converged on the Common and set up dwellings to ride out the heat wave. While most people were cordial and pleasant, criminals once again saw this as an opportunity to exploit the situation. Many went to sleep and woke to find all of their personal items gone. In one case, "a man's shoes and socks [were] stolen off his feet as he [slept]."

Inside Boston Common the temperature hit 100 for the fourth time that week. Part of the problem was that as the land dried, the asphalt and concrete became absorbent and spongelike, soaking up the sun's rays and heat. In turn, the earth turned into a radiator, essentially banking the sun's heat during the day and redistributing it at night. In certain sections of the city, the night brought little or no relief—which, experts knew, could mean only one thing.

More deaths.

▲ ▲ ▲

For an aging Franklin Andrews, leaving the confines of his friend Howard Francis's house and heading into Hartford gave him a sense of not having a permanent place to hang his hat. Franklin felt as if he was living the life of a gypsy. He'd find a place to settle for a time, then move on when he felt maybe he wasn't wanted anymore. After seeing those ads in the newspaper for the Archer Home, Franklin had been seriously considering calling on Amy. He had the money. What was stopping him?

Upon arriving in Hartford, Franklin's sister Nellie Pierce convinced him that her home was as good a place as any to stay—at least for a while. He didn't need to run off anytime soon. Nellie was concerned about her brother. She wanted what was best for him.

As Franklin settled into Nellie's, he learned there was no work available for him at Hartford Steam Boiler after all. Just as well, Franklin confided to Nellie. It was great simply to be around kin again. In one respect, family was important to Franklin. Yet, in another, he did not want to burden anyone with his lameness or housing issues. It's clear that nothing made Franklin Andrews happier than to connect with relatives and friends. Here he is writing to his former neighbors, whom he lovingly referred to as his grandparents:

> *Dear Gramps and Gramma,*
> *Your letter came this morning. I was supposed to hear the news*
> *that you had a granddaughter but it's nothing strange . . .*
> *sorry to hear about [a neighbor who died] and glad to hear*
> *you are both better. . . . How is that little granddaughter*
> *getting along? . . . [H]ave not heard from Robert [the child's*
> *father] in a long time but hope thay are . . . getting along all*
> *right, and have thay found a name for her yet? . . .*

Quiet and unassuming, Franklin Andrews was a man "who had very little to say," his cousin Samuel Hall once commented. Yet Franklin was one of those turn-of-the-century men who took great pride in looking his best wherever he went. "His appearance was good as far as anything," Hall added. "I . . . never [heard him] complain of ill health." In addition, he was a man of habit. Rarely did Franklin leave his house without donning his favorite two-piece dress suit, white ruffled shirt, and black vest. His scraggly black mustache was combed down, covering the sides of his mouth.

Since moving to Hartford, Franklin had told many of his friends and family that he had never felt better. It was something about being around the city and visiting with everyone that made him feel alive again. Seeing all of his nieces and nephews. Attending family functions.

The truth was, however, Franklin's rheumatism was beginning to bother him. Maybe the excessive heat had taken a toll on Franklin's aging body? That July, Franklin started to feel sluggish and lethargic. Most around him thought it was his lameness—arthritis that had taken over his joints. Instead, it was rheumatism, a condition often wrongly associated with arthritis, and something that affected Franklin's entire body. He had lived with the condition for decades, and knew which treatments worked best.

Near this time, in fact, Franklin decided that he needed to go back into the hospital to get a handle on this recurring bout of rheumatism. After a brief stay with Nellie, he checked himself into Meriden Hospital, taking the train once again back toward his former hometown. This hospital stay would set Franklin Andrews on the path toward a growing desire to allay the burden he felt he was placing on his family.

▲ ▲ ▲

At the Archer Home Amy was in dire need of a man around the house. Those routine chores James had taken care of were beginning to pile up. Normal, everyday things, like painting, weeding, minor fence and home repairs, general cleaning. Amy couldn't do it all herself. To top it off, she now had a severe bedbug problem, which was not routine, she later said. So she sent one of her inmates down to W. H. Mason's Drugstore to purchase some arsenic.

"From time to time," a report later filed by Amy's attorneys stated, "bedbugs got into rooms in the Archer Home and caused trouble and annoyance . . . [Amy] at times used arsenic to get rid of bedbugs and other small vermin in the house."

Indeed, bedbugs were a common problem during the early twentieth century inside institutions, whether public or private, and arsenic was a surefire way to kill the pesky vermin, along with all sorts of other problematic insects. Moreover, Amy's attorney added, "the Archer Home and, in particular, the barn and yard were infested with rats, and arsenic was used to rid the place of these rats and was stuffed into rat-holes in the barn and yard for that purpose."

By this point talk around town had shifted. As Carl Goslee worked his end of the investigation, the *Hartford Courant* had now become fundamentally involved on many different levels. Townsfolk started to wonder what to do about Amy and her home. It had become a burden to have her in town. Windsor didn't need this kind of trouble, or notoriety. Whether or not Amy was guilty, well—that was beside the point; she was causing friction. And no one wanted a nuisance to contend with.

At W. H. Mason's, Carl Goslee uncovered another series of arsenic purchases by Amy that coincided with several death notices he had written. The purchases were not made on the day of the deaths; even more curious, they were made a few days—or *the* day—before.

Amy insisted the poison was for her rat and bedbug problem.

"Look," her attorney recalled, "the arsenic bought for use at the Archer Home was obtained openly and without concealment." Indeed, it was. Amy wasn't trying to hide the fact that she was buying arsenic. Yet when Carl realized that many of the dead were embalmed almost immediately after death—per Amy's request— and taken to the cemetery for burial, the circumstances seemed too coincidental. There was a pattern. An evil portrait was slowly coming into focus. Here was a woman, Carl believed, who was possibly trying to cover up murder.

Still, Clifton Sherman encouraged the reporter to keep looking. Circumstantial evidence wasn't enough. The answer was out there. There was a witness somewhere: a former inmate, a relative. a scorned friend or lover. Find someone willing to talk on record about what was going on inside that house, and then you'd have a story.

Chapter 11

COLD STORAGE

THEY STOOD OVER ONE HUNDRED STRONG. Men and women, depleted and emaciated, banding together in unity and defense of their sick and dying children. The heat wave was now in its twelfth day, and the temperature had not dipped. Ice was being sold at a premium—if you could find it. The reservoirs in New York and Connecticut were now so shallow that New York's water commissioner had issued a proclamation that the future of clean drinking water had turned "very precarious," and was at an extreme risk of being wiped out. In a press release, the commissioner warned, "During the past week the reservoirs were lowered by the enormous amount of two billion gallons. Unless heavy rains come in the near future, it will be absolutely necessary for us to take the most radical measures conserving the supply."

Imagine: two *billion* gallons.

No one could believe what was happening. Water rationing was mandated. Fines for excessive water use were issued. A state directive on how much water each family would be allowed to use per day was in the works.

The men and women converging on the East Side of New York that morning in defense of their children were not necessarily upset about the water—at least, not in its liquid state. They were there to protest the price and availability of ice. While water was one major problem, ice was just as troublesome. Without ice, the food supply would be stressed. The price of ice in the city had gone up almost 300 percent since the start of the heat wave.

The crowd had gathered outside the Knickerbocker Ice Company, which had sent out word that it was now refusing to sell any ice to retail outlets, where the average man would normally acquire the small amount of ice he needed for the daily upkeep of his family rations. For infants, this decision would mean a sure death sentence if the heat continued.

A few angry bystanders in the crowd approached a *New York Times* reporter on hand to cover the event and explained that many of the people there had children at home who were dying for lack of fresh milk, food, and water, and it was ice that tied the three together. The crowd began to chant, "Ice, ice, give us ice" as company personnel flocked to the doors and windows, staring out at the people, wondering what to do.

"Smash the windows," a protester yelled.

Managers from Knickerbocker tossed buckets of water at the crowd from the second-story windows, hoping to quell the riot.

Finally, a manager met with several leaders of the group. It was explained that the crowd would not leave without a promise of ice being made affordable and, at the very least, available, to *everyone*—not just a chosen, select few.

Tickets, said the company manager. He would distribute tickets, which could then be exchanged for fresh ice at the company's pier. First come, first serve, however. When the tickets were gone, so was the ice.

Three cheers rang out. It was a small victory, but a victory nonetheless.

As the day went on, the heat index rose yet again. In some regions the temperature on the ground was up to 110 degrees. In fact, it had been so hot for so long in Canada, as it was in many parts of the Northeast, that the ground turned into a tinderbox, finally igniting in Ontario on July 11, killing close to 200 people, with dozens more drowning in nearby lakes as the fires drove them back into the water, their only hope to swim for safety.

▲ ▲ ▲

Heat as a ferocious killer was much more of a reality for Americans in the first half of the twentieth century than it is today. Air-conditioning wouldn't become truly affordable until the 1950s. The heat wave of 1911—along with a similar event ten years prior—would serve as precedents for a series of heat-related, catastrophic events, killing nearly 50,000 Americans before the introduction of air-conditioning. Some estimates claim there were over 65,000 heat-related deaths in the United States alone during the twentieth century, many of which were attributed to the early part of the century.

A single wave of heat could not last forever; there had to be an end to it at some point. A heat wave is considered a prolonged period of temperatures 90 degrees and over, with high amounts of humidity, for three or more days in a row. As New Englanders entered the evening of the twelfth day of July 1911, there was nary a soul alive who would debate the fact that this particular heat wave was the most persistent and unrelenting anyone alive at the time had ever experienced. Yet, out of Washington, the Weather Bureau was perhaps just as persistent in spewing its rhetoric, doing its best to downplay a rather shoddy forecasting of the event.

Earlier that day, Weather Bureau chief Willis L. Moore issued a statement to reporters, personally speaking out and promising an end to the "hot wave," adding that it was important to give his professional opinion and assessment of why the heat had lasted as long as it did. He wanted Americans to understand why this particular event had been so difficult in predicting.

"For a prolonged period the barometric pressure has been above normal over the Atlantic Ocean and low over the northwestern portion of the American Continent," Moore told the *New York Times*. It sounded as if Moore was making excuses, trying to say that the Weather Bureau could not control the weather anymore than a pagan Greek god.

Despite Moore's explanation, Americans were upset because the Weather Bureau had blown so many forecasts over the past week. Many insisted that bureau officials would have been better off if they had simply kept their mouths shut. Still, Moore wanted to assure the nation that regardless of what his forecasters had said previously, the heat was going to be leaving the region anytime now.

He had proof, he insisted.

"The international weather map," Moore explained, "of Wednesday"—July 12, 1911—"showed a reversal in this pressure distribution—an extensive area of high barometric pressure appearing over Alaska, while the pressure over the middle latitudes of the Atlantic Ocean has fallen to below normal."

What did all this "science" actually mean in terms of relief?

Moore described a change in the barometric pressure that was "indicative of the dissipation of the warm weather over the Eastern States and Middle West in the immediate future . . ."

A cold front, in other words, was moving into the regions most affected by the heat. It was finally coming to an end.

Moore didn't know exactly when, he said, but certainly within twenty-four hours, a rather violent and dramatic storm was going to arrive. Batten down the hatches, he said; keep the kids away from the windows, make sure the sandbags were placed in those areas where flooding generally occurred—because the coming together of these two charged fronts was going to give birth to one hell of a super thunderstorm.

Senate members were a bit standoffish and quiet after Moore gave his little supposition. It was hard to trust the head of a group of scientists who had been so wrong in the recent past. Inside Senate chambers, the official temperature machine kept inside a glass case in back of the Senate hall had disappeared. In its place was a note. Someone had handwritten the words on paper and pasted it to the empty spot where the machine had been:

> *The temperature has gone so high that the self-recording thermometer refuses to register and the machine has been put into cold storage for a few days to reduce its temperature and regain its normal condition.*

After Moore's rather sketchy speech, many wondered if the Weather Bureau was just blowing smoke again, trying to cover up its incompetence.

In Hartford, near 8:00 p.m., the temperature was still hovering in the high 80s, with humidity levels creeping up toward the 90s, making breathing conditions "unbearable," one report claimed.

As bad as that seemed, though, this was a good sign. Because as the humidity climbed upwards, this meant more moisture was in the air—and moisture, in the form of rain, meant relief.

Then, just fifteen minutes later, at 8:15 p.m., with the parks in Hartford still packed with people, the streets so crowded you'd think a parade had just ended, a group turned and saw the sky light up in the distance. Several quick flashes, like strobes, flickered on and off.

A cheer rang out.

Then another series of flashes, as bolts of lightning miles away could now be seen by the crowds.

And yet, with such a wondrous "electrical storm" taking place in front of everyone, where was the rain? Heat lightning had been appearing all week. Where were the rainstorm and cool temperatures Washington had promised? Had everyone gotten their hopes up for nothing?

Chapter 12

RED SKIES AT NIGHT

THE SKY WAS PINK, LIKE A TONGUE. LIGHTNING continued for over an hour outside downtown Hartford as thousands of hot and sweating state residents watched in anticipation of rain.

Where in the hell was it? The waiting went on . . . and on . . .

The lightning continued for another hour. Then the sky darkened, and for sixty minutes straight the rains unleashed, buckets of water pouring down on throngs of people as if they were being baptized. If there had been music, many surely would have danced in the streets. Still, far too many people had died. A celebration seemed bittersweet.

Instead, the rain was a quasi-sign of renewal. An indication that a normal way of life was returning—a life which had been in a holding pattern for nearly two weeks.

"The storm," the *Courant* reported, "began [at 8:15] after hope was almost dead, people believing that the gathering clouds and distant artillery meant nothing more than disappointment and that Hartford would be surrounded by a rain belt without getting any benefit."

For fifteen minutes it rained so hard in downtown Hartford and Windsor that people sought shelter under awnings and overhangs. The street gutters ran about four feet wide because the rain had fallen so hard and so quick. "Trolley cars were practically deserted," said one report. "The thunder peeled and ripped throughout the whole storm and the lightning flashes and bolts were brilliant."

When the rains finally stopped and the stars and the moon shone brilliantly in the night sky, the saturated sidewalks dried as quickly as they had been drenched, cement and asphalt still soaked with so much heat that the water didn't have a chance. The streets turned into mud baths. Electrical wires for the trolleys hung in certain sections and sparked, while telephone lines swung wild like the tails of cats—all from the damaging winds and lightning that had accompanied the rain.

In other parts of the state, hail had fallen. In Windsor and Suffield, some of the tobacco fields still surviving because of their proximity to the Connecticut River were destroyed by large ice pellets falling from the sky like musket balls.

And yet, as residents looked out their windows and emerged from their hot houses as the storm passed, no one seemed to care. The heat had been broken. Temperatures were back to normal. The *Courant* probably put it best a day later in a little article stuffed on the bottom of the front page:

> *Although there was no danger of a frost anytime yesterday, the temperature was nearer the kind that a civilized community has a right to expect, the mercury, while reaching the near uncomfortable mark, being thwarted in its attempts to make people miserable by a cool breeze....*

The day had started out at 75 degrees and, at its peak, had reached 95 by noon, but as the storm approached, the mercury began a slow decline, from 88 degrees at 1:00 p.m., to 82 by 7:00 p.m. By the time the front arrived, it was 78 degrees, without, of course, that wet-shirt humidity. Federal reports claimed that 919 people had died in New England and New York alone, broken down into 654 in Massachusetts, and 265 in the other states (New Hampshire, Vermont, Rhode Island, Connecticut, Maine, and New York). This estimate was, at best, irresponsible, and at worst, a gross misunderstanding of what constitutes a "heat-related death." Drownings, for example, could account for well over 200 more deaths in the Northeast. Add to that the amount of unreported or undiagnosed deaths related to the heat, and the numbers are likely staggering. *Yankee* magazine, in a 1997 article titled "The Worst Weather Disaster in New England History," was probably more accurate with its estimate of 2,000 heat-related deaths.

The bottom line is that heat kills more people than any other natural disaster, and yet heat waves go unnamed. They do not blow in with 100-mile-per-hour winds, a blistering, swirling shadowlike image on radar with a defined eye, or shake the ground in an intense display of drama. No. Heat is a *silent* killer. It slowly and stealthily moves into a region like a ghost, targeting the vulnerable and unsuspecting. Yet as the heat wave left the region, another killer emerged—one who had been hiding, riding out the heat best she could, using the time to plan her next move.

Chapter 13

THE BEGINNING OF FRANKLIN'S END

FRANKLIN ANDREWS STAYED THREE WEEKS in Meriden Hospital and then moved back to Hartford to once again board with his sister, Nellie Pierce, after she insisted. However, arriving in the late summer of 1911, Franklin knew that his stay would not be long. It was time that he started to fend for himself. He needed to move on and have a go at life alone.

In January 1912 Franklin boarded the train in Hartford and made the long trip to New Haven to see his brother. While there, Franklin became ill. His rheumatism, according to Nellie Pierce, "was . . . worse, and he went to Grace Hospital . . ." Franklin spent an additional three weeks at Grace while doctors tended to his "arms and his shoulders," Nellie later explained. His general health, however, was "very good."

After recuperating, Franklin took the train from New Haven to Meriden to stay with yet another sister and brother-in-law. By now it was clear that he did not want to be a bother any longer. As a fifty-nine-year-old man, Franklin couldn't stand having to depend on family.

"Well," Nellie Pierce said, "he wanted to be independent and have a home for the rest of his life."

Traveling all over the state was not good for Franklin's health. He needed to settle down. He reached out to Nellie and asked her to inquire about the Archer Home on his behalf. Franklin told his sister that he had a bank account with plenty of funds saved for this eventuality.

It was September 1912 when Nellie took the trolley into Windsor from Hartford, stepped off the train, and made the two-minute walk to the Archer Home. She had placed a call to Amy a few days prior, alerting the matron to her brother's needs. Nellie explained that Franklin had cash (which would have certainly piqued Amy's interest).

"[Under] what conditions will you take my brother?" Nellie asked Amy after they greeted each other.

"One thousand dollars for his lifetime, or seven dollars per week."

Nellie was not surprised, as this was the going rate. She looked around the house and noticed that the interior was a bit dumpy and run-down. When asked, Amy explained that her husband had died unexpectedly a few years back, and with his death she had lost her handyman.

The talk shifted to what would happen if Franklin was displeased or unhappy with the way in which he was treated; would he get his money back?

Amy thought about it. "If at any time he is dissatisfied here," she said, "I will charge him the rate of seven dollars per week and pay him that balance, and he can leave when he chooses to."

Nellie asked who ran the place.

"It is an institution incorporated among the members of my family."

Nellie was pleased with the answers Amy provided. It wasn't the Four Seasons, but it was full of people Franklin's age, all of whom were in seemingly good health and spirits.

Nellie wanted to know how the agreement would be legally bound.

"I will give him a written contract to take him for one thousand dollars," Amy replied, "and in the event of his death, I [would] pay funeral charges, and in case he became dissatisfied at any time, I [would] charge him the rate of seven dollars a week and pay him the balance . . ."

It seemed to be a fair deal—not to mention exactly what Franklin was looking for: a way to break out on his own, fend for himself, and not be a burden on his friends and family any longer.

Nellie said she would report back to Amy in a few days. She wanted to discuss it with her brother first.

PART TWO

INVESTIGATION & INNOVATION

Chapter 14

THEY COME AND THEY GO

THE YEAR 1912 STARTED OUT ON A COLORFUL, childish note. Lifesaver candy hit the shelves, and the motorized movie camera replaced the tiring hand-crank model generally depicted in silent films of the day. Meanwhile, the Wright brothers were in and out of court, battling a patent infringement lawsuit they had brought against the Herring-Curtiss Company, when Wilbur died unexpectedly of typhoid fever.

Such interesting interludes of pop culture were usurped, however, by an international tragedy that ultimately set the tone for the remainder of the year.

The *Titanic* tragedy was such an overwhelming, loss-of-life story that both the American and British public were still consumed by it that fall. Months after the incident, the death toll and the stories of survival still dominated front-page headlines. So many people had died. So many had suffered. But many had also found a strength within themselves they had not known existed. In one instance, Chicagoan Constance Willard told the *Chicago Tribune* on April 21, 1912, six days after the terrible accident, how she had left the *Titanic* only twenty minutes before she sank: "When I reached the deck after the collision, the crew were getting the boats ready to lower, and many of the women were running about looking for their husbands and children. . . . [T]wo men took hold of me and . . . pushed me into a boat. . . ." Ironically, even Marconi's invention wasn't enough to save the masses.

As the *Titanic* story faded and the leaves changed color amid the cold weather moving into the Northeast that October, things at the Archer Home were fluid. Amy and her inmates had made it through the heat wave—only one death recorded during that time, which Amy later claimed she had nothing to do with. In one respect,

Amy had begun to feel the pressure of a town closing in around her; in another, she was managing to wade through the accusations and finger-pointing quite calmly, thwarting attempts to kick her out of town.

Regardless of the public image she projected, however, Amy Archer, the widow, was a far different person from Mrs. Archer, the wife. Now, she was viewed as unusual at best, suspicious at worst. With no man around the house to help with the chores, and trying to stave off the hits the business was taking because of rumors churning at every social event in town, Amy found herself in a terrible spot as time moved on. Her business was failing. She was forced to manage it alone, with only the help of her daughter, Mary. As inmates checked in and subsequently checked out—in body bags—Amy kept tabs on Carl Goslee's repeated inquiries. Carl was digging for that one nugget to convince *Courant* editor Clifton Sherman there was enough to run a disparaging story about Amy and her alleged "death house," and finish the woman for good. In just over four years since she'd opened, there had been twenty-nine deaths at the Home. That number was staggering.

For now, Amy was safe, what with most of Carl's reportage devoted to the *Titanic* story, and his day job as an insurance man keeping him busier than ever. As Amy struggled to keep the Home financially stable, she focused on rewriting current contracts and making sure that any new inmates she checked in had signed over their livelihoods, whether or not they were aware of it.

Back on April 15 (the day of the *Titanic* disaster), several months before Franklin Andrews had settled the minor discrepancies in his own contract with Amy and made preparations to move into the Home, Amy sat down with Margaret Reynolds, an aging and rather burdensome New Britain, Connecticut, resident, who desperately needed a place to live.

Reynolds was old and ill when Amy met with her family. It was decided the sooner the woman got a bed, the better off *everyone* would be.

If there was one fixed item in all of Amy's contracts that she flat-out refused to bargain with, it was that part of the inmate's estate would eventually go to Amy at some point. Each contract was geared toward Amy's best interests—and rife with incentives to make a potential inmate worth a hell of a lot more dead than alive. Most people would have clearly seen this as a motive for murder, but Amy was good at hiding it.

In Reynolds's contract, for instance (and every contract was different, depending on the oral agreements that Amy had made with each family), Amy called herself "the Matron of the Archer Home." This particular contract also included the name of Lewis Reynolds, Margaret's son, and read as follows:

> *Margaret Reynolds has been admitted into the Archer Home for the remainder of her natural life . . . She is said to pay Mrs. Archer the sum of $700 cash . . . and her pension granted her by being a soldier's widow now amounting to $12 per month, payable quarterly, and should the pension be increased, said additional pension must also be paid to Mrs. Archer. Mrs. Reynolds' watch and jewelry will be returned to her son or his wife at the death of Mrs. Margaret Reynolds. In consideration of the foregoing, Mrs. Margaret Reynolds is to receive kind care and all the requirements of a respectable home, nursing during sickness, and have all bills paid by the home or by Mrs. Archer from this date; also her funeral expenses . . .*

In the "fine print" section of the contract, Amy placed the value of the Archer Home at $7,700, hoping to convince Margaret Reynolds that she was stepping into a respectable business establishment of great worth. In other contracts, Amy valued the business and home at far less, perhaps forgetting to cover up previous lies. One has to assume that the harder the sale, the more frosting Amy put on the cake. Same with the price of life care. In a contract she signed with an inmate months after the Reynolds deal, the price she charged for life care was $500. It appeared that each inmate had his or her own separate deal with Amy.

And yet, even amid swirling rumors and tiresome accusations that would not go away, there were still those in town who saw fit to stand behind Windsor's most popular (and some would say, most hated) business owner. "Poor soul!" said one supporter. "It breaks my heart every time one of her old folks dies. But you can't expect them to live forever."

♠ ♠ ♠

It was September 12, 1912, when Franklin Andrews walked into the Archer Home—this, after handing over $2,500 in cash to Amy. Franklin was tired and beaten down by having moved all over the state. An extended hospital stay for his recurring rheumatism problem and his sincere desire to avoid becoming a burden to his aging family members had helped him decide to enter Amy Archer's facility.

Franklin took to his caretaker almost immediately. Amy needed help, and Franklin was not an old man at fifty-nine, considering that the mean age around him inside the Home was somewhere around seventy-five. He wasn't frail and looking to sit in a rocking chair all day with a quilt over his legs; he was still a strong man, having worked on a farm and inside a shop most of his life. He could do things around the Archer Home, he explained to Amy.

So Amy put Franklin to work.

Throughout the winter of 1912 and into the spring of 1913, Franklin painted fences and rooms. Raked leaves. Fixed things around the property and inside the house. Ran errands for Amy. Many later said that they still saw Franklin Andrews, cane in hand and dragging that lame leg, taking his usual five- to six-mile daily walk, as he'd done all his life.

A year into his stay at the Archer Home, Franklin began to develop a bit of loneliness, so he put pen to paper. During the month of October, Franklin initiated what quickly turned into a voracious appetite for human connection on the outside. Franklin wrote to his cousins, brothers, sisters, old friends, and in-laws. On the one hand, the letters were short and to the point; on the other, they were sincere and, in some ways, an avenue for Franklin to wrestle with some of the serious issues that had been plaguing him ever since he'd moved into the Home.

On October 13, 1913, Franklin wrote to his cousin George Johnson, who was in his sixties. George lived in Cheshire, and he and Franklin had been close all their lives.

There were eighteen inmates at the Home as Franklin began writing. He had been there a little over a year by this point, and, as he described to George, seventeen had died during that short time. It was clear Franklin was concerned about the death rate. He had been carefully—if not sneakily—keeping an eye on his fellow inmates and their health. He encouraged George to pay him a visit. "If you ever get a chance, Come up this Way and see me. Would like to have you very much. I don't think of Much More to Write."

In early November, Franklin wrote to his brother, Wesley, who lived in Waterbury. After greetings and salutations, Franklin got right to his point: "There [have] been some deaths here lately. Have been 18 died . . . there [are] 15 here now, and she expects some more before long." In what would become one of Franklin's signature sayings, he added, "They come and go, one after another."

Further along in the same letter, after he talked about how "dull" (slow) the "shops" were in Windsor, Franklin mentioned how long it had been since he had seen the old farm in Meriden. "Most 5 years," he wrote. Then he talked about a fair he had attended in town recently. Like a young buck, Franklin said he had walked to the fair and watched a "fine horse trot," where "one horse went a half mile in 1.4 [minutes, and] one mile in 2.17."

In December Franklin Andrews wrote to his sister, Julia Bennett. Julia had taken Franklin in when he'd first left the family farm many years ago. When asked later why her brother had moved into the Archer Home, Julia said, "He was getting into his years and thought he would have a home for life."

Julia would later confirm an important fact of Franklin Andrews's life at this time: He was *not* under the constant care of a doctor. When Franklin Andrews felt his rheumatism act up, he checked himself into the hospital and got it treated. Here it was, a year after moving into Amy's home, and he had not suffered any recurrent bouts of rheumatism, or any health problems at all. Julia had visited Franklin that summer. "He looked happy and healthy," she said later. He did not complain once about his rheumatism, nor did it seem like he was having a tough time adapting to his new life inside Amy's world. Quite to the contrary; Franklin was "contented and well," Julia said.

Franklin said he had gone to visit their other sister and her husband in Hartford recently, and he'd even visited with several other old friends and relatives during the same trip.

"Got Home Tuesday night Safe and Sound."

He said he was hoping to go to New Haven and Waterbury to spend some time with other friends, but "Winter is coming on."

As the letter continued, Franklin spoke of how he was starting to question Amy's behavior and what he had witnessed inside the Home—but then he went on to say that he wasn't sure of himself. "Well, things don't seem quite the Same here as they did at first, but they may come on all Right. I hope so, for my Sake, and the Sake of the others." He failed to give specifics, only reiterating that the Home was not the place he'd once thought it was.

Near the end of the letter, Franklin encouraged Julia to tell her husband to visit when he could. "If [he] comes to Hartford tell him to come up and See me and Old Mike Gilligan," a man in town Franklin had met and befriended.

Despite the mixed feelings he had about living in the Archer Home and what was going on around him, Franklin Andrews toughed it out.

"Fun-loving Andrews," reporter Joseph McNamara wrote, "considered himself a youngster [at fifty-nine years of age] to the ancients who lumbered about the place." McNamara also wrote that Andrews had started to notice "that many of [the inmates) were dying off and were quickly replaced by others . . ."

It was such a strange set of circumstances that Franklin continually talked himself out of what appeared to be happening. It was downright chilling to even consider the idea that Amy could be murdering inmates.

Chapter 15

DEATH AT FIRST SIGHT

MARGARET EGAN AND PATRICK GILLIGAN WERE BORN in Galway, Ireland, migrating with their countrymen to Connecticut alongside an influx of Italians, Poles, Germans, and Lithuanians during the mid-1800s. Their son Michael Gilligan was born and raised in East Windsor. At a young age Michael relocated to nearby Windsor. When Michael Gilligan moved into the Archer Home during the summer of 1913, he was fifty-seven years old and in perfect health. As one friend later described him, "Why, he was a man, I should say, in the neighborhood of five foot ten, rather stout in build, probably weighed 180 or 190 pounds, somewhere around there."

From the moment Michael Gilligan met Amy Archer there was a pang of need, unspoken and salient, between the two of them. A divorced father of three sons and two daughters, Gilligan needed a place to live out the remaining years of his life. He had worked on farms his whole life and had even been a fireman in town, but had since retired. As luck would have it, Amy was in the market for a hired handyman—or, rather, someone to take care of things (including her own needs) around the house. Gilligan was a strapping, strong man, in far better health than the general aging and ailing clientele Amy catered to inside the Home. And so, no sooner had Gilligan showed up at the house to inquire about a room to live, did Amy Archer and Michael Gilligan realize how much they needed each other.

Within a few weeks of cutting the lawn, painting the house, and playing the role of general handyman, Michael Gilligan was involved in a romantic relationship with Amy. On November 25, 1913, Amy Archer became Mrs. Amy Archer-Gilligan. Michael Gilligan, twenty years her senior, was Amy's new husband of convenience.

Neighbors were happy for Amy and Michael. Maybe Michael was the answer to all of Amy's problems; perhaps she wasn't a killer after all. If Michael Gilligan had seen enough good inside of Amy to want to spend the rest of his life with her, how could she be evil?

"They were sweet as pudding and twice as soft," one woman who lived nearby later said of the two of them. She'd watch Amy and Michael as they sat on the veranda together or walk the grounds, hand in hand.

On their marriage license, Michael called himself a fifty-eight-year-old farmer. Amy listed her age as thirty-nine. They married just up the block from the Archer Home at St. Joseph's Church, Michael's parish. As an addendum to the license, Michael listed his assets, which Amy had found out about only days before the idea of marriage ever came up in conversation between them. In outward appearances, Michael Gilligan might have come across as a rough type, a man of little means. He dressed like a farmer and was said to have made a beeline from the Archer Home to the hotel saloon just about every day. On paper, however, Michael was anything but a poor, destitute drunk, looking for a place to live. His total net worth was close to $5,000—incidentally, just enough money to get Amy out of the financial sinkhole she had found herself in since James's death. That nagging McClintock lawsuit was still shaking the fiscal foundation of the Home.

Around Windsor Michael was illustrious and well liked. One man called him a "genial, good, neighborly sort of man ... liked by everybody ... and popular."

"He was an agreeable man and always spoke, and seemed, exceedingly agreeable and always strong and well," said a friend, Dr. Charles Perkins, who lived two houses down from the Archer Home on the same side of the street. Perkins often waved Michael over for a chat whenever he saw Amy's new husband working in the yard or walking by.

"Full-blooded," one man called him.

But then there was that part of Michael that favored whiskey. The Windsor Hotel was a three-minute walk from the Archer Home and, according to some, as the bar became a daily stop for

Michael, his reputation and standing in the community began to falter.

"He dropped over to the Windsor Hotel, on and off," a local said, "made a daily call there . . . he took a drink . . . liked to drink."

▲ ▲ ▲

Amy paid close attention to how much money her inmates had stowed away in the bank. She even demanded to see bank records and assets before an inmate moved in. Where Franklin Andrews was concerned, Amy saw a lonely man who had been stumbling through life, drifting from relative to relative; now, he was secure in his new home, perhaps just biding his time, waiting to die. Here was a guy who had worked hard all his life, had no wife or kids, had saved his money, and was now enjoying his golden years alone, inside an old folks' home. What did he need all that money for? It wasn't doing anybody any good in a bank vault.

Franklin Andrews was, Amy Archer-Gilligan realized, the perfect mark.

Quite out of character, Amy sat down by a dim light in her bedroom on the night of January 6, 1914, while all of her inmates were sound asleep, and wrote Franklin Andrews a letter.

"I think you will be surprised to hear from me in this way," she began, "and it is with a heavy heart, I assure you."

If there was one attribute Amy had learned throughout her years of taking care of old people, it was a way to draw the attention away from herself and place it on the person she was trying to cajole. She was an expert manipulator. She could, with just a few terse words, make a person feel as though he or she owed her something.

Her letter continued: "Mr. Gilligan's bills I went to pay at once— and I am writing to ask you, as I consider you my dearest friend in need as you have proved so thus far, could you, or, rather, will you please let me take a few hundred dollars as near to a thousand as you can for a few months until I can get money I have loaned?"

Michael Gilligan's father had passed away, and apparently— although no record exists to prove as much—Amy was trying to convince Franklin that she and his new close friend, Michael Gilligan, were in a terrible financial jam because of the debts Michael's father had left behind.

"I have but little cash and our bills just now are very heavy, but as you know he left ten times [more than] what they [add up] to, only every one seems to want Cash and I don't want any trouble."

There was a certain panache of guilt-weaving throughout the letter. It was ladled on, of course, with the poise and prowess of a pro, but Amy had a way of making it seem so genuine.

> *I will pay you 6% in advance as you know it is safer than any Bank. I thought as a friend you would accommodate me. I would rather you would <u>please not</u> speak of this to <u>any one</u>. I appreciate your confidence or I would not ask you, as I have friends whom I know would lend it but I would rather not ask them. Please let me know if you could get it tomorrow morning. I could use it in the afternoon and I <u>assure you</u> on my honor you won't be sorry. I will give you my note so there can be no possible way for you to lose. [underlined text is Amy's]*

As the letter drew to a close, Amy added how pressing the loan request was on her part, but also, rather sneakily, how she wanted Franklin to answer.

"Please let me know by note tonight, and kindly say nothing about this to <u>any</u> one. I have $2,900 out on real estate besides our home, but I want the money to use tomorrow. If possible please let me know."

Unfortunately, there is no written record of Franklin Andrews's reaction to this letter. Yet there's little doubt that Franklin asked himself the same question many would pose in the coming months, as this letter became one of the focal points of Amy's criminal life: Why wouldn't Amy go to Michael Gilligan for the money, seeing that if what she claimed to be true was in fact so—that she needed the money to dig out of a hole *his* father had put them in? And why on earth would Amy hide this from her new husband, who was by now close friends with Franklin Andrews?

Chapter 16

THE LAST GOOD-BYE

WITH OR WITHOUT REALIZING IT, AMY ARCHER-GILLIGAN had revealed her cards to Franklin Andrews. She had taken a chance and reached out to the man for a loan—and why not? Franklin and Amy had known each other now for over a year. What would be the harm in asking her favorite inmate for a personal loan to get her (and the Archer Home) out of pecuniary ruin?

In doing this, however, Amy had exposed the fact that the Archer Home would be in dire straits, financially speaking, if beds weren't continually filled. With such long intervals between new inmate check-ins, Amy had seemingly designed a business to fail on its own merits—that is, of course, unless she stepped in and played God herself.

The day after he'd received that rather strange letter from Amy, Franklin Andrews met up with his sister, Julia Bennett. It wasn't a cheerful social call. Franklin's brother-in-law, William Pierce, had died. The man had been old, sick and frail. Nellie was a wreck. Franklin met the family on Garden Street in Hartford to attend the funeral.

Afterward, Julia encouraged Franklin to return to Meriden with the rest of the family, have a few good meals, and stay the night. In fact, she said, he could stay as long as he liked. And so he did. It was great to be around family and friends again.

"You look good," Julia said at one point during his stay.

"I feel better," Franklin answered.

"He looked better, too," Julia recalled later. "He had a good appetite."

What Julia meant was that living at the Archer Home had been just what the doctor ordered for Franklin Andrews. He was in tip-top spirits, considering the sorrowful nature of the visit, and he appeared stronger, healthier, more alive than ever. He had more energy. He smiled. Laughed.

Franklin stayed the night at Julia's and returned by trolley to the Archer Home the following morning.

A few days later, Franklin wrote to his cousin, George Johnson. It was January 19, 1914. Once again, he was in a great mood. It had been unseasonably warm over the past week, a strange treat for the middle of winter.

> *Dear George,*
> *Glad to Hear from You. Hope you are well. I am quite well.*
> *Are having some cold weather for a change. What the Ice*
> *Men will like! Let's hear from You again.*

Not even the temperature changes had impacted Franklin's temperamental rheumatism or his recurring joint pain; he hadn't spoken of any health problems for months.

The one thing that kept Franklin going while at the Home was the friendship he had developed with Michael Gilligan. They were inseparable, working on projects around the house, walking into town together. They played cards and visited at night, chatting like old war buddies.

As Franklin got to know Michael better, Amy's husband began to talk about his children, whom he adored. There were many stories, all of which put a smile on Michael's face. He had lost his first wife, but not his kids.

Since 1903, Michael's twenty-seven-year-old son Frank Gilligan had worked for the Henry Souther Engineering Company in Hartford as a metallurgical chemist. He was not married, and lived in Windsor. Before Michael married Amy, he had lived with Frank. Michael was probably closer to Frank than any of his other kids—not because he didn't care for the others or favored Frank, but because Frank was the oldest and lived nearby. After Michael moved in with Amy, Frank and his dad ran into each other quite often. Frank had Amy and Michael over for "Sunday dinner" during the holidays and other times of the year when he wasn't so busy traveling for work.

On February 13, Michael Gilligan was at the Windsor Hotel, having a few drinks and talking to the bartender, when Frank walked in.

"Hey, son," Michael said, turning to look at his boy.

"I'm going away for a few weeks," Frank said. It was a business trip. He knew where his dad would be and had sought him out to say they wouldn't be seeing each other for a while. He wanted to say good-bye before he left.

Frank needed to catch a trolley into Hartford so that he could board the train. He asked his dad to wait with him at the trolley depot outside the hotel. It was cold—that dry, frigid air only February can bring. They could see their breath like smoke in the air. Frank thought his dad looked great, saying later, "Why, he appeared to be in good health. He had fleshed up a bit." Amy was obviously feeding her man quite heartily.

"How are you feeling?" Frank asked his father as they waited for the trolley.

"Fine—fine, son," Michael answered.

With that, as the trolley squeaked into the station, Frank Gilligan said his good-byes to his dad and left town.

Michael Gilligan went home to Amy.

Chapter 17

DEATH BY MARRIAGE

NEAR THE TURN OF THE TWENTIETH CENTURY, the common household concoction of hot water, sugar, and fresh lemons—warm lemonade—was considered a remedy for a host of ailments, but mainly for colds and the flu. Going back seventy-five years earlier, doctors had prescribed lemonade as an antidote to a more serious illness called *purpura*, which is, according to the American Heritage *Stedman's Medical Dictionary*, "a condition characterized by hemorrhages in the skin and mucous membranes that result in the appearance of purplish spots or patches." It has also been referred to as *peliosis*. The *American Journal of Medical Sciences* even cited lemonade in an 1827 article as a treatment for *cutaneous ecchymosis*, a nasty skin condition, writing, "Three cases . . . accompanied by swelling of the legs from effusion of lymph, and other scorbutic symptoms, are noted as cured by the acid and tonic treatment—viz., by lemonade, elixir of vitriol, tincture of the chloride of iron, port wine, and abundant vegetable diet."

As the middle of February 1914 brought with it more bitterly cold weather and snow, word around Windsor was that Sister Amy, under terrible financial distress, had been mixing up batches of homemade lemonade in her kitchen—but not for the sake of curing ailing inmates of colds or the flu. No, indeed not. Instead, some of the more cognizant and curious in town were starting to speculate that Amy was spiking her lemonade with a (deadly) distilled form of arsenic acid.

Although he had no proof, Carl Goslee had to concur. The evidence all pointed to it.

During the second week of February 1914, W. H. Mason's registry of poisons recorded a purchase by Amy of ten ounces of arsenic, an enormous amount—which, when added to the additional amounts she had purchased recently, made an entire pound of the poison acquired since the beginning of the year, only six weeks prior.

What in God's name was the woman doing with so much poison—during winter, no less?

Years later, when Amy reflected on this period of her life in Windsor, she considered it nothing short of a witch hunt initiated against her by a group of women who were beginning to take Carl Goslee's fictions as fact.

"Some of the inmates of the Home told me from time to time that they were liable to be poisoned if they remained in the Home," Amy said. "And one of the old gentlemen, over 90 years of age and ailing, went so far as to intimate that a glass of lemonade served to him when he was suffering from a severe cold had been drugged. The physician in attendance on him at the time was requested to make an analysis of the drinking lemonade and did so by drinking it in the presence of the old gentleman, who suspected it was drugged; [and] the man still lives!"

▲ ▲ ▲

On February 15, 1914, Roscoe Nelson, the respected pastor of the Congregational Church in Windsor, and one of Michael Gilligan's closest friends, ran into Michael on the steps of the post office. Nelson had not seen Michael all that much since his marriage to Amy. When asked later how often they spoke after Michael's marriage, Pastor Nelson said, "I should say not so very frequently; I had no conversation with him. After his marriage I think I must have seen him, passed him upon the street, but I had no conversation with him until . . . [that day, February 15, 1914]."

Michael "appeared in good health," Nelson explained later. Their conversation stuck with Pastor Nelson, even years afterward. "Perhaps it might be interesting, I happen to recall the conversation because it was a little out of the usual." The main reason he felt this way, the pastor added, was because he and Michael had not talked in so long. On this day, they chitchatted about life in general and how things were going. Michael said he was doing great, and Pastor Nelson agreed that he looked good, too. It had been a blessing to see his old friend and to have the chance to speak with him.

Two days later, another friend of Michael's ran into him at the hardware store. Isaac Filkins had known Michael for two decades. "He looked good," Filkins reported. "I saw him going towards [the Archer Home] . . . between three and five o'clock . . . he appeared to be walking along the same as I would be . . ."

On the night of February 19, Amy called Michael downstairs and asked him to sign a document she had laid out on the kitchen table. Michael wondered what it could be.

He looked down at the heading on the page: LAST WILL AND TESTAMENT.

Huh?

They had been married three months; it was time to get their legal matters in order, Amy asserted.

But tonight? Now? Why the urgency?

Michael Gilligan did not look so well. He was white and pasty, and sweat was pouring off his brow. He had a fever. His hands shook. Did he need to sign the document at this very moment?

Yes. Amy encouraged him to get it over with.

Michael leaned over the table, and, "while suffering awful agony," one report later noted, signed the will, "leaving his whole estate to"—of course—"his wife."

The next morning, February 20, Dr. Charles Perkins bumped into Michael outside on the street, near the Archer home. Apparently, whatever "bug" Michael had been suffering from the previous night was gone.

"Why, he appeared to be normal," Perkins said, "as I had known him and seen him and observed him."

That night, Amy and Michael were sitting and talking in the kitchen. According to what she later said, Amy was getting breakfast ready for the following morning.

Once again, Michael didn't look so great. That paleness was back; in fact, he had a green tint to him. Headache. Dizziness. Confused.

The flu?

"Have a glass of whiskey," Amy suggested. Whiskey was one way to either bite the hair off the dog, or calm a brewing cold or virus. Amy prepared it for him.

Michael Gilligan took the glass of whiskey, saying, "I'm going upstairs to lie down."

While upstairs, Michael couldn't get comfortable. He tossed and turned in his bed. Covers on, covers off. Several inmates later reported that he started to moan and hold himself around the area of his stomach. After a time, Michael dragged himself from the bedroom to the bathroom, where he began to vomit profusely.

Amy was still downstairs. There is no record of her running to Michael's side to help him.

♠ ♠ ♠

Michael Gilligan's good friend Ralph Frost worked at the Windsor Hotel as manager, but also moonlighted as an undertaker for Smith and Son Undertakers. Michael and Ralph Frost had seen each other just about every day, as Michael was pretty much a regular at the hotel bar. Earlier that day, February 20, before Michael had become so ill, Ralph had seen his friend inside the hotel. Two days prior, Michael and Ralph had taken the trolley into Hartford together to run a few errands.

Near 2:00 a.m. on what was now Friday morning, February 21, 1914, Ralph was awakened from a dead sleep by the subtle buzz of the telephone rattling against the wall. It was odd that someone was calling in the middle of the night. Ralph didn't know of any emergencies in the business of undertaking. Dead people had a way of waiting.

"Yes, yes," Ralph answered, half asleep, he later said, "who's calling now?"

"It's Amy Gilligan, Ralph."

"Amy?"

"Come over to the house right way—it's Michael. He's very sick."

Ralph didn't even answer Amy. He left the phone receiver hanging, got dressed quickly, and ran to the house.

Moments later, Ralph burst into the kitchen where Amy was waiting for him.

"He's in bed," she said.

"Where?"

"Ground floor." (It appears that Amy had managed to get Michael from the upstairs bathroom to a downstairs bedroom. Why—or how—she did this was never determined. One can only assume that Mary, or several of the inmates, had helped her.)

The house was quiet and dark and cold. Ralph walked into the bedroom, located off the dining room, on the opposite side of the staircase that led to the second floor. As he walked through the "lounge," or parlor, he said later, he saw Mary Archer sitting there. Mary was sixteen at this time. She had a look about her, but she didn't say anything.

Ralph entered the room. Amy was behind him with her hands over her mouth in an *oh my goodness* gesture, Ralph later said, as Michael appeared to "lay in bed asleep." As Ralph stood and looked at his friend, he was confused and bewildered. Michael was "in and out of it," or "dozing," Ralph explained. He seemed to be extremely ill, groaning and mumbling and sweating.

Ralph grabbed his friend by the hand—Michael's eyes were closed at this time—and shook him, trying to startle him awake.

"Mike? Mike? Wake up!"

Michael Gilligan opened his eyes slowly.

"Hello, Mike . . . Do you know who is talking to you?"

Michael nodded a yes. ("He recognized me," Ralph recalled.)

But Michael Gilligan could not speak. He didn't have the energy, or, it seemed, the psychological wherewithal to put two words together.

"What seems to be the trouble with him?" Ralph turned and asked Amy.

"He was taken after supper," Amy answered unabashedly. "I think it was an acute attack of indigestion."

Indigestion? If that was true, it was some case all right.

What appeared odd to Ralph later, after he sat and thought about it, was that as he and Amy had stood there in the room and watched Michael Gilligan essentially die, Amy did not once call

Dr. Howard King or any other physician in town. Why hadn't she called someone who could help this suffering man? Why had she called Ralph first? Why not a man of medicine?

"Call a doctor, Amy," Ralph insisted angrily.

What was the woman waiting for?

Amy walked out of the room.

Finally, about a half hour after Ralph had arrived and begun helping his friend, Amy picked up the phone and called for medical help.

Chapter 18

SWEET LITTLE AMY

INTERVIEWED IN 1986, LIFELONG WINDSOR RESIDENT Jane Nearing spoke about a particular day when she visited the Archer Home as a child. Jane and her fellow choir members used to go to Amy's house and sing hymns to the inmates. She remembered Amy as an amiable woman. Quite likeable. Extremely nonthreatening.

"She was well respected and very highly thought of," Nearing said.

A nurse who later took care of Amy described the matron as "an almost saintly woman," one who *always* dressed in black, "always" carried a Bible in her hand, prayed incessantly on her knees, and obsessively read the Scriptures throughout the day. "She was a sweet, little old lady," Amy's caretaker added. "You'd look at her and you'd be amazed to think that she had ever hurt anyone."

Although she had a frequently changing (or evolving) public image in town, many still believed Amy was running what amounted to a slaughterhouse. The death rate inside the Archer Home became public knowledge as Carl Goslee used the numbers to convince those few supporters Amy had left that the deaths inside the Home were no common, probable occurrence. Come to find out, the ratio of dead to living in the Archer Home was six times higher than any other home in the state. For example, Amy had *ten* (living) inmates during the year 1911 measured against *two* deaths. A home in Hartford that same year housed 59 inmates against *thirteen* deaths. In 1912, Amy had *ten* inmates and an additional *fifteen* deaths.

More death than life that year.

The Hartford home studied for the same period came in with 67 inmates against *three* deaths. The following year was nearly the same for Amy: ten to thirteen.

In Hartford, 67 to *four*.

Carl Goslee finally got the attention of Clifton Sherman with these revealing numbers and convinced him to act. Sherman promised Carl he would put an additional reporter on the story and call the governor and state's attorney.

It was time to stop the madness. Something needed to be done.

And quickly.

▲ ▲ ▲

Ralph Frost was flummoxed during the early morning hours of February 21, 1914. His friend Michael Gilligan was dying in front of him, and Ralph could do nothing to help the poor man. Even worse, Amy was just now calling Dr. Howard King, days after her husband first started getting sick.

"Please, Doctor, he's very sick. You must step over to the house at once," Amy said.

"I'll be right there."

It was nearly three in the morning, King later recalled, when he hung up, got dressed, and rushed over to the Archer Home.

Amy returned to the bedroom after making the call and told Frost that Dr. King was on his way.

But Ralph Frost knew it was too late. As he and Amy stood at his bedside, Michael Gilligan, the fifty-eight-year-old otherwise healthy superintendent of the Archer Home, took one last breath and drifted toward eternity.

It was strange, Ralph Frost later clarified. It was almost as if Michael died the moment the doctor arrived. "The doctor didn't get there until he passed away. I think he had passed away when the doctor came in."

Twenty minutes had gone by between the time Ralph told Amy to call Dr. King and the time King arrived.

The doctor was surprised. "I'm shocked . . . why didn't you call me earlier?" he asked Amy as Ralph stood by and listened. "I should have seen him earlier."

Amy did not respond.

Dr. King used a stethoscope and listened to Michael's chest as he checked his pulse.

He was certainly dead.

At that moment, as King and Amy talked, Ralph Frost learned that King had, in fact, been at the Archer Home earlier that night. He had not only attended to Michael Gilligan, but had left specific instructions with Amy regarding how to treat him. On top of that, he had also given Michael some pills for indigestion (a mixture of cocaine and bismuth).

King had told Amy her husband was going to be just fine when he'd left after that earlier visit, but if he didn't improve, to be sure to call right away.

"I called Dr. King and he checked out Mr. Gilligan and said he was sick," Amy told Ralph when he asked about the earlier visit by King. Ralph even wondered why Amy hadn't called on Michael's priest. It was standard practice for a Catholic to have his priest anoint him as he lay sick in bed, and maybe, if he started to slip away, to give the man last rites. It was something Michael had talked about with Frost.

Amy claimed she had, adding, "He was away, so I called on a priest from Hartford." But he'd never shown up, either.

Dr. King later insisted that the indigestion pills were still sitting atop the dresser in Michael's room on a saucer plate when he arrived later that next morning. For some reason, Michael had never taken the medicine.

Franklin Andrews awoke at some point while the commotion was taking place in Michael Gilligan's room and asked what had happened.

Amy explained.

After King left and Michael's body had been removed from the Home by an undertaker, an astonished and saddened Franklin Andrews went up to his room, sat down, and wrote a postcard to his brother in New Haven, who also knew Michael Gilligan:

Dear Brother,
Hope you are Both well. I am quite well this winter. Mr.
Gilligan died this morning at 3:30 o'clock with indigestion

*very Sudden. Seems very Sad. He seemed to Be a very Good
Sort of a man. So They Go one after another. From Frank.*

As the moon reflected off the frost on the front lawn outside the
Archer Home later that same morning, Dr. Howard King made
out Michael Gilligan's Medical Certificate of Death. Prior to that
night, the doctor had not treated Michael for any ailments during
the three months he and Amy had been married. Michael had
rarely seen a doctor, simply because he was so fit. Yet, on his death
notice, Dr. King put "valvular heart disease" as the primary cause
of his death, with an additional note that he had an "acute bilious
attack"—gastritis, in other words. A stomachache. But the doctor
gave no indication as to where he had obtained this information.

According to the medical assessment, Dr. King—a physician
who had treated Michael Gilligan only occasionally before Michael
moved into the Archer Home—had *not* conducted an autopsy, nor
had he even consulted with a coroner. The healthy husband of Amy
Archer, who just happened to sign his last will and testament the
day before, giving his life's assets to Amy, had dropped dead of indigestion. And for some strange reason, Dr. King added that Michael
Gilligan, a patient he had never treated, had heart disease, too.

Later, when Dr. King's feet were put to the flame by state's
attorney Hugh Alcorn regarding his diagnosis and final assessment of Michael Gilligan's cause of death, the doctor admitted
that Michael was "in generally good health . . . was very active . . .
[and was] a hardworking man." More important, during the past
three months that Michael had been married to Amy, Dr. King—
who had treated him at various times throughout his life for stom-
achaches, and, as he described it later, "acute bilious attacks and
indigestion"—never knew the man to "be sick in bed while he was
at the Archer Home."

When King showed up earlier on that evening before Gilligan
died, after Amy had called around seven o'clock and summoned
him, he said Michael was sicker than he had ever seen him. "Why,
he was complaining of extreme nausea and pain, burning, and was
vomiting into this receptacle on the floor," King recalled.

Amy had Michael on the couch in the dining room on the

first floor. Most of the burning and pain was confined to "the pit of his stomach," King reported. But there was "some burning in the throat" also.

All symptoms consistent with arsenic poisoning.

King asked Amy how long Michael had been ill.

"A short time," she replied. Furthermore, he had no temperature and his pulse was "up."

Checking Michael over that evening, Dr. King made the prognosis that he "expected him to recover," despite how ill he seemed. The medication he left on the plate for Amy to administer was "nausea tablets," which were made of, King said, "Cerum oxalate, bismuth" and "1/12 grain cocaine." They would have helped Michael deal with the pain.

In addition, before leaving the house King gave Amy ten calomel tablets, which were supposed to settle his stomach and make him feel better, and instructed her to give one to Michael every hour until the pills were gone. Leaving, King explained to Amy, "If he doesn't get better, call me immediately."

Not difficult directions to follow.

♠ ♠ ♠

Word of Michael Gilligan's death shocked the small Windsor community. Save for a propensity for good whiskey, Michael was as healthy as a twenty-year-old man. He had done much of the heavy lifting for Amy around the Home. Shoveled the snow. Built things. Worked on the outside of the house. Many saw the guy walking through town the day before he died.

A few days after Michael's death, Franklin Andrews wrote to his brother, Jack. Franklin was still in shock, on top of now being distressed. He was full of uncertainty and sorrow, and didn't know what to do.

> *Jack,*
> *Mr. Gilligan died last Thursday morning with indigestion. He had not been married quite three months. Died very sudden. Was buried last Monday. Was taken to the Catholic*

Church. I went to the funeral. Was a large funeral. It seems very sad. He was a very nice kind of man.

And then Franklin made what would become an important point:

So they go one after another—that makes 21 that's died since I came here. Don't know who will be next. There [are] 18 here now and she expects more soon.

Full capacity at the Archer Home was twenty-one, and there were already eighteen in beds. Amy explained that "more" were getting ready to check in. How many more? And where, exactly, were they all going to fit, Franklin Andrews wondered.

Yet Franklin didn't completely distrust Amy. He felt at times as if he was being pulled in two different directions. In that same letter to Jack, he added, "Well, you must come up when you get a chance and see the place. Mrs. Archer Gilligan is certainly a splendid woman. She likes to have folks come see relatives."

⁂

Michael Gilligan's body was embalmed twice. "This was done," law enforcement speculated, "because the body required more than the usual amount of preservative"—an indication that Gilligan's body might have been brined in a preservation solution. Arsenic, given over a period of a few days, would certainly have done the trick.

One of the problems for Amy became her inability to keep track of the lies she had told. In speaking with a friend regarding Michael's death, Amy said, "[Michael] was a big, strong, healthy fellow up to the night he died . . . I went the same as usual and made a cup of tea and we had tea together and crackers, and after that he took these terrible cramps and groaning and he only lasted an hour . . . he died of double pneumonia."

This was in stark contrast to what Ralph Frost and Dr. King knew and witnessed. Amy had told them that Michael had become extremely ill after dinner and she had given him a glass of whiskey and sent him to bed.

Now it was tea and crackers? Pneumonia? Where had that come from?

Explaining his death to a friend, in hopes of perhaps trying to cast Michael in a negative light and take the focus off herself, Amy said, "My husband was practically no good to me. He never done anything, only just to work around the lawn and pick up the leaves and things like that. He was sick one morning. The morning before he died. I gave him a drink of whiskey and told him to go upstairs and lay down. He went up to the bathroom and it was a short time later that he died."

Amy was backing herself into a corner. She knew people were watching and talking, yet she continued to steadfastly deny any wrongdoing as she conducted business as usual at the Archer Home. She insisted that she was serving a specific clientele of aged and otherwise sick, elderly people. Of course there were going to be deaths! Of course men and women would die suddenly, without good cause. It was an old folks' home, for crying out loud. Death was an inherent part of the business.

Still, a bell had been rung with the death of a relatively young and healthy Michael Gilligan—and Amy needed to do something about it.

Succumbing to the pressure, Amy sat down and wrote a postcard to state's attorney Hugh Alcorn, encouraging him to stop at the Home anytime he wanted to observe for himself the type of business she ran. She feared a grand jury investigation was under way, and wanted to address several concerns. By striking first, Amy believed, she could beat law enforcement and the town at their own game. What murderer would be stupid enough to invite the state's attorney into her home?

♠ ♠ ♠

It was early March 1914. The air was still cold. That crack of spring had not yet opened. It had been so cold for so long that grave diggers could not break ground; Michael Gilligan's body was being preserved in the vault at St. Mary's Cemetery to be interred in the Gilligan family plot as soon as the ground was soft enough. Amy said she couldn't believe what was happening. She missed her husband and wanted people to stop making judgments about her.

On the front side of the postcard Amy had sent to Hugh Alcorn was an eerie black-and-white image of the Archer Home, which made it look haunted and dreary. The house looked contorted somehow—faded, run-down, and downright spooky. On the opposite side she had written:

> *Dear Mr. Alcorn,*
> *When you find the opportunity—When you go through here*
> *in your Auto, will you please call to see us? It is not necessary*
> *to let me know the time as I am rarely away.*
> *We have eleven (11) here between 80 and 102 years of*
> *age. Six are over 87 years. All have been here between three*
> *and six years.*

Hugh Alcorn was not interested in stopping by the Archer Home for a friendly chat and a tour. A walk around the house and a meet and greet with Amy's aging inmates would not explain anything away. There's no doubt she cleaned the place up and made sure the inmates had what they needed and were not crammed into rooms and made to fend for themselves. But as far as explaining the increasing amount of deaths in the Home, Hugh Alcorn was going to handle things his way.

♣ ♣ ♣

Franklin Andrews wasn't about to allow the death of his friend Michael Gilligan to dampen his spirits—although, in nearly every letter and postcard Franklin wrote after Michael's death, he felt the need to mention it. To his sister-in-law in Waterbury, for example, Franklin wrote a lengthy letter near the end of March, opening with the same story he had told everyone else, referring to how Michael had died so "sudden," before mentioning once again how many had died since he'd moved into the Home. It was as if Franklin was keeping track of the new arrivals and deaths. Perhaps he was waiting for someone else to point out the obvious, or maybe he was talking things through in his own way. Whatever the case, he never once made a direct accusation against Amy. Instead, quite shockingly, he continued to praise the woman, the town, and the Archer Home: "Windsor is a very Pleasant Town. Is 6 miles above Hartford."

He talked about several other deaths in the family, along with losing friends and neighbors. It seemed everywhere Franklin Andrews turned, someone was dying. But, as his postcard continued, at least he could take a bit of comfort in the fact that his health had improved:

> *Mr. Archer died 4 years ago in February. Mrs. Archer Gilligan as she calls her name has one daughter . . . A fine young lady. They are Catholics here But I don't mind! That everything Goes along All Right. It Goes by the Archer Home Just the Same. I hear from Mary [Franklin's sister in East Hartford] once in a while. Have been to see her once or Twice. . . . I came here September 12, 1912, [almost] a year and a half [ago]. Have improved a Good deal Since I came. Did not think I should ever Be any Better. When I first came I [thought I] may Stay as long as I live. I do some Errands for her [Amy] to the post office and the Stores, and I think Come Spring, I can do quite a few things around the Place.*

Days later, writing to his cousin George Johnson, Franklin responded to a letter in which George had talked about several more deaths in the family.

"I am quite well," Franklin said in response. "Sorry to hear of so many deaths. Someone all the time. I have got a splendid Home."

▲ ▲ ▲

Amy wasted little time in filing a petition with the Probate Court for the District of Windsor to have Michael Gilligan's estate divvied up. In early March of 1914, the court reported that Amy had put in a claim against the Gilligan estate for $1,500, alongside several other businesses looking to divide Michael Gilligan's $4,500 worth of assets. Judge D. Ellsworth Phelps appointed Amy the adminis-trator of "said estate."

So Amy had control over Michael Gilligan's property and assets—at least for the time being. Before she could touch any of the money, however, Amy would have to extend a grace period. She had to make the notice public so any potential creditors could come forward and make a claim.

But Amy was sinking. She needed cash quickly. Michael's death had not opened up a bed that she could fill with a new inmate (thereby providing additional funds). Her actions, no matter what she did, seemed only to cause the woman more problems and spread additional stories about how dangerous a place the Archer Home had become. Yet Amy never backed down.

"For a period [of time] . . . I was constantly informed that the authorities had examined . . . the conduct of the home," Amy com-mented later, referring to this crucial period in her life when the walls in the house began to close in on her, "but knowing that I had done no wrong and that there was nothing that I should fear as a result of the investigation, I continued to manage the home and solicited patronage."

Chapter 19

THE CON

MICHAEL GILLIGAN'S UNTIMELY DEATH removed any doubt Carl Goslee might have had that his former friend and neighbor was no more a God-fearing Christian than Lucifer himself. In studying Michael's death and the affairs of the Archer Home, Carl's growing suspicions were solidified: Amy had plenty of motive to kill.

And it was all about money.

After reporting to *Courant* editor Clifton Sherman that Michael Gilligan had suddenly dropped dead after reportedly being sighted by several people in town only hours before his death, Carl talked it over with Sherman and made a decision to collect all the evidence together and put it in a neat little package. If what Carl was reporting turned out to be true, Sherman would be compelled to now show the evidence to Hugh Alcorn and get some sort of official law enforcement investigation initiated, in tandem with what could be a major exclusive story for the *Hartford Courant*. Now Sherman could demand that his friend, Alcorn, get the police involved. Sherman encouraged Carl and other reporters working on the case to write stories. They could bank them, and then, when the time was right, Sherman said, they would publish.

"He was a close friend of Michael Gilligan . . . ," *Courant* reporter Bob Zaiman wrote in 1954, praising Carl Goslee's role in breaking the story, "and when Gilligan died suddenly under strange circumstances, Goslee knew something was definitely amiss."

It was 1953 when Carl sat down and spoke to Bob Zaiman about this important moment in the Amy Archer-Gilligan investigation, in which Carl had played such a pivotal role.

"Sherman had me check the vital statistics at Town Hall for a long time and bring him all the death certificates of the people who died at the Home," Carl told Zaiman. "Then he had me check the drugstores to learn when Mrs. Archer-Gilligan purchased the poison."

Carl had been snooping around in those records already. He knew Amy was purchasing more arsenic than a pest control company. And when those records were finally presented to Clifton Sherman, the editor in chief could not deny the obvious any longer. Sherman, however, did not want to run an incriminating story without the endorsement of law enforcement. He needed quotes and background from the State Police. He also didn't want to meddle with the investigation and destroy any chance of justice being served. After all, the evidence was still only circumstantial. Sherman wondered if he should take the information they had and bring it to other state officials, besides Alcorn.

"Why, yes, I've heard rumors about the Windsor Home for two years," Connecticut governor Marcus H. Holcomb told reporters, "but no newspaper, state official, or private citizen ever approached me on the matter."

As Carlan Goslee built a case against Amy, and Clifton Sherman piqued the interest of law enforcement, Amy was busy filling up open beds.

Charles Smith had met Amy in September 1912. Smith had lived in Waterbury, twenty miles west of Hartford, for the past forty years, making his living as foreman for the Scovil Manufacturing Company in town. The thirty-man crew underneath Smith had adored the old man. Smith stayed on the job right up until 1910, shortly after celebrating his eighty-fifth birthday.

Charles could have retired a much younger man, but with his health intact, he had kept on working. Only when his wife became extremely ill did Charles leave his job to care for her. If not for his wife's sudden illness "of the mind" (probably Alzheimer's or dementia), Emily Smith, Charles's sister, later explained, he probably would have died on the floor of that manufacturing company.

"He would have continued," said Emily, "so doing, but his wife, being very ill at home and her mind failing and her not desiring a housekeeper, he had to stay at home to take care of her for the next two years, until she died, when he was eighty-seven."

Upon her death, Charles Smith was "left without a home," Emily said, but gave no explanation as to why, leading one to believe that he probably couldn't afford to live in it by himself.

From Waterbury, Smith traveled to New York City in 1911 to stay with his son, a druggist. Smith had sold all of his "silverware, linen, household furnishings, etc.," Emily explained, "and expected to spend the remainder of his days there," in New York, with his son and daughter-in-law. But that daughter-in-law objected harshly to the old man living with them for an extended period of time. She demanded that he leave at once. Apparently, her health wasn't the best. She needed her space.

Leaving New York, Smith traveled back to Connecticut and moved in with his sisters, Mrs. Agnes E. Henderson and Emily, and his brother, James Smith, where he stayed for nearly a year.

Pushing ninety years old by the summer of 1912, Charles Smith was "remarkably rugged," Emily recalled, as he contemplated the idea of moving into the Archer Home to take any pressure off of family to care for him. His brother lived in East Hartford and had told him about the Home. By all accounts it seemed like a great idea. Furthermore, Charles "had a good appetite," Emily said, "slept well, and read the papers and could play cards and walk about; he enjoyed life." He would bring a bit of spunk to the old folks' home.

It was the middle of September 1912 when Charles Smith was in East Hartford visiting with his brother and sister-in-law. He spotted an article in the newspaper regarding the death of a local man. In connection with the article, there was a "piece," Emily explained, "recommending the [Archer] Home highly, and my brother James's wife . . . knowing that [Charles] was looking for a quiet boarding place, went to the Home and looked."

When Smith's sister-in-law returned to East Hartford later that day, she told Charles she approved of the place, encouraging him. "You should go look for yourself. It's a nice place."

So Smith and his sister-in-law took the trolley into Windsor that afternoon.

Amy was waiting. She smiled, welcoming all of them, and played her part as the happy and lovable matron—the consummate saleswoman. "Look at the wonderful brightness of this man," Amy said, looking Charles over, "especially a man of his years!"

She was taken by Charles's health of mind and body, Emily later said. Amy seemed to be intrigued by the idea that he was close to ninety years old, but had the resolve, energy, and sharpness of a man twenty years younger.

Charles looked around, shaking his head in agreement that the place was quite nice. Amy followed, commenting as they walked. "I would be glad to take you. You are so different from any of my other inmates. We could play cards together. Walk together."

Charles Smith liked what he heard.

"There's a ten-dollar room upstairs," Amy said, "but I'll let you have it for seven because you are such a bright man. You won't be any trouble."

"She thought he would [take] less care," Emily recounted, "comparatively, and he didn't wish to pay any more, and wouldn't have taken it if she had asked any more."

Charles Smith thought about Amy's offer.

"I will come in about a week and try the place for a month," he said. "If I like it here, I [will] send for my trunk and will stay indefinitely."

Seven dollars a week for room, food, and care. Who could argue with such an arrangement?

That November, after Charles had been in the Home for about a month already, Emily returned for a visit. She needed to bring Charles his money, some cash he had left behind at the house in East Hartford. She handed him a $100 bill.

"Now, shall I pay the forty-two dollars," she asked, "and take home a good part of the remainder?"

The $42 was for back room and board Charles owed Amy.

"Oh, now, Emily," Charles said rather contemptuously, "you leave it with me and I will pay my own way. I will settle the bill myself." Charles Smith was working on a century of life; he didn't appreciate being treated like a child.

Months passed and Emily visited Charles again during the spring of 1913. It seemed that Charles had found himself a nice little place to live out the remainder of his life. He wasn't complaining of anything in particular and enjoyed the company around him. He had even taken walks with Franklin Andrews and gotten to know several of the other inmates quite personally.

Over the previous Christmas holiday, when Charles had returned to East Hartford to be with family, he had picked up his bank book and brought it with him back to the Archer Home. If he needed money, Charles figured, he wanted to be able to go and get it himself.

"I heard of a life contract," Charles explained to his family after having dinner one night in East Hartford, "and want to engage in one for $1,000 with Amy myself." He said he was happy at the Home. Why waste money paying weekly when he could get such a good deal? It was obvious Amy had been working on him, talking him into signing a life contract.

As Charles headed back to the Home, Emily called Amy. She wanted to discuss this so-called life contract.

"Please wait before you engage in a life contract with my brother," Emily said. "I want to talk it over with my other siblings first. I am sure they will think it is not wise." After all, an eighty-six-year-old man could drop dead at any moment. What if Charles paid the $1,000 and died the next day? The family would get nothing.

Amy said, "Why, certainly. I can wait."

A few days later, Charles's brother and sister-in-law went up to talk to Amy about the life contract and explain to her in person that they had thought about it and talked it over, but decided it wasn't something they wanted Charles to engage in. Didn't matter what Charles said. They had always taken care of his business and would continue doing so.

Amy said it was too late. She and Charles had made (and signed) a contract. She had even made a trip with Charles to his Waterbury bank to withdraw the $1,000 in cash. What Amy failed to mention during this conversation with Charles's siblings was that Charles had withdrawn *all* of his money—every last cent—and handed it all over to Amy.

When Emily heard about the life contract and what she thought had been a $1,000 withdrawal, she made another visit to see Charles and speak with Amy. For one thing, she wanted to explain to Charles in person that she had taken some of his money (from the cash he had left behind in East Hartford) to purchase a stone monument for his wife. There was some change left—about sixty dollars. He could use it for pocket money.

Amy stood by and listened as they talked. Finally, she interrupted to say, "He doesn't need any spending money. He has a ten-dollar bill in his pocket at the present time."

Emily was astonished by this comment. "Where did he get it?" she asked. "I thought all his money [was] tied up in your contract?"

"There is no contract!"

"No contract? But you told my sister and her husband that there was . . . when they came up to see about it."

"I couldn't afford to do it for that," Amy said.

Emily was confused. What was the woman talking about? She asked Amy where all of Charles's money had gone if he hadn't signed a contract.

"I am keeping that money," Amy explained, "and I am paying board to myself, taking out board myself, $10 a week!" Not quite the deal they had made the previous year.

"Ten dollars?" Emily queried sternly. "But you took him for seven."

"Well," Amy said, "I found I couldn't afford to do it for that—he is becoming more of a care to me, and I am keeping track of all the expenses, doctor's bills. He has had over a $40 doctor's bill this winter—and he is spending more money."

The woman standing in front of Emily on this day was a far cry from the saintly creature that Charles, Emily, and the other family members had met when they'd looked at the Home a year prior. Amy was calling the shots now. She had the man's money and said she was keeping it. No two ways about it.

In total, Amy had withdrawn $2,300 of Charles Smith's money. He was broke. Completely busted. Emily was not only incensed at the woman for taking advantage of such a nice old man, but even angrier that Amy thought she could get away with such a thing.

Emily went back to East Hartford and discussed the situation with her family. Something had to be done.

In August, she returned to the Archer Home to check in on Charles and see how he was faring.

"Not bad," he said. Then, "As soon as it gets a little cooler, Mrs. Archer is going down to New York with a lady friend and she will fix things down there at the bank so that I can have a little money for spending when I want it."

Once again, this was an odd remark. What did Charles mean by it? Emily was taken aback. Was he saying Amy was in financial trouble and was heading to New York for a loan? And part of the money was going to be used to pay him back the money she had, quite frankly, stolen from him?

In fact, no. Amy was heading to the Immigrant Industrial Savings Bank in Manhattan to withdraw a stash of $1,042.48 that Charles had in *that* bank. It was the last of his life savings. His siblings had not known anything about this money.

Amy was cleaning the guy out.

When Amy's attorney, Benedict Holden, later spoke of this rather strange arrangement that Charles had made with Amy, he pointed out that Charles Smith was a grown man and free to make his own decisions.

"[He] was there in the Home apparently satisfied," Holden said. "He gave [Amy] money to keep for him. She was charging him ten dollars a week; he was drawing his spending money; he was paying such expenses as he incurred; and if [Charles Smith] didn't make any charge that she had any money belonging to him, certainly we must assume that the money was . . . given to [Amy] by [Charles] to keep for him, which sum was charged with his board and his upkeep and other expenses."

Emily Smith and Amy Archer-Gilligan butted heads over Charles Smith's money throughout the next six to seven months. In a way, Charles was stuck, Emily finally concurred. He couldn't leave the Home; all of his money was tied up in the place. And it was clear that Amy was in no financial position to pay him back.

Chapter 20

RED FALCON

FRANKLIN ANDREWS HAD ALL HIS SENSES FIRING as the spring of 1914 dawned. The letters he wrote to family and friends were longer, more detailed, and had a certain urgency about them. Franklin was still backing Amy, talking about how kind the "splendid woman" was to everyone in the Home. But his lavish praise of her made it seem as if he was trying to convince himself more than anybody else.

> *Dear Cousin,*
> *I am Getting along nicely for me. Am a Great deal Better Than when I first came. I have Got a nice Home and a fine Mistress, Mrs. Archer. The Mistress was married last November To a Mr. Gilligan and he died the 20 of February very sudden with Indigestion. It Seems Very Sad. He was a Nice kind of Man. Mr. Archer died 4 years ago. Mrs. Archer-Gilligan as she calls herself is certainly a Splendid Woman. . . . I get around and do quite a good many errands for her. To the Post Office and Store and meat market and I am Going To Try and help Some around The Place This Coming Summer if Nothing Happens. . . . Seems sad to hear of so many Deaths. Seems someone all the Time . . .*

Franklin went on to say that he had not been back "home" to Meriden or Cheshire for five years by this point, and truly missed the old farm, hanging out with old friends. It was clear by his missives that he was beginning to think about his own mortality.

Two weeks later, he wrote again to the same cousin.

*I am Getting along quite well now [but] have had a hard
cold, But am coming on all Right I Think. Are you having
a long spell of dull weather? Will Seem Good when Warm
Weather comes again.*

The ailment Franklin referred to was more than a common runny
nose and cough. His throat burned at times, but not every day. He
suffered dizzy spells and lethargy, but again, not for an extended
period of time. It was strange, he insinuated. The condition came
and went.

With the warmer weather of late April came outside work,
which Franklin welcomed. He picked up the slack Michael Gilligan's death had left behind. Soon he was raking rotted leaves and
amber pine needles from the previous fall, cleaning up the yard,
getting it ready for mowing. Amy told him that as soon as the grass
grew, it would be his job to keep it cut.

Franklin Andrews liked that. A job. Anything to keep him from
the tedium of sitting around an old age home waiting to die.

▲ ▲ ▲

Emily Smith received a call from Amy that same April that
Charles had taken ill. He was pretty much bedridden by now, Amy
explained.

How sick was he?

"He had failed very much," Emily recalled later. In fact, when
Emily next visited, Charles was "hardly able to speak." When she
arrived, to her shock and concern, Amy had made Emily wait
downstairs in the parlor, telling her, "We'll fetch him."

There was a maid with Amy on one of Charles's arms, Amy on
the other, both helping him walk down the stairs. Emily could not
believe this was the same man she had seen a few months prior.
For the first time in his life Charles Smith looked his age. Tired,
wrinkled, and pale. Slouched over. Sluggish. Drooling on himself.
Unable to put two words together that made any sense.

What the heck had happened to the man?

Emily sat in silence for twenty minutes with Charles, who could not speak or communicate in any way.

Amy said nothing.

▲ ▲ ▲

Franklin Andrews complained once again of a sore throat in a letter dated April 8 that he had written to his good friend, Elsie E. Royce. It was a nagging cold, he explained—one that wouldn't let go. A day later, Franklin wrote again, this time noting a bit of anxiety he was beginning to have.

> *I am quite well. An old Ladie died Sunday night. That makes 20 that's died Since I come here. There [are] 18 here now and she expects more Soon. I Guess things will go on all Right. They did not Seem quite the Same at First.*

Franklin grew deeply concerned that his sleep was all too frequently disturbed by somebody else being taken out of the Home in the middle of the night in a body bag—and it seemed that Amy had the person's bed filled even before the sheets turned cold.

The next night, Charles Smith began coughing and choking; he was unable to breathe properly, and by now was entirely unable to get out of bed by his own accord.

"Oh, he was far gone," Emily Smith said later.

On Friday morning, April 10, Emily took a call from her brother.

"Yes," she asked, "what is it?" There was a bit of melancholy apparent in his voice after a moment of silence.

"Mrs. Archer gave me word that Charles died suddenly last night."

"Of what?"

"She said it was 'shock.'" More commonly known today as stroke.

Dr. Howard King had already been to the Home to pronounce Smith dead and to fill out his death certificate.

Charles Smith, born in England, was dead at the age of eighty-nine, Dr. King wrongly reported (he was eighty-seven).

Primary Cause of Death: "Old Age."

Secondary or Contributory: "Epilepsy."

During the weeks leading up to his death, Hugh Alcorn later said, "Charles Smith . . . ate his meals at the table with the other inmates and his food was served to him in the same manner. He was a remarkably well-preserved man, of strong physique and vigorous health for a man of his years . . ." When Smith expired, Alcorn continued, "[Amy] had the body removed at once to Smith and Sons' Undertaking [no relation to Charles] rooms in Hartford, and it was there embalmed with Red Falcon embalming fluid."

This had turned into a common practice for Amy. When an inmate died, she demanded the body be taken away immediately *and* embalmed. And the choice of embalming fluid would turn out to be of great consequence. Red Falcon did *not* contain arsenic. Most embalming fluids of the day—although it was illegal—did.

Chapter 21

"I Can Fix That All Right"

THE PRACTICE OF PRESERVING THE HUMAN BODY POSTMORTEM is nearly 8,000 years old. Preservation after death was invented, of course, by the Egyptians, who mummified their dead. Ancient Greek historian Herodotus wrote of how the Egyptians believed that the soul could achieve immortality if preserved in the proper spiritual manner. That procedure might seem rather grotesque today. Early Egyptians cored out the body's innards and removed the brain—through the nose, mind you, with "a crooked piece of iron"—during the process of embalming. Explaining this gory method, Herodotus spared no detail:

> First they draw out the brains through the nostrils . . . then with a sharp Ethiopian stone they make an incision in the side, and take out all the bowels; and having cleansed the abdomen and rinsed it with palm-wine, they next sprinkle it with pounded perfumes. Then having filled the belly with pure myrrh pounded, and cassia, and other perfumes, frankincense excepted, they sew it up again; and when they have done this, they steep it in natrum [salt], leaving it under for seventy days. . . . At the expiration of the seventy days they wash the corpse, and wrap the whole body in bandages of flaxen cloth, smearing it with gum. . . . After this the relatives, having taken the body back again, make a wooden case in the shape of a man, and having made it, they inclose the body; and thus, having fastened it up, they store it in a sepulchral chamber. . . .

Some of the chief ingredients in nineteenth- and even early-twentieth-century embalming were strychnine and arsenic, which preserved the body, organs, and tissue better than any other compound. Arsenic also had the advantage of being accessible and inexpensive. But the experts learned quickly, as murder trials in the mid- to late 1800s and early 1900s became more fashionable, dramatic, public, and perhaps even ostensibly centered around justice, that using arsenic to preserve the dead posed several investigatory problems—namely, that if one had poisoned a fellow with arsenic and was ultimately charged with that crime, it would become an open-ended argument in a court of law. Not only did embalming fluid contain arsenic, but traces were also contained in ground soil minerals, rock, and limestone. Criminal cases of men accused of poisoning their wives with arsenic became almost laughable. It was difficult enough to draw the conclusion that if one found arsenic in a dead man's *organs*, as opposed to *tissue*, there was indeed a chance he was murdered; but if the poison was found only in the *tissue*, well, there was a good chance the landscape into which he was interred or the mortician's choice of embalming fluid had been the culprit.

"I have advocated for years," said one prominent coroner in 1902, "the discontinuance of the use of embalming fluid containing poison. If such fluids are used they destroy the value of a postmortem"—an argument that fell on deaf ears for nearly two more decades.

⁂

The ground was soft enough by April 18, 1914, for Michael Gilligan's embalmed corpse to be put into its final resting place in St. Mary's Cemetery. In no way, however, would Michael Gilligan rest in peace.

Amy was still waiting for the probate court to release Michael's $4,660 estate. According to Amy, she wanted to use the money to take care of the debt Michael had left behind. What exactly that debt included was never made public.

Despite having to live with a woman who was going mad from all the anxiety, stress, and finger-pointing going on in her life, Franklin Andrews appeared to be quite content. As the month of May broke, the grass began to grow, tree buds burst with dark green leaves, and the mood around Windsor seemed to shift from the doldrums of a dark, lingering winter to a new spice of fresh smells and an energized community. Franklin was out and about, taking his general walks around town, waving to friends, running letters and telegrams to the post office for Amy, clipping the hedges, edging the lawn, and writing to friends and family.

For Franklin, a new day had dawned.

Nellie Pierce was Franklin's preferred sibling. Franklin seemed to communicate with Nellie more than he did with the others. Nellie later talked about her brother and this period of his life, when things seemed to be going better for Franklin Andrews than they had in almost a decade—despite the nagging questions surrounding why so many of his fellow inmates were dropping dead around him.

"He [never] complained of any trouble . . . ," Nellie later said. She had been to the Archer Home to see Franklin on numerous occasions, and he never once mentioned a problem: with Amy, an inmate, or his own health.

On May 15, Franklin wrote a short postcard to Nellie after she had written to inquire how he was getting along that week.

> . . . *glad to hear from you. Hope you have a good Place and getting along well. I am getting along fine. Come up when you can. I will Try and come down Some Time . . .*

Nellie lived in Hartford, which was probably one of the reasons why she and Franklin were so close. But Franklin was a bit too busy for regular visits. He had work to do around the Home for Amy, he said. He was even helping the woman he now called the "wonderful matron" with the other inmates. Cooking. Cleaning up. Playing cards. Keeping everyone occupied and busy. It all gave Franklin a new lease on life, a reason to wake up everyday.

On May 18, Amy received more frustrating news. Judge D. Ellsworth Phelps said he would hear the case of Michael Gilligan's estate—his children were, of course, fighting Amy—on May 28, 1914, at 10:00 a.m. The bottom line in Phelps's decision was for all of the parties to show up and hash things out. The money wasn't going to be released until the judge was confident everyone was going to get his or her deserved share.

Amy was furious. How dare they try to take away what was rightfully hers! She was a widow, two times over. She would fight that family right up until the end.

Two days later, on May 20, Franklin wrote a short note to his brother in New Haven. He just wanted to say hello and, "Hope this finds you all well . . . I am getting along fine . . ."

▲ ▲ ▲

Alice and Loren Gowdy were married in 1893, when both were close to fifty years old. Twenty-one years later, now well into their seventies, Alice and Loren realized that life had caught up with them; they needed help doing those everyday things which had come naturally during their younger years. In reading the newspaper one morning that May of 1914, Alice saw an ad for the Archer Home and realized that here was a place the two of them could go to live out the remainder of their years—together. Even better, the Archer Home was close to Enfield and Somers, where Loren and Alice had lived most of their lives. Alice was a nurse at one time, and a schoolteacher; she had grown up in Hartford, and had taught grammar school in the city for years. Many of their relatives lived nearby. Moving into the Archer Home was, in the complete sense of it, the best logistical choice for a place to live out their final years.

Shortly after inquiring about a room, and being told by Amy that none were available at the time, the Gowdys started searching for another home. There were other elderly homes like Amy's in Hartford, Springfield, and New Haven. Yet no other home seemed to offer the deal the Archer Home had been advertising. The Gowdys were not wealthy people by any means; and, like most elderly couples, they lived humbly off what little money they had put away throughout their lives.

So Alice wrote to Amy near the end of May, asking once again if she had an open room with two beds. Alice wasn't going to give up just yet. Amy had impressed Loren and Alice. They had visited the Archer Home and appreciated the atmosphere, how the establishment was run, and the clientele Amy housed. It was an ideal situation.

Amy wrote back to Alice on May 26. By now the Gowdys had moved out of their home in Enfield and were living with friends in Hartford.

"Your kind note is before me," Amy wrote, "and I most sincerely wish I was with you to help you out."

Apparently, the Gowdys were in a terrible jam. They couldn't stay where they were much longer, and they needed someone to cook their meals and tend to their basic needs. What was more, they had nowhere to store their life's belongings and wondered if Amy would take their things and store them in her barn until a room became available. They would wait as long as it took and move between various relatives' houses, similar to what Franklin Andrews had done.

"Try not to worry, or take things hard," a seemingly comforting Amy Archer-Gilligan wrote. "Send along your things just as you wish, the easiest way for you, and do not worry about anything."

Apparently, Amy had a plan.

When the Gowdys had visited the Archer Home the previous week, it was Amy who had shown them around. It just so happened that on the day they'd arrived for a tour, Franklin Andrews was out and about, probably taking his daily walk through town or running an errand for Amy. Perhaps she had even sent him out for this reason.

In any event, Amy showed the Gowdys Franklin's room. "This will be vacant very soon," she said to their surprise.

Franklin had boarded with another man, who Amy and the Gowdys had referred to as "Ramsey." It was spacious, one of the larger rooms in the Home. Perfect, in other words, for Mr. and Mrs. Gowdy.

Loren Gowdy walked into the room and immediately brightened up. Then, seeing Franklin's belongings sitting there, he said sharply, "Oh!" It appeared Franklin Andrews was well established in the room. "This room is occupied, ma'am."

"I can fix that all right," Amy said smugly, shaking her head, as if she knew something they did not.

"But it looks to be occupied," Alice Gowdy repeated.

"I'll take care of that, ma'am, don't you worry," Amy responded.

In her May 26 letter, after she'd made a point to tell the Gowdys not to worry about a place to stay, and that she was in the process of taking care of all their needs, Amy added, "You will do me a favor if you will please send the check for $1,000 on the 28th of this month. You can mail it to me if it is now convenient for you to come, and I will sign the contract to care for you during your life when you come . . ." Her letter continued:

> *I write this so that it will certify for the check in case you cannot come with it. I would rather you would come when you find it convenient; it makes no great difference to me. If convenient for you to wait a few days, it will [be] just as well, but you do as you wish—only I want to use the money to advantage and I can save $200 by having it the 28th, so if you will please mail it to me on or before that day, you will favor me and I don't suppose it will make any difference with you.*
>
> *Always your sincere friend,*
> *Amy E. Archer*

Amy was still in a deep financial pinch, and needed that $1,000 to pay off creditors who were now calling every day. Also, Amy had to look responsible in front of the probate court if she had any shot at getting a hold of the lion's share of Michael Gilligan's estate. Any outstanding debt—well overdue on her part—would make her look weak and unable to handle her finances in the eyes of the court.

Amy ended that May 26th letter with a postscript: "I know you will be very happy here and I will do all I can to make you so."

Chapter 22

THE WRONG VICTIM

AMY FOUND HERSELF IN A BIND ON MAY 28, 1914. She had a married couple with plenty of cash waiting for a room, but no room available. She also had a court date that would ultimately decide Michael Gilligan's estate.

Decisions, decisions . . .

It was two days after she had last heard from Mr. and Mrs. Gowdy that Amy wrote a second letter, which sounded a bit more frantic, maybe even urgent. If Amy had devised a plan of any kind, it was clear that it was not working out the way she had intended. With the Gowdys basically living out of a suitcase in Hartford and no other potential clients waiting in the wings, Amy had to act fast, or forfeit what was essentially $2,000 cash, $1,000 for each, the $1,000 she mentioned in her letter being a down payment.

> *My dear Friend,*
> *I hope I will not disappoint you too much if I ask you to please wait for a few days before coming as the lady who is to go away cannot go away for a few days.*

Amy promised to call or write as soon as the inmate's "mother came" to take her away. She promised to pay "any expenses" the Gowdys accumulated during this waiting period. She encouraged them to send their furniture, anyway.

"I tried my best to have it so you could come," Amy wrote, "and I long to have you with us for it is just lonely here now."

Continuing, Amy explained that she was busy as ever and had no room in the Home because her sisters had come for a visit and other relatives of inmates had also showed up.

"We have a full house."

She was buying time.

"So please try to come next Thursday," the first week of June; "we will have your room all ready and everything settled as near as we can . . ."

At the close of the letter, Amy nudged the Gowdys once again regarding the money. "If you kindly mail me a check tomorrow so I can get it cashed before the banks are closed I will greatly appreciate it."

▲ ▲ ▲

On the morning of May 29, 1914, Franklin Andrews was engaged in painting a fence outside, in the front yard of the Archer Home. It was a white picket fence running the property line. Franklin was whistling and a having a grand old time, enjoying the beautiful temperatures of a gorgeous pre-summer morning. Several neighbors saw him and waved, tipped their hats, or said hello as they made their way by.

"There were no signs of sickness or [emaciation] about him [on that day]," said a friend.

That night, Franklin sat down at the dinner table in the main dining room and ate his supper as usual, "taking his food from individual dishes placed before him" by Amy, a report later claimed. He was alone. Amy had cooked his meal separately from the other inmates, who had already eaten.

Franklin's roommate, Seth Ramsey, a sixty-two-year-old former farmer himself, had lived near Franklin, in Southington. At the time Ramsey entered the Archer Home, his wife had been dead two years. It was December 17, 1913. Ramsey had been paying by the week, having refused to sign a life contract. The room he and Franklin shared—that same room Amy had since promised to the Gowdys— was the only two-bed accommodation in the Archer Home.

Ramsey and Franklin got along well. Later, Ramsey said of his former roommate, "Why, he was a cripple, lame, but never complained of any illness."

Ramsey and Franklin's room was in the back end of the house, on the first floor, next to the veranda. Ramsey's bed was in the southeast corner, Franklin's in the northeast. No doubt it was the best room, with the best view.

Like Franklin, Ramsey generally retired around nine o'clock. They would lie in their beds for a time, talking about the day and what was ahead for the next. After dinner on May 29, both men sat around downstairs and talked with the other inmates for a time, and then went to bed.

Franklin was fine, Ramsey said later. He went to bed like any other night, cheerful and talkative and his same old self.

Near "five or six" the following morning, which happened to be Decoration Day (Memorial Day), Ramsey was startled awake. There were sounds coming from Franklin's side of the room. Moans. Low-pitched groaning. Shuffling.

At first, Ramsey didn't know what was going on as he opened his eyes and oriented himself. Looking across the room, he noticed that Franklin was sitting up in bed—"vomiting profusely," Ramsey later recalled. All over himself.

"What's wrong?" Ramsey called out.

"I am sick to my stomach."

"I'll get Miss Archer," Ramsey said, rushing out of bed. She would know what to do. He knocked violently on Amy's door. "Miss Archer? Miss Archer?"

"What is it?" she said groggily from behind the door.

"Mr. Andrews is sick. Come quickly."

Amy and Ramsey rushed back into the room together, Amy putting on her bathrobe as she walked. Franklin was on the floor by that point, holding his midsection, drool and vomit sliding down the side of his mouth. He was pale and green and sickly looking.

"You ought to have a doctor," Ramsey said sternly.

"I will call on Dr. King," Amy responded.

Ramsey couldn't take the sight or the smell of his poor friend apparently getting sicker as the minutes progressed, so he walked outside to get some air. He figured Dr. King would be arriving at any moment. He could greet the doctor, fill him in.

To Ramsey's surprise, however, Dr. King never came.

All day long, Franklin Andrews continued to vomit and dry-heave; he was unable to eat or even take fluids. He stayed in the room as Ramsey monitored the situation from time to time, spending most of his time outside in the "piazza," as he described the north side of the house, where a small grotto of grapevines and other plants adorned a small garden.

As the day went on, Franklin never saw the doctor. At one point, Ramsey went in to check on Franklin to see how he was feeling. Amy said Franklin was doing better. "Why, I didn't think he was so very sick," Ramsey said later. "I talked with him. He seemed to be [lying] in bed, quiet."

Throughout the day Franklin was in and out of it. He had not gotten better by any means, but more or less had found a way to contend with his illness.

Just after eight o'clock that next night, Ramsey was outside once again when he spied Dr. King walking up to the front door. Ramsey had just gone in to see Franklin before King arrived. Amy was standing at his bedside, monitoring the situation, making sure that if Franklin needed fluids, she would offer.

Especially lemonade.

Ramsey looked at Franklin. He was in bed, eyes closed, his breathing labored. Franklin couldn't even acknowledge that Ramsey or Amy were there. He was completely out of it.

"I just stepped up to the bed and looked at him," Ramsey said later. "He was insensible."

At that moment, Dr. King walked into the room.

▲ ▲ ▲

Howard Frost King had lived in Windsor since 1899. He had been on Amy's payroll for nearly four years by the time he visited the Home on the night of May 30, 1914, responding to Franklin Andrews's now two-day-old illness. Before that night, King admitted later, he had never treated Franklin. Franklin had called Dr. King by phone "about four or five" times during his stay at the Archer Home, twenty months before this particular incident, to ask the doctor how to treat a sore throat or cold.

"Trivial things," King called them.

When King arrived that night—he claimed later it was "six

o'clock" and he had responded "immediately to Amy's call"—he found Franklin Andrews knocking on death's door.

"The patient was suffering with what appeared to be an acute indigestion," a popular diagnosis from the doctor. "There was gastric pain and nausea and vomiting."

King asked Franklin where, exactly, the pain was centered.

Franklin managed to point to his stomach, where, King added, "He complained of [a] burning pain."

While King was there, Franklin asked for water, which Amy ran into the kitchen to get for him.

Facing Amy, King said, "Look, I am prescribing several medications, and if anything goes wrong, I suggest you call me at once."

What more could he do?

The doctor gave a nausea tablet comprised of cerium oxalate, bismuth sub-nitrate, and cocaine hydrochloride, a common remedy King had been giving out to various patients in the Home complaining of the same symptoms. The main thrust of the prescribed medicine was to counteract any nausea Franklin had and to make him more comfortable, which was all King felt he could do for the guy.

King would say he gave Amy specific instructions to give Franklin the tablets every hour, and to continue after he felt better. King believed Amy was a trained nurse, based on what she had told him. He felt confident whenever he gave her instructions and medicines that she would carry out his orders with perhaps more precision than a layperson.

King left, but near nine o'clock Amy called on him again. "I need you back."

Then Amy called Franklin's sister, Nellie Pierce. "Your brother is sick and I am afraid he will not get well," Amy told Nellie over the phone.

King had not given Amy any sort of prognosis. She was making this call on her own.

Nellie was startled. She had seen Franklin just a few days earlier and had spoken to him less than twenty-four hours ago. He had said he was fine. He had painted a fence, and was going to cut the lawn. Rake some leaves.

"What's the matter with him?" Nellie asked.

"You know how he has been having boils on his neck. Well, I am afraid they have affected him internally."

Who had said anything about boils?

Nellie was astounded by this revelation. It was the first time she had ever heard of Franklin suffering from boils of any kind.

"Do you consider him serious?" Nellie wanted to know.

"I am afraid he is not going to get well."

"Will I come right up tonight, then," Nellie said, which was more of a statement than a question. She said she was going to make the trek from Hartford immediately.

"No!" Amy shot back. "It will not be necessary."

"Mrs. Archer, will you please call on a doctor? Don't spare anything. Do everything possible. I will come up there first thing in the morning."

It had taken King five minutes, he later calculated, to get over to the Archer Home after Amy had summoned him that second time. When King walked into the room, he saw Amy standing bedside. According to King, Franklin was "practically dead." There were "no signs of life" in the man at all.

He was beyond pale, beyond unresponsive. And beyond, certainly, any medical treatment King could administer.

"There was nothing I could do for him," King said.

It was an hour or so later that Franklin Andrews gave up the battle and took his last breath. King and Amy were in the room with him. Dr. Howard King cited the "primary cause" of death as "gastric ulcers." Franklin Andrews was sixty years old. Up until the day of his death, the man had never complained of stomach problems. Franklin walked with a limp, and admittedly suffered from rheumatism. But ever since moving into the Archer Home, he had stopped complaining of those ailments. Furthermore, not once had he mentioned a condition having anything even remotely to do with his stomach—nor had he suffered from any problems having to do with boils.

Amy Archer-Gilligan ordered Franklin's corpse to be removed at once—before daybreak—and his body embalmed. Then Amy asked Seth Ramsey to move promptly into another room. She needed to get this one ready for Loren and Alice Gowdy.

Chapter 23

"FIT AS A FIDDLE"

NELLIE PIERCE HAD NOT SLEPT WELL. The last she knew, her brother was close to death—a death that was as surprising as it was sudden.

When Nellie Pierce awoke the next morning, May 31, there was a suspicious butterfly fluttering in her stomach. Nellie was not the only one, in fact, feeling that Amy Archer-Gilligan and her home needed a quiet exit out of Windsor. It seemed that those who had stood behind Amy up to this point, and the town itself, were now ready to bid her farewell.

And the sooner the better.

Far too much had happened. Far too many people had died.

In an article he wrote for *The American Weekly* two decades after the problems began at the Archer Home, George Vedder Jones noted this change of heart in Windsor, saying, "Neighbors felt that the presence of an old people's home . . . cheapened the neighborhood. They got up a petition to have it closed. When this failed, they began writing letters to . . . [Clifton Sherman] in nearby Hartford alleging improper care of the inmates and urging an investigation."*

---

* From this point on I will refer to George Vedder Jones's article in the present tense so as not to disrupt the narrative. The article Jones wrote, "The Case of the Hearse at Midnight," published in *The American Weekly*, January 8, 1950, was part of an *American Weekly* column that focused on true crime. Readers appreciated well-written true crime stories as much then as they do today. As a researcher and author, I feel that Jones did a terrific job of interviewing those connected to the Amy Archer-Gilligan case who were still alive, which is one of the reasons I give so much credence to the piece. Without Jones's fine reporting, at a time when some of those who experienced this terrible tragedy firsthand were still alive and able to tell their stories, we would have lost an important—if not dramatic—piece of this history.

That night, someone in town had seen the coroner come and take Franklin's body. That same person sent an anonymous note to Clifton Sherman the following morning: "A black hearse comes at midnight to spirit away their bodies."

What could not be denied, no matter how you looked at it, was the fact that so many had died over the course of the past several years. Clifton Sherman had estimated eleven per year. Nearly one per month.

This startled him.

When Nellie Pierce showed up near seven o'clock the next morning, she ran into Seth Ramsey and had a quick conversation with him, asking him at some point, "Where is Mrs. Archer?"

"In the parlor," Ramsey said.

Nellie walked into the room where Amy was sitting with Dr. King, who had arrived shortly before Nellie. Dr. King took one look at Nellie, said he was sorry for her loss, tipped his fedora, and left the house.

"How long had he been ill, Mrs. Archer?" Nellie asked. She wanted facts, details of her brother's sudden death. Why had Amy waited and called at the last minute, for example? "How did he die? What were the circumstances surrounding his death?"

"He was painting the fence," Amy said.

Painting the fence, indeed. In fact, that was Nellie's point. "He didn't complain of being ill until [later on that day]," Amy continued. "He said he wanted to finish painting and I told him he couldn't do it. He went out but came back and said he couldn't go."

"That's it?"

"He never complained of any pain until about ten minutes before he died," Amy said.

Liar.

Nellie was bemused. Amy's comment made no sense. How does an otherwise healthy man simply drop dead?

"I asked him," Amy added, "if he had wanted me to phone you and he said no. He thought he could get well."

This didn't sound like the Franklin Andrews Nellie had known—the same guy who had written her postcards describing the weather in a town neighboring her own.

"Where is his body?" Nellie asked.

"Smith and Sons in Hartford."

"Why?" Nellie snapped, inquiring about the hasty removal of Franklin's body.

"I don't keep a body in the house after a death."

After leaving the Archer Home, Nellie Pierce made two separate trips to Windsor over the next two days, although the order in which she made those trips is not clear. Nonetheless, Nellie stopped in at Smith and Sons to view her brother's body. It was awful, seeing him like that, especially after she'd just spoken to Franklin and visited him a few days earlier. Nellie cried, her face in her hands.

How? Why?

"He looked natural," Nellie recalled later, speaking of standing there staring at her brother's corpse. "I recognized him all right. He showed no [emaciation]." Perhaps the most devastating part of it for Nellie, was that Franklin didn't appear sick. He looked to be sleeping, Nellie thought—like he'd dozed off for a nap, never to wake up.

Nellie also visited the offices of the *Hartford Courant* at this time. She was in need of a good reporter who wanted to hear her story. She felt there was something going on at the Archer Home— something murderous and violent and altogether evil. She was fed up with Amy's answers. She was tired of Amy telling her things that were entirely out of character for her dead brother.

"I've come," Nellie said to Clifton Sherman, "to report a murder at the Archer Home."

"A murder?" Sherman asked. Standing, looking at Nellie, Sherman thought she was merely one more in an increasing number of disgruntled neighbors looking to get Amy kicked out of the neighborhood once and for all, and asked Nellie about this.

"No," Nellie explained. "My brother, Franklin Andrews, lived at Mrs. Archer's." She described Franklin as "strong, healthy . . . he just turned sixty."

Sherman was interested, to say the least. He had Carl Goslee and another reporter, Robert Thayer, out there stealthily working on this story. Listening to Nellie, witnessing such sincerity, he sensed that the story was about to get a heck of a lot bigger.

Sherman knew the accusations weren't going away. Every time he turned around, lo and behold, there was another piece of the puzzle.

What sparked Nellie's concern was that Franklin had not been ill, or even sick enough to warrant the night of vomiting that ultimately led to his death. She couldn't figure it out. Sure, he could have eaten something that made him ill, or caught some type of "bug." But it seemed that he had been fine one minute, and dead the next. Furthermore, Amy had waited until Franklin's final moments before calling her, Nellie said. Perhaps Clifton Sherman and his team could get to the bottom of what was going on in that house of horrors.

Later, in his *American Weekly* article, after interviewing several of those present, George Vedder Jones described this meeting between Nellie Pierce and Clifton Sherman:

> *"Well, I went to Windsor to visit [Franklin] just last [week]," [Nellie told Sherman]. "He was fit as a fiddle then. But Tuesday evening I had a phone call from Mrs. Archer, saying that he'd been taken seriously ill. But she told me not to worry, because the doctor would be there any minute. She said there was no point in my coming so late at night." [Nellie explained that the doctor said Franklin had died of gastric ulcers.] "Nobody can tell me he died of ulcers . . . He had them as a young man, but they hadn't bothered him for years. And another thing, when I got there at seven in the morning his body was already gone! The undertaker had taken it during the night."*
>
> *"At midnight?" Sherman asked.*
>
> *"Yes, I believe that's what they said. Mr. Sherman, there's something about this that's not right. Why wasn't I called when he died? Why [couldn't] I see him until after he was embalmed?"*
>
> *"You're quite right to feel the way you do, Mrs. Pierce," Sherman said. "We'll investigate the matter and get in touch with you very soon."*

Early in the morning of June 1, Amy sent a telegram to Loren and Alice Gowdy, who were unknowingly about to move into a dead man's room.

> *Please let me know if you wish to take the room; it is ready to-day, please mail me the contract I let you take.*

Perhaps feeling the need to explain herself, Amy wrote a longer letter later that afternoon. She began: "I am very sorry to have caused the delay but I could not possibly avoid it." She went on:

> *After receiving your letter [in which the Gowdys basically wanted to know one way or another if and when a room would be ready], I was about to get your room ready and call you at once, but one of our dear loved-ones here was taken very ill and I had to be with him. You may know he needed me when I tell you he passed away . . . with ulcers in the stomach. He was very, very dear to us and you must try to forgive me if I am causing you any unpleasantness.*

Astute when it came to using the sincerity of others to support her own agenda, Amy was once again playing to the Gowdys' obviously kind sensibilities and sympathy. How could they respond to such a letter?

The Gowdys were not happy, but they bought it; they were finally moving into the Archer Home. No more would they have to worry about where they were going to hang their hats. Although they were quite unhappy about how Amy had handled things, she was now taking care of all the arrangements. In the same letter, hoping to allay any fears or disagreements, Amy said, "I know my dear Friends from the tone of your letter, I have not had your confidence, [and] this I very much regret—but I do not blame you as there is much deception in this world. [A]nd yet, when you consider the Home offered you, and the ½ price rate, do you blame me if I should feel a little hurt?"

Mr. and Mrs. Gowdy had no idea, of course, seeing how they had signed one of Amy's all-inclusive life contracts, that they were (however reluctantly at this point) moving right into a death trap.

▲ ▲ ▲

Amy and her business were part of a rapidly growing number of private-sector elderly care homes opening up across America just after the turn of the century, helping to spawn what would become a massive, multibillion-dollar monster of commerce. In the early part of the twentieth century, elderly housing and nursing homes weren't viewed as the saving grace they might be seen as today. Before the establishment of homes like Amy's, the elderly and/ or disabled were sent to what were called "poor farms" or "alms-houses," privately funded homes for the destitute that put a roof over the heads of those without money or family. The elderly were packed in, and care was substandard and even abusive. Most people were expected to take care of their own medical needs. The stigma attached to being sent away to such an establishment was that you were being cast out of society—there was something *wrong* with you. Regardless of the accusations against her, Amy had helped to change that image, even if in a small way.

From all accounts, it's clear that Amy grew up in a fairly well-mannered household in a suburb of Litchfield, Connecticut, a little borough known as Milton. Amy was one of five children raised by James and Mary Duggan. According to a town history of Milton, Amy taught at the "Milton School, and in early 1890 attended New Britain Normal School [and later] became a bookkeeper for a New Haven firm."

It seemed that the Duggan family's wholesome reputation was slipping away as the family of Franklin Andrews—and the town of Windsor—were closing in on Amy, demanding answers. Amy's best bet was to keep a low profile. She could not draw attention to herself any more than she had already. It was bad enough that more people were asking questions, and Carl Goslee and the *Courant* had ratcheted up their investigation.

Nellie Pierce, along with Franklin's other sister and brother, went through his belongings and were quite stunned after reading a letter Amy had written to Franklin just days before his death. In the letter, Amy had asked Franklin for a loan, and he'd refused.

So she killed him.

To Nellie, this seemed like as good a motive as any.

The letter was vague, however. Nellie needed to find out for certain if Franklin had refused Amy the loan. So she and her siblings made a trip to the Archer Home on June 5, 1914, to inquire about his death and to demand answers to a few open-ended questions.

Franklin's brother spoke first, asking Amy, "Did he give you a loan?"

"He [did] not," Amy responded. She was firm.

"Did you ever—by writing—ask Frank for a loan?"

"I did not." Again, unbreakable.

"Ma'am, would you recognize your own handwriting if I were to show it to you?" Franklin's brother reached into his pocket and took out the letter Amy had written.

Amy thought about this while looking down at the letter. Where was the conversation going? They apparently had more information.

"I would," Amy said, acknowledging that she recognized her handwriting.

Franklin's brother pointed to her signature, and then showed Amy the section of the letter where she had asked Franklin for the loan, and also asked him to keep her request on the down-low.

"Oh, this . . ." Amy said, acting surprised, realizing she could not deny it any longer. "I forgot about that. But he never gave me the money, anyway."

"Couldn't you have let us know?" said Franklin's sister, talking about the moment he became ill. Why had she waited until Franklin was so close to death to call Nellie?

"My dear," Amy said sharply, not backing down, "I would have had I known myself. I didn't know!"

Franklin's siblings asked Amy about paying for his funeral arrangements, seeing that his contract had stipulated the expense would be hers. As it happened, Amy had sent a nice bouquet of flowers for Franklin's burial, with a card that read WITH DEEPEST SYMPATHY FROM THE ARCHER HOME.

Amy looked at them. Said she would think about it.

Chapter 24

PUBLIC SERVICE

CLIFTON SHERMAN HAD ENOUGH INTUITION TO KNOW that he was sitting on the story of his career. Whatever was going on inside the Archer Home would be front-page news. Better it be the *Hartford Courant* that broke the story instead of the competition, the *Hartford Times*, which, as far as Sherman could tell, didn't have any reporters covering the investigation.

Carl Goslee was still working his sources and making progress, if only a step at a time. He had a family and a full-time job that were also keeping him busy. Behind the scenes, Sherman and state's attorney Hugh Alcorn talked about Carl as being someone who would ultimately play a larger role in the case than any other private citizen. But for now, Carl wasn't being told of this recent development; he was still working as a freelance reporter. Clifton Sherman had Robert Thayer, one of his full-time reporters, on the job, too, picking up his pace on the Archer investigation after hearing about Franklin Andrews's death. Thayer was as objective as they come, and the perfect newspaperman to take control of the story.

By speaking to Sherman, Nellie Pierce ignited a firestorm of suspicion in the longtime newspaperman, who then went to Thayer and gave him the letters and notes Nellie had dropped off, along with several bits of information Carl Goslee had dug up.

"A stomach complaint, sudden death, and a body carried out at midnight," Sherman told Thayer. It sounded like whatever had made Franklin sick had come on all at once.

Same as in all the other cases.

Thayer wasn't buying the premise of murder just yet; he wanted more solid proof than simply personal anecdotes from family and friends. He told Sherman, "It could be acute indigestion." Then mentioned the possibility of an appendicitis attack. "Or [it could be] murder by poison," Thayer allowed. The fact was, no one knew for certain what had happened. And no one had positive proof other than wild speculation that it was anything other than one more in a long line of unexplained deaths.

"I think we owe it to the public and to Mrs. Pierce to find out," Sherman said. He wanted Thayer to hit the bricks, ask questions. Make his way around Windsor and see what he came up with. Maybe even go right to Amy and see what she was willing to talk about. Thayer agreed that a visit to the Archer Home couldn't hurt.

So one afternoon, during the second week of June, Thayer knocked on Amy's door and asked if he could have a few moments of her time. He introduced himself, according to George Vedder Jones, and explained the reason for the visit. "We're planning a story about the Home."

Amy opened the door. "That's nice," she said. "Come in."

Walking with Thayer in the downstairs parlor, Amy spoke of how she and James had opened the Home in 1907. She was calm and willing to help out in any way she could. She even gave Thayer a quick overview of the Archer Home's history. "[James] died in 1910," she said somberly. "We have been fairly successful financially, however. Our capacity is fourteen and we are always filled up."

This was a strange comment, seeing that the Archer Home had twenty inmates at any given time. Why would Amy downplay the number of inmates she could house?

Amy talked about how her payment scale had been set up— that she liked it that way. "A lump sum," as she called it, was best for everyone. Family, she said, often neglected their aged and left them to fend for themselves, so it was good to have the money up front.

As they walked around the downstairs rooms and Thayer took notes, Amy told him that things had become a little easier once she'd met and married Michael Gilligan. He was great, she said. He'd helped out a lot. But then, of course, he had also died and she was back to being a widow with a business to run.

"It's difficult without a man around the house," Amy told Thayer that afternoon. And it was in this capacity that Franklin Andrews had picked up a lot of the slack.

It seemed—at least, when one looked at this conversation later and weighed it against the evidence piling up against Amy—that she was trying desperately to let Thayer know that killing strong men who could help her out around the Home would not be in her best interest. Why would she even consider doing such a thing?

"Poor Mr. Andrews," Amy added. "He helped me for a time. But now he's gone and I have nobody."

Thayer later said that a "look of disappointment crossed Mrs. Archer's face." She looked down. Seemed to be genuinely hurt over the notion that she was all alone and running the business by herself again.

When Thayer began to talk about the community and the rumors swirling around town, Amy stood erect. "So my neighbors have been talking again," she exclaimed sharply, shaking her head. "I was afraid that was why you had come."

Yes, Thayer agreed, there was "talk" around town. He asked what she thought about Franklin Andrews and the rumors circulating that she had done something to him—that perhaps Franklin's death had been facilitated, like some of the others.

Amy said she wanted to clear things up. There was too much speculation and wild talk. The facts needed to be put forth.

"[Franklin] spent the afternoon helping me around the yard," Amy told Thayer. "And at dinner he ate much more than usual."

It seemed every time Amy was asked about Franklin's final hours, she added one more small detail that was either never mentioned previously, or totally contradicted what she had said already. Now she was claiming that Franklin had eaten too much and it had caused him great discomfort.

"Shortly after he went into his room he began to complain of violent stomach pains," she said. "I helped him to bed and sent for our regular doctor. But he was sicker than anyone thought. He passed away before the doctor could help."

Thayer asked for Dr. King's address. He wanted to verify what Amy was putting on the record.

Amy obliged. King lived right up the road.

"Can I look around the house a bit?" Thayer wanted to know.

She told Thayer it was okay to inspect the place, and added, "I do hope you'll write something nice about the Home."

Thayer then walked into Amy's office and asked to see a list of the inmates' names. Amy balked at first, but then allowed the newspaperman to copy down the names from a master list.

As Thayer walked out the door, he turned to Amy and asked one more question: "By the way, we had a report that Mr. Andrews's body was taken away in the middle of the night. Is that correct?"

"Yes," Amy responded, "it's our usual procedure."

She was a peaceful woman, Thayer reported. At ease with her responses. Before he walked through the gate leading to the street, she said, "It's difficult in an old people's home when death occurs because everyone is so depressed, wondering who'll be next."

⚜ ⚜ ⚜

On June 11, 1914, Loren and Alice Gowdy signed a life contract with Amy Archer for $1,000, which Loren paid in cash. Compared to what she was charging others, Amy had given the Gowdys a great deal. Fifty percent off! It was the same clear-cut contract Amy had signed with several of the other inmates who chose the life-care package over weekly payments—only the Gowdys were charged $500 a piece, half of what most others paid. Alice and Loren were comfortable with the contract. They now had a home with their own room on the first floor. Exactly what they had wanted all along.

A couple days after the Gowdys had moved into the Archer Home, Alice began making regular visits to her friend, Nellie R. Clark, who lived in town. Alice had known Nellie Clark for twenty-seven years. Alice loved the walk. It was good exercise for both mind and body, and she enjoyed getting out.

Alice would spend "two hours" or more at the house, Nellie Clark said later, and she often visited without calling first.

"She was in good health, certainly," Clark remembered. They talked, and enjoyed tea and crackers. They took walks together through the garden in the backyard and west side of the Home, giving Loren Gowdy some time by himself.

Before he'd met Alice, Loren had lived in Albany, New York, where he clerked at a carpet store. As a young man, he had been strong, and eager to move from town to town, state to state, in order to find the work that suited him. Three years later, before moving back to Connecticut, Loren went into the liquor business. Then he met Alice.

Now Loren was living out his golden years in what he presumed to be a comfortable, safe environment, with the love of his life by his side. The Archer Home, Loren commented later, was the perfect place for them. Being around people was important, as was having someone capable to turn to—a service he'd never before realized that they needed.

▲ ▲ ▲

After speaking with Amy, Robert Thayer walked from the Archer Home to Dr. Howard King's residence just around the corner. King opened the door and "seemed irritated" by Thayer's cold call.

Thayer asked King about Franklin Andrews, and how it happened that under his professional medical guidance, Franklin Andrews had just up and died. What did King think about Franklin's sister, Nellie Pierce, asking questions and pointing a finger?

Thayer described King as a "gray-haired man with a brisk, professional manner." Some called King ornery and mean-spirited. Here, both of those character traits stood out to Thayer. King was upset that someone—especially a newspaper reporter!—was digging into the way he practiced medicine. What business of the *Hartford Courant*'s was it how King handled his medical practice?

"There was nothing unusual about Andrews's death!" King raged as Thayer stood on the front doorstep of King's house, pressing him for a quote. "True, he appeared a well man, but he had a history of ulcers." King went on to say that Franklin likely "severely overtaxed his stomach" during dinner, "which caused a violent recurrence and put too great a strain on his heart."

Franklin Andrews ate himself to death, in other words. It was an odd explanation. The notion that overeating had caused Franklin Andrews's heart to give out was preposterous. It was a diagnosis that educated men would never buy. King was putting his

131

reputation on the line—and for what, Thayer wanted to know; Amy Archer-Gilligan?

"What about poison?" Thayer queried a moment later.

"Ridiculous!" King said. "I'd have noticed the symptoms."

Thayer went back to the *Courant* office scratching his head, wondering what to do next. He'd found nothing to back up Nellie Pierce's suggestion that Amy had murdered Andrews to avoid having to pay him back for money she had either borrowed or stolen from the dead man.

▲ ▲ ▲

By mid-July, Loren Gowdy trusted Amy enough to "quit-claim" two parcels of land he owned—the last of his and Alice's assets—over to her. Loren never gave a reason why he did this—for example, if he was simply lending Amy the asset so she could borrow against it. There was nothing in his contract to stipulate that the $1,000 the Gowdys had paid Amy was a down payment, per se. Nonetheless, by the end of the summer, Amy had in her possession two pieces of land the Gowdys had once owned.

In early September, Mrs. Lena Peterson, a lifelong Hartford resident, took the trolley to Windsor to call on Amy. Peterson was representing her friend, a woman she called "Mrs. Rand" from New Britain, who needed a place to live right away. Rand and Peterson had been friends all their lives, and Rand was in no position to make the trip herself, because she was so ill.

It was just after eleven in the morning, Peterson recalled, when she arrived at the Archer Home.

"I am inquiring about giving my friend room and board," Peterson asked Amy. "Would you have any rooms available?"

Amy thought about it. "Not right now," she said. Then, after a brief pause, "But I will in a few days' time."

"How much?" Peterson wanted to know.

"Well," Amy said, "I would rather have a life contract than any other type of payment."

"I am not so sure [she can do that]," Peterson said of her friend. "She is living on charity now. I would need to speak to her brother."

Amy asked about the potential new inmate. How was her health?

"She is not good," Peterson said. "If you take her by lifetime or by week contract, you ought to be good to her, because she has been suffering and has had lots of troubles."

"Why, I know suffering," Amy said stoically. "I have been having troubles myself."

"You have?" Peterson said, somewhat surprised. It seemed that Amy was doing just fine for herself.

"Well, yes. I have been married twice. My first husband was sick for a long time." (Not true.)

"What seemed to be the matter?" Peterson asked.

"Well, that rheumatism got him. My second husband was a big, strong healthy fellow up to the night he died."

"What seemed to be the reason there?"

"I went the same as usually," Amy explained, "made a cup of tea, and we had tea together, and crackers. And after that he took these terrible cramps and groaning and he only lasted an hour."

Chapter 25

Too Late

PORTER BACON AND HIS WIFE MINNIE LIVED IN Springfield, Massachusetts. The Bacons were related to Loren and Alice Gowdy by marriage. The Bacons' niece, Doris Gowdy, was also Alice's niece. On the afternoon of November 26, 1914, Porter Bacon, his wife, and niece took the trolley from Springfield to visit Alice and Loren at the Archer Home. The ride was short and pleasurable. The Gowdys had spent a better part of their lives in Springfield, just over the Massachusetts line, above Enfield and Somers.

When they arrived that evening, Amy answered the door. "What do you want?" she asked. Amy seemed unnerved by the visit for some reason. Irritated and offensive.

Porter Bacon explained. "We are the Gowdys' people—we would like to visit with them."

"Do you know them very well?" Amy queried.

"We do," Porter said.

"Wait here," Amy responded. "I will go and see if they are in any condition to see you."

Surprised by the cold reception, the Porters still waited patiently.

Some time later, Amy returned. "Yes, you can come now."

Upon entering the room, Minnie and Porter noticed that Alice did not look good. She was in bed, pale and sluggish. When she saw her visitors, Alice forced herself to sit up. Soon, she got out of bed and walked around the room, while complaining of a terrible "pit in her stomach," a common complaint around the Archer Home.

After just a short walk about the room, Alice was exhausted and had to sit back down. The Porters asked what the problem was, to which Alice responded, "I feel pressure in my stomach. I am very ill."

After some small talk, they all agreed that it must have been the Thanksgiving meal that had beaten Alice down so badly. Alice had eaten too much. She had a terrible case of indigestion.

They talked for a while. Alice said she couldn't understand how her illness had just come out of nowhere after dinner. One minute she was eating, and the next she was bedridden with these horrible pains in her stomach, far beyond anything she had ever experienced before.

The Porters spent a few hours at the house, and when it was time to leave, Alice said that she and Loren would walk with them to the trolley depot.

No way, said the Bacons. Alice was not at all up to it.

But Alice insisted—and she got dressed and led them out the door.

"Well," Porter said later, describing the short walk, "she was weak going down there, and we walked slow. She said she couldn't walk fast—that she was weak—and . . . when we got down [to the depot], she said she didn't feel as if she could even stand up." Nearly falling down, Alice sat and rested on the steps of W. H. Mason's Drugstore.

"What is going on?" Porter asked, concerned, walking over to Alice. "How is Mrs. Archer treating you?"

"Well," Alice said, "she tried to have me take some medicine, but I told her I didn't need it. I told her I was a well woman and that I didn't need anything."

They said their good-byes—Alice did not get up—and parted ways.

Sixty-nine-year-old Alice Gowdy had never had any problems with her stomach, or any other major health issues. She had taken frequent walks to her friend Nellie's house ten minutes away, had eaten dinner with her husband, and had never had any adverse reaction to Amy's food in the past.

What in the world was the problem?

Near nine o'clock on that same evening, things took a turn for the worse.

"She vomited profusely," state's attorney Hugh Alcorn later said. "Complained of severe pain and a burning sensation in the throat and in the region of the stomach."

Amy was right there to help Alice after Loren called out for her. Amy again asked Alice if she wanted to take that medicine, but Alice again refused.

Throughout the night Alice's condition grew worse. The burning and pain continued, but she managed to hold on after begrudgingly agreeing to take a bit of Amy's "medication."

The following morning, upon waking up, the pain was worse.

Two days later, Alice was still in bed trying to work through whatever it was she had picked up on that Thanksgiving afternoon. Maybe it was a bug? Or the flu virus?

No one knew.

As the days went by and Alice grew sicker, Amy did not call a doctor—that is, not until the following Tuesday, December 1, a cold and windy day in Windsor. Amy phoned Dr. Emma J. Thompson, who had been Alice Gowdy's primary care physician for what Thompson described as "several years."

Thompson's practice was in downtown Hartford on Trumbull Street, where she had lived and worked for the past sixteen years. Thompson was educated at the Woman's Medical College of the New York Infirmary. She did most of her postgraduate work-study in Boston before settling in Hartford. Thompson was admired by her peers, as much for her persistent desire to succeed in what was surely a man's world as she was for her progressive views of medicine.

"I am Amy Archer, speaking for Alice Gowdy," Amy said when she called Thompson on that Tuesday. "She is ill . . . we wish to have you call over here to the Archer Home . . . [W]ould you come?"

Thompson said of course she would, and jumped on the trolley down the block from her office. It was near ten in the morning.

When Thompson arrived, Amy said, "Mrs. Gowdy is a hearty eater, ma'am, and she sometimes has attacks of acute indigestion. This seems to be that very sort of attack. It came on Thanksgiving night after she had eaten a very hearty Thanksgiving dinner."

Amy showed Thompson to Alice's room and left them alone.

What the doctor found when she entered was a weak woman on her death bed. And the first thing Thompson wondered was, *Why hadn't someone called me earlier?*

"[Alice] was lying in bed, apparently very much prostrated. When she saw me she held out her hand and began to weep," Thompson recalled.

Tears of pain and joy and relief. Finally, someone to take care of her.

Thompson sat down on a chair beside her patient. "How are you?" she asked. "Did you have too much Thanksgiving dinner, Alice? What is it? What's going on?"

Alice continued to cry. "She couldn't speak much," Thompson recalled.

Thompson checked Alice's pulse, which was "very weak and thready." Her heart was failing. "It was a quick, small pulse," Thompson said further, "one which is light under the finger . . . she had no rise in temperature—her temperature was normal." This was another dangerous sign to Thompson that Alice's body was shutting down; no fever meant that Alice's immune system had given up, stopped working. "I found that she had been . . . very profusely vomiting, and [had] very profuse diarrhea, but she didn't vomit while I was there, nor were the bowels evacuated while I was there."

Thompson stood up and, bending over Alice's midsection, "palpitated the abdomen." She placed her hands together and put light pressure on different sections of Alice's stomach, feeling around to see if there was any swelling or "special tenderness."

Nothing.

"Has there been any blood in her stool?" Thompson asked Loren, who was sitting in the room.

"Not that we know of."

Alice started to feel better as the night progressed. Thompson stayed with her. When she could talk, Alice said her "stools [were] like water" and her vomit was the same. She could not take most liquids—all profound signs and symptoms of poisoning, by the way—but was able to keep small sips of orange juice down.

The doctor could find "no further symptoms" to explain what was causing Alice such discomfort and pain. It seemed that the longer the doctor spent at the Home, the better the woman felt.

"I gave her a tablet for nausea." It was the same medicine Dr. Howard King had prescribed previously to several other inmates suffering from what was the same condition. Speaking to Loren as Alice dozed off, Thompson said, "See that she does not take any food other than liquid for two to three days."

Loren nodded. That was easy enough.

Dr. Thompson later described her diagnosis as "cholera morbus." According to most medical dictionaries, *cholera morbus*, an early-twentieth-century term, was more or less a seasonal condition, what most doctors of the day believed was an "acute gastroenteritis occurring in summer and autumn and marked by severe cramps, diarrhea, and vomiting," all brought on by indigestion.

Looking at Alice, Thompson was sure that her patient would improve and be back on her feet in a few days. She had seen this condition before. "Well, I thought her condition was serious . . . but I thought she would also recover."

Thompson collected her things and said her farewells to Alice and Loren, encouraging them to call if she was needed.

"Thank you, Doctor," Loren said.

On her way out, Amy stopped Thompson. "What do you think of this case?" Amy asked.

"I think she seems to be over the worst of it," Thompson responded. "Be careful, though. Give her a simple diet for the next two to three days—malted milk, and no other food."

Amy said she would.

"Now," Thompson continued firmly, giving Amy specific instructions, "she will probably get better, but if she doesn't get better by tomorrow, telephone me, please."

Throughout the following day, December 2, Thompson did not receive a call from Amy Archer. For Thompson, no news was good news.

Late the next morning, near noon on December 3, Amy called Thompson. "Come at once, Doctor, to see Mrs. Gowdy. I believe she's dying."

"Why didn't you call me sooner?"

Amy said she'd tried, but could not reach the doctor.

Why not call another doctor? Thompson would ask later. Why wait until the last minute, when the poor woman was ready to breathe her last? What could she do for her then? Dr. King was just down the block, his office directly across the street from another doctor. Why hadn't Amy called either of them if it was such an emergency? Thompson was in Hartford, a good hour-long trip.

Dr. Thompson's description of what she found and did upon entering Alice's room that afternoon, shortly after Amy called, needs no further explanation:

[T]he patient [was] ashy, blue—her extremities, her hands and feet were cold; there was no pulse at the wrist, and she was restless, although she was too weak to move. She could not get up and yet she made the effort to get up, as if she were under some kind of distress. I tried to make out what her distress was, but she could not articulate very well, but I judged that she wished to empty the bladder, and when a vessel was presented to her she could not evacuate the bladder. There was no result. I gave her hypodermic morphine one-quarter of a grain and waited till she got quiet, seemed comfortable. I left five or six tablets of one-eighth morphine and asked Mrs. Gilligan when the patient, when the effect of the morphine wore off if she still seemed restless, to dissolve two of those tablets in starch water and give it as a rectal injection to make her comfortable.

Thompson knew Alice Gowdy did not have a lot of time left. She was going to die. There was no hope for recovery this time. The only thing the doctor could do at this point was to make the woman feel as comfortable as possible.

In her office later that night, Thompson was finishing up some paperwork near seven o'clock when her phone rang.

It was Amy.

"Yes, what is it?" Thompson asked.

"Mrs. Gowdy has died, Doctor."

Chapter 26

DONE TO DEATH

ROBERT THAYER FOUND HIMSELF TAKING over an investigative role for Carl Goslee as the noose around Amy's neck began to tighten. It was discussed privately that Carl's new role in the case was going to be in the judicial realm, although nothing had been said publicly as of yet. As for Thayer, here was a man who was now in his element. As Thayer himself would later put it, "[hard] news was more than canned corned beef, 'and it took a man to get it.'"

Once Thayer had proved to himself that the death rates in the Archer Home far exceeded any of the other homes in the immediate Hartford region, he was resigned to getting something done. No more talking about it. After speaking to Nellie Pierce himself, a woman he said he didn't "think was pipe-dreaming . . . I got the idea she might know what she was talking about . . ."

Thayer had decided there was a murderer inside the Archer home, so he asked for an "editorial meeting" with Clifton Sherman to decide what path they would pursue. Thayer was convinced that something criminal was going on inside the Home; whether Amy had anything to do with it was another matter. He had Carl's information regarding the purchases of arsenic by Amy, sure; but a majority of the purchases had been made by inmates inside the Home. No one knew yet if Amy had been sending inmates on errands, or they were making the purchases on their own. He had a new, refined graph comparing the death rates in the nearby homes. But perhaps more than any of that, Robert Thayer was working on his own instincts.

As Thayer outlined the recent developments in the Amy Archer story, Sherman became convinced that they were on the periphery of the "greatest journalism coup" of his career. Yet the moral, conservative reporter in Sherman suggested it was probably time to bring in Thomas Egan, the superintendent of the Connecticut State Police. If nothing else, Egan would have something to say about what the *Courant* had uncovered—and perhaps share a suggestion or two as to what to do with the information. Sherman knew Egan well, having dealt with the Connecticut State Police on different levels for years. He could trust him.

By the time Sherman and Thayer were on their way to Egan's Hartford office that afternoon, the Connecticut State Police was already an active arm of the department of justice (Hugh Alcorn's office). Up until the State Police's inception in 1903, investigation on any large-scale effort was left to local police precincts, which, it was no secret, had been beleaguered by corruption and incompetence. It was 1901 when the idea for a statewide police force actually came into being in Connecticut. The Connecticut State Legislature "authorized the appointment of a state fire marshal to investigate fires of suspicious origin." John Russling, appointed to the position by elected officials, "became the state's first public safety officer." Then, in 1903, officials decided that the state should also have its own police force, which was then signed into action by Governor Abiram Chamberlain. On that day, House Bill Number 247 gave birth to what is the oldest state police force in the United States.

The need for a state-run police department stemmed from a widespread problem in Connecticut with "commercialized vice, liquor, and gambling crimes, as well as prostitution." There were only five officers on the force when the State Police started, each covering a different section of the state: Frank Brown (Norwich); Henry English (New Haven); James Huntington (Woodbury); John Perry (Southport); and Marcus Holcomb (Southington).*

In those early days, all officers wore plain clothes. Today, of course, state troopers in Connecticut wear Stetson-like Western hats and flashy blue, gray, and gold uniforms, while detectives don traditional suits and ties. During Amy's day, the State Police

---

* Incidentally, this early idea of splitting the state up into jurisdictions and having a "unit" set up in each area has not changed in over 100 years. Today the State Police is split into (12) "Troops," the letters A through K, and (3) "Districts," Eastern, Western, and Central.

investigated cases based "on the discretion of the governor, state's attorney, coroner, or any other legally appointed prosecuting officer . . ." So going to Superintendent Egan was a smart move on Sherman's part. If Egan thought the *Courant* had something, he would take it to Hugh Alcorn, the state's attorney, who could then sanction a full-scale investigation. It didn't matter that Alcorn had heard reports of weird things going on inside the Home; if Egan came to him, it turned into a law enforcement matter.

Clifton Sherman had been adamant when he'd told his reporters to secure solid findings backed up by facts. True, acting quicker may have saved lives inside the Archer Home (if something was indeed going on), but it also may have led to problems down the road when it came time to prosecute the case in a court of law. Whenever high-profile murders such as the Archer case made waves in the community, it was standard practice for newspaper reporters working the story to meet with police and discuss their findings. As it was, murder investigation in the state of Connecticut was in its infancy, the State Police, with its skeleton crew, just getting started. The local police did not have the resources or manpower to dedicate officers exclusively to murder cases. It was natural for reporters to aid in police investigations and share their findings—providing they were given the scoop when it was showtime.

One of the first State Police officers to be appointed to a ranking position was a brutish-looking man some said was as crass and ill-tempered as a rabid raccoon (when he needed to be), but as gentle as a falling leaf when duty called for it. The man had pudgy cheeks, a tar-black walrus mustache hiding his lips, and small, beady eyes. They called him "the captain," but his name was Robert T. Hurley. The forty-five-year-old policeman worked directly under Thomas Egan, and had lived east of Hartford in Manchester for several years before moving to the capital city in 1910. Born in Plymouth (Connecticut) in 1869, Hurley had worked in a factory in Bristol before becoming a professional trotting race driver, or harness-racing jockey. Just a few short years after ending his career as an investigator, he would go on to become Commissioner of the State Police. One of Hurley's most famous cases—that is, before he crossed paths with Amy Archer-Gilligan—was built around his suspicions regarding a house fire in the early 1900s that presumably killed a family of five. Although it had first appeared to be a routine fire, Hurley bet on his gut feeling and stayed with the case. After sifting through an enormous pile of ashes, he discovered that all five victims had been shot before their bodies were burned. It became known as the Shuttle Murder Case.

The information Sherman and Thayer brought forth would have to pass muster with Egan first, before it got to Hurley. But there was a good chance that once Egan had heard what the men had to say, Hurley was going to be knocking on doors, initiating an investigation of his own.

Thayer gave his pitch to Egan as Sherman sat and listened, backing up his reporter where he could. Egan listened closely, staring "at them in amazement," George Vedder Jones reported.

After hearing both men out, Egan asked, estimating, "Are you telling me that forty Archer inmates have been murdered?"

The number was low (the actual number was fifty-three recorded deaths between 1908–1914), which was even more astonishing. Fifty-three human beings. Dead. With an estimate of forty by the hand of *one* person?

Later, Egan would claim that the first time he had heard of any wrongdoing possibly going on at the Archer Home was several weeks before this meeting. When asked who had first brought the "Archer matter" to his attention, Egan responded, "Governor Holcomb."

Nonetheless, during the meeting Egan played along as if it was the first he'd heard of the case.

Sherman spoke next, saying, "Probably not all forty, sir. If averages mean anything, five died naturally. The rest were somehow done to death."

Egan was taken aback. He had not considered the idea that the two newspapermen had spent months investigating the case already. They weren't walking in out of the cold to simply point an accusatory finger at a woman who was obviously losing popularity in the town where she'd lived and worked.

"But it's too fantastic to believe," Egan said, taking a firm objective stance.

While the men waited, Egan picked up the phone and called Hugh Alcorn. Although Alcorn had been hearing rumors about the Archer Home for the past few years (Amy herself had written Alcorn a letter, inviting him into her home), Egan believed it was time to get the state's attorney involved on an inherent level; it was time to open an official investigation.

Children are marched down a Manhattan street during a parade. It is July 4, 1911—the beginning of the deadliest heat wave in New England history. One boy off to the right wipes the sweat from his brow as the girls in white go by. *Courtesy of the Library of Congress*

On July 5, 1911, crowds numbering in the hundreds of thousands flocked to Coney Island beaches to beat the heat. By day's end dozens of New Englanders will go "crazy from the heat" and commit suicide—drowning themselves, slashing their throats, jumping off buildings—while thieves begin to work the crowds, and ice and water become as scarce as a cool breeze. *Courtesy of the Library of Congress*

Thirsty children crowd around a public drinking fountain in hopes of re-hydrating with fresh water, which became so scarce during the 1911 heat wave that riots for it broke out in Hartford, Boston, and New York. This as the dead began to pile up. *Courtesy of the Library of Congress*

With horses dropping dead in the streets due to the excessive heat, the expensive luxury of shower baths were given away for free. *Courtesy of the Library of Congress*

Children did anything they could to stay cool, as this photo shows a group of kids in New York wetting their heads in a horse drinking trough, unconcerned about cholera or any number of waterborne diseases. *Courtesy of the Library of Congress*

Horses needed constant watering, as the temperature continued to rise against a humidity level that hovered in the high eighties and low nineties for two weeks straight. *Courtesy of the Library of Congress*

This rare image shows Carlan Hollister Goslee, in his early twenties, as the Military Band Major for the town of Windsor, Connecticut. Many residents considered Carlan one of the most honest, caring, and respected men of the town. By the time this photo was taken in 1914, Carlan had already suspected that fellow town resident Amy Archer, the owner/operator of the Archer Home, a one-of-a-kind nursing home opened in 1907, might be harming patients. *Courtesy of Spencer Moore and family*

When this cartoon image of Carlan was published on the front page of the *Windsor Town Crier* in March 1916, Carlan was planning on exposing Amy Archer with a series of stories he had investigated and written as a freelance reporter for the *Hartford Courant*. Although this article accompanying the portrait of Carlan did not mention the many untimely deaths at the Archer Home, it did report that Carlan had a "keen news sense," calling him a "loyal citizen with a strong civic spirit." *Courtesy of Spencer Moore and family*

Later in life, Carlan avoided talk of his heroic involvement in bringing down Connecticut's most notorious serial killer, Amy Archer-Gilligan. He instead focused on his role as Mae Goslee's husband and the large family they had nurtured during their storybook marriage. *Courtesy of Spencer Moore and family*

Carlan Goslee was treasurer of the "Windsor Rogue Detecting Society," a quasi-detective agency that investigated robbery, burglary, suspicious fires, and the occasional murder. Here he is showing off the detailed, meticulous records he kept for the society. *Courtesy of Spencer Moore and family*

Officially called the Archer Home for Elderly People and Chronic Invalids, this red-brick colonial owned by Amy Archer had some twenty beds. Elderly clients (or, as she called them, "inmates") paid either a lump some of $1,000 (for life care), or between $7 and $15 weekly. Billed a "Murder Factory" by the *Hartford Courant* eight years after opening, records indicate Amy Archer could have poisoned well over fifty inmates—and two husbands—in this house, events that later inspired Joseph Kesselring to write the hit Broadway play *Arsenic & Old Lace*. *Courtesy of the Windsor Historical Society*

One of only a handful of known photographs of Amy Archer, this undated, poorly reproduced photo depicts a mild-mannered, grandmotherly type of turn-of-the-century woman. Amy is stoic and unemotional. She seems to be captured by the mere idea of having her photo taken. Behind a saintly façade she portrayed in town, however, was a drug-addicted sociopath who started killing out of greed and soon turned into one of the nation's most prolific serial killers in history. *Author's collection*

In these rare mug-shot photographs taken in 1916 after her arrest on murder charges, Amy appears more feeble than sinister. She was said to be thirty-eight years old when these photos were taken, but no record of exactly when Amy was born is available. *Author's collection*

Town greens are a traditional New England staple, whereby a space near the center of a town is set aside for picnics, parades, and social events. This is the center of Windsor, only a few years after Amy opened the Archer Home. For years, neighbors and friends referred to the Windsor caretaker as "Sister Amy" because she was often seen wandering about town with a Bible in the fold of her arm. *Courtesy of the Windsor Historical Society*

W. H. Mason's general store became the focal point of the investigation into the suspected murders at the Archer Home. Carlan Goslee and the Connecticut State Police uncovered that Mason's was selling copious amounts of arsenic to the Home. Amy was so callous and cold-hearted she actually sent some of those she was about to poison "on an errand" to Mason's to pick up the arsenic she would later use to kill them. *Courtesy of the Windsor Historical Society*

In this century-old photo, Windsor residents stand around the Post Office. One of the many clues that helped authorities realize Amy might be murdering inmates were the letters Franklin Andrews, a boarder at the Archer Home and friend to Amy's second husband, Michael Gilligan, wrote to his brother and sister, detailing the suspicious numbers of inmates dying inside the home for no apparent reason. *Courtesy of the Windsor Historical Society*

State of Connecticut — Bureau of Vital Statistics

Medical Certificate of Death

1. Full name of deceased _Maud Howard Lynch_
2. Primary cause of death _Epilepsy_ 3. Duration _____ days
4. Secondary or contributory _Pernicious Anemia_ 5. Duration _____ days
Remarks

I hereby Certify that I attended the deceased in her last illness, and that the cause of death was as above stated.
Signature _H.H. King Attending Physician_
Capacity in which he signs
Dated _Feb 2_ 19_16_ Address _Windsor Ct_

Undertaker's Certificate — Personal and Statistical

1. Full name of deceased _Maud Howard Lynch_
2. Place of death—Town _Windsor_ No. _Prospect Ave_ Street _____ Ward
   [If death occurred in a hospital or institution, give its name instead of street and number]
3. Number of families in house
4. Residence at time of death _Windsor_ _Ct_
   Town _____ State or Country
5. Occupation _At any_
6. Condition (state whether single, married, divorced or widowed) _Married_ _Lynch_
7. If wife or widow, give name of husband _James E Lynch_
8. Date of death—year _1916_, month _Feb_, day _2_
9. Date of birth—year _1883_, month _____, day _____
10. Age _33_ years, _____ months, _____ days
11. Sex _F_
12. Color _W_
13. Birthplace—Town _____ State or Country _Penna_
14. Father's name in full _George Howard_
15. Father's birthplace—Town _____ State or Country _Penn_
16. Mother's maiden name _Nellie A Wheeler_
17. Mother's birthplace—Town _Wyoming_ State or Country _R.I._
18. Place of burial _Windsor_ Cemetery _Palisado_
19. Name of informant _Mrs Archer_ Address _Lakeville_
20. Was body embalmed _Yes_ If so name of embalmer _Frank L Archer_ License No. _123_
Signature of Undertaker _Smith & Chase_ Address _Hartford_

One of the only known inmates Amy murdered with strychnine (rather than arsenic) was Maud Lynch, who died inside the Archer Home on February 2, 1916, at the young age of thirty-three. Clearly written on Maud's death certificate, the cause of death—"epilepsy"—was to become a talking point among detectives investigating Amy. Questioned later about this, the doctor who signed off on the death certificate said Amy had told him what to write. *Author's collection*

This is a rare photo of Franklin Andrews, one of the only known images available. As Andrews watched inmate after inmate die around him inside the Archer Home, he suspected that the lovely caretaker who had been plying him with favorable comments and chores around the home, could be a cold-blooded murderer. Andrews would ultimately spark the investigation that sent an undercover officer into the home posing as an elderly inmate. *Author's collection*

In this undated photograph, Dr. Howard King, Windsor's medical examiner at the time many of the deaths occurred inside the Archer Home, stands tall and trim, decked out in a fedora and overcoat. The state's attorney, Hugh Alcorn, would later question the doctor's ethics, saying he should have seen the signs of death by poisoning in the patients he tended to inside the Archer Home. *Author's collection*

They called him "the captain." Former race car driver Robert T. Hurley was forty-five years old when he was brought into the Archer Home investigation. This undated, grainy photo shows the man who was the first Connecticut State Police officer to use a motor vehicle during an investigation of this nature. Hurley questioned Amy on the night of her arrest, and ultimately took her into custody as her daughter, Mary Archer, protested her innocence and cried. *Author's collection*

"We Will Fight for Mother," Says Mrs. Gilligan's 18 Year Old Daughter

MISS MARY K. ARCHER.
She Engages Counsel for Her Mother's Defense.

"WE'LL FIGHT FOR MOTHER."

Mrs. Gilligan's Daughter, Pretty, And An Accomplished Musician, Says She Knows Her Mother Is Innocent.

This rare photograph of eighteen-year-old Mary Archer, Amy's only child, ran with an article in the *Hartford Courant* after Amy's 1916 arrest for murder. Mary, a piano prodigy, was certain of her mother's innocence and vowed to prove she was being railroaded and set up by an overzealous state's attorney. *Author's collection*

This blurred image of forty-two-year-old high-profile defense attorney Benedict Holden shows the man who took Amy's case immediately after her May 1916 arrest. Holden's first job out of law school was a private practice he opened with a friend, Marcus Holcomb, the governor of Connecticut at the time of Amy's arrest. *Author's collection*

This *Hartford Courant* artist's depiction of the courtroom during Amy Archer's first trial shows Dr. Howard King on the witness stand, while the wife of a man who died at the Archer Home under Amy's care sits in the gallery looking on. Howard King finally admitted he should have had a better handle on the patients under his care at the home and should have realized that many of the dead had shown signs of poisoning he missed. *Author's collection*

In the illustration: DR. H·F·KING, MEDICAL EXAMINER OF WINDSOR

Opened in 1827, the Wethersfield (Connecticut) Prison where Amy Archer-Gilligan was initially sent to be executed was modeled after Auburn State Prison in New York. In 1963, Wethersfield prisoners were transferred to a brand new "state prison" in Somers, Connecticut. By 1965, Wethersfield Prison was torn down. *Courtesy of the Connecticut Historical Society, Graphics Collection*

Not far from Amy's cell inside Wethersfield Prison, this "hanging room" would have been where Amy's sentence of death was carried out had Governor Marcus Holcomb not stepped in and stayed her execution until an appeal could be argued. *Courtesy of the Connecticut Historical Society Museum*

After a second trial, Amy was housed in one of these state-of-the-art cells at Wethersfield Prison—that is, before she started talking on the phone to nobody on the other end of the line and playing funeral music on the prison organ. Re-evaluated after reports of "bizarre behavior," Amy was judged to be insane and shipped to a Middletown, Connecticut, mental asylum, where she lived until her death in 1962 at the reported age of eighty-nine. *Courtesy of the Connecticut Historical Society Museum*

Chapter 27

MAY THE CURSE OF GOD
COME DOWN ON YOU

HUGH ALCORN WAS FIRM: IT WAS ESSENTIAL that the *Hartford Courant* not publish any stories in the near future about the Archer Home. Alcorn had advised Clifton Sherman after being briefed about the allegations that Amy Archer-Gilligan could be a sadistic serial killer. Alcorn said he needed time to look into the matter himself with his investigators.

The managing editor was, of course, disappointed. He had a vested interest in the story. It was his newspaper, after all, that had broken the case.

Not to fear, Alcorn advised. The *Courant* would get the scoop once the State Police knew where the case was headed. On top of that, Alcorn had several questions he needed answers to before he would sign off on an indictment. Alcorn had heard of these "murder" rumors for years; however, he warned, just because they were persistent, it did not mean they were true. He asked everyone to be careful. A wrong move now could seriously damage a court case, if it came down to it. Truth be told, how did any of them know, Alcorn suggested, that there was not a "homicidal maniac" running wild inside the Archer Home and that Amy was innocent?

The woes of circumstantial evidence.

"Was some mentally unbalanced neighbor trying to get rid of the Home by murdering its inmates?" Alcorn asked rhetorically.

It was clear that a majority of the Windsor community was totally against Amy and her Home. Was it a case of sabotage? Hugh Alcorn had heard "things" about Amy from various neighbors in and around Windsor, he explained. The neighbors were fed up with getting no help from the law.

This discussion then led to one of the most important questions of the case thus far: How could such a high death rate inside the Home "fail to attract the notice of the [in-house] physician?" Was Dr. Howard King killing his patients?

It was not at all probable, Alcorn insisted, but still possible.

While Hugh Alcorn and the Connecticut State Police began working on how to further facilitate the investigation started by the *Courant*, Franklin Andrews's sister, Nellie Pierce, was waging a war of her own against Amy. Nellie could not simply sit back and wait for the authorities to act and do something. Nellie didn't need any more convincing: She was certain that Amy had murdered her brother, and would murder others. Now Nellie was going to do everything in her power to prove it.

Nellie had gone through more of Franklin's records and found that an additional $500 in cash was missing from his bank account. Coupled with the loan of $1,000 that Franklin had apparently (willingly) given Amy, Nellie decided there was enough money involved to hire a lawyer and sue Amy to get it back. Who was this woman to think she could steal Franklin's money and get away with it? Nellie was livid. What's more, when Nellie heard that Alice Gowdy and Michael Gilligan had both died under circumstances that were suspiciously similar to Franklin's, she became entirely convinced that Amy was a murderer who needed to be stopped before more inmates lost their lives.

"My brother's death," Nellie said near this time, "and Mr. [Michael] Gilligan's, too—one day they were well, the next dead!"

To intelligent people, Nellie suggested, the writing on the wall was clear.

Beginning in June 1914, Nellie started making accusations against Amy in a series of letters she sent to the woman. Could she rattle Amy's cage enough to get her to respond in kind?

It worked.

In one of her return letters, Amy invoked the "spirits and memory" of the recently departed to "bear witness that she [spoke] the truth." In other words, Amy was calling on those from the grave to strike her down if she was telling lies.

Nellie's attorney, R. H. Deming, contacted Amy and threatened a lawsuit, in addition to a bitter and humiliating public scandal that would eventually follow—all of which could be avoided if Amy paid back the money she rightfully owed the Andrews family.

Another lawsuit was certainly not what Amy needed right now; she was already in enough of a bind with the community, who were all but lighting torches and sharpening pitchforks, as it were.

So Amy caved—but not without first speaking her mind.

"Mrs. Archer-Gilligan returned the $500," the *Courant* reported years after the incident, "explaining that although she could have kept the money, she did not feel it was worth quarreling over." Amy did not give up the money easily, however, and it took Nellie and her attorney months to recover it.

At one point, Amy attacked Nellie, writing, "I am no little surprised in the attitude you take in trying to injure my Home. If a man ever sets from the grave, Mr. Andrews will. He certainly would never allow you ... to do as you are."

From that point forward, Amy raged about how well treated Franklin had been during his stay at the Home, and how much he would have disapproved of Nellie taking issue with his funds and attacking Amy as such. How dare Nellie make a claim that Franklin did not want Amy to have what was lawfully and rightfully hers? Franklin had given Amy that $500, Amy suggested in her letter, to help the Home. It was a donation.

After sending Nellie the $500, Amy could not let it go. She had to have the last word. In her next letter, she lambasted poor Nellie Pierce, calling her a greedy relative of a dead man, who wanted to take what "Mr. Andrews gave to our Home." It was avarice driving Nellie, Amy suggested. Nothing more than plain old greed. She was so sure that Franklin had wanted the money used for the "beautification of the Home," she said, that she "[hoped] God [would] afflict me, as I know he will, if these were not the *exact* words [your brother] used [emphasis added]." She continued:

I will pray this morning that Almighty God, who knows how you and yours tried to destroy my Home, may the curse of God come down on each one of you and punish you by doing for you what you never had the slightest cause to try to do to us: destroy

147

your home, your name (if you have any!), take from you your
means of livelihood, separate you from your relations and
friends. [M]ay this Curse come on you at once so that you may
be made an example of. . . . I trust he will haunt the wicked
wretches who would tell the terrible falsehoods they have.

The letter went on for another two pages as Amy conjured the name
of God several more times as she cursed Nellie and her sister and
brother for what they had done to her in demanding the money
through a lawsuit.

It was pure hatred driving Amy—she was more upset over the
fact that Nellie had beaten her than she was at having to pay back
the money. She believed that God would see it her way and penalize
Nellie for her dastardly deeds. There was vengeance and anger and
obviously scorn in the letter. Amy wasn't used to losing.

"May God punish you all," she ended the blistering missive,
"and make example of your work. Now you will see who is right.
May Mr. Andrews haunt you until you make public your conduct."

☙ ☙ ☙

After several meetings and long discussions, Hugh Alcorn and Thomas
Egan decided that the best thing to do was to beat Amy Archer-
Gilligan at her own game. If she was killing her inmates and stealing
their money, the only way to nail her was to catch her in the act.

But how?

The State Police called on Zola Bennett, an "elderly" woman,
according to one description. Bennett was probably in her late fifties, early sixties, and had been working for the Connecticut State
Police as an "undercover private investigator" for many years. The
idea was to send Bennett over to the Archer Home to ask if there
was an open room for rent.

"I'm a wealthy, friendless widow," Zola Bennett explained to
Amy when she showed up a few days later.

With her trademark genteel reverence, Amy took one look at
Zola Bennett—*a wealthy widow?*—and opened the door wide, saying eagerly, "Come in, come in . . ."

Chapter 28

POISON CONTROL

D R. EMMA THOMPSON SIGNED OFF ON ALICE GOWDY'S death certificate on December 4, 1914. The primary cause of death: *cholera morbus*, a condition, the doctor estimated, that Alice had suffered from for "six days" before succumbing to it. According to what Dr. Thompson wrote, Alice's "acute gastric intestinal condition wore out the heart."

Alice died late into the night of December 3. The death certificate was signed and filed the following day. Interestingly enough, Thompson noted on the certificate that Alice's body had been embalmed not twenty-four hours after her death by Frank P. Smith, an undertaker Amy frequently used.

"Mrs. Gowdy's body," Hugh Alcorn later explained, "was at once sent to the undertaking rooms of Smith and Sons in Hartford, and there embalmed with Red Falcon embalming fluid. The arterial process was used. The stomach was not punctured, nor did any of the embalming fluid enter the stomach."

More important, the death certificate specifically stated that "permit for burial is FORBIDDEN, if 'heart failure' or a synonym is given as the only cause of death."

Despite this, Alice Gowdy was readied for interment and buried.

As talk in Windsor centered on how the townspeople were going to get Amy kicked out of her home, by March of 1915 Amy felt pressured into responding to new allegations surrounding her behavior and the business. Amy understood that if she didn't fight back, it was only going to be a matter of time before she was forced out of town like a common criminal, either by legal means or a disruption in her business.

Unbeknownst to Amy, Zola Bennett, now firmly ensconced as an inmate of the Home, began reporting to Hugh Alcorn and Thomas Egan via secret letters about Alice Gowdy's last week of life. Bennett conducted interviews with inmates when Amy wasn't around. She uncovered documents—letters, diaries, real estate papers and bank account information—and read through them.* Somewhere in her correspondence, Bennett suggested that it might a good idea for someone to interview Dr. Emma Thompson, so as to find out exactly what she knew and how she felt about the last few days of Alice's life. Bennett was fully convinced that Amy had played a role in Alice's death, simply because *cholera morbus* was such a common condition in the Home, and the fact that Alice had been on the mend when Thompson left Amy with specific instructions regarding what to do if Alice's condition changed. By all accounts, Alice should have recovered.

Although Amy soon got wind of Alcorn's latest investigation, Bennett's identity had not been compromised. So Amy wrote to the attorney once again and offered him access to the Home, saying, "I trust you will forgive me if I appear presumptuous in writing you as I do; but I feel bitterly grieved and hurt in being accused of that which is so blatantly false."

Amy went on to clarify that the main thrust of the accusations against her came after Robert Thayer's visit, and after Carl Goslee had become interested in speaking with family members of dead inmates.

Part of Alcorn's investigation focused on the monetary agreements and contracts Amy had made and signed with her inmates. In Alcorn's view, the contracts alone were designed to create a situation where the business depended on frequent deaths. An inmate was worth more dead than alive. During periods of time where no one died, no new income came in.

It made sense to Alcorn that greed was the motivating factor.

"You hurt my feelings very much," Amy continued in her letter to Alcorn, talking about the rumors, "when you said you did not

---

* Sadly, I could not locate any of these documents; instead, I found only written descriptions of their existence. Having Bennett's report during her time inside the Archer Home would have explained a lot.

like the way I had for taking money from these people—altho I am glad to tell you the case—We have <u>never</u> taken a person under contract when the chances were not <u>always</u> against us—these at the most were very few—I took one woman for $450 who was with us 8 yrs. But the people here are not under contract as a rule or very rarely. . . ."

This statement on Amy's part was categorically false—a downright lie. Amy *pushed* inmates to sign life contracts.

Alcorn wrote back to Amy, laying out his concerns and the possibility that an investigation was already under way.

To that, Amy responded with one of her longer diatribes, belaboring several points which made little sense when the facts were taken into account:

> You spoke of Mr. Andrews's death being "very suspicious." It may have represented to you as such—but there was nothing of the kind about his death. He loved our Home [and] everyone about here knew this and his own people knew it. He met death anything but suddenly. He came from the Hospital here alone—hardly able to walk—and his body was one mass of boils and ulcers for months before he died. Now, his sisters knew this. On the day of [an Andrews friend's] funeral, [Franklin's] neck was broken out with three great abscesses and he was not able to go to the funeral, tho he went. His sister, I very well don't remember her name [she certainly knew Nellie's name] was here a week or two before he died, and she well knew he was in a very feeble condition. The poor man suffered terribly so before he died. . . . To people who know me, they actually laugh at the charges, knowing the sacrifices I have made. Only last Sunday night a man who knows what I suffer—by these false statements—said, "Mrs. Archer, why don't you send for Att. Alcorn to visit you . . . Someone has lied . . . and I know if he came here and saw for himself your work he would feel differently." What more can I do?

The reality of the situation for Amy Archer was that Hugh Alcorn had an investigator inside the Home and Amy knew nothing of it.

She could lie all she wanted to, but in the end, Amy was going to have to explain herself.

▲ ▲ ▲

Following the suggestion of Zola Bennett, Captain Robert Hurley interviewed Dr. Emma Thompson, who said she had "decided to go to the police" herself because "Mrs. Gowdy's attack on Thanksgiving seemed a severe one . . . but she had responded so well to treatment that I stopped seeing her after the third day, leaving Mrs. Archer to telephone me if there was a change for the worse."

"Did she?" Hurley asked.

"No," Thompson explained. "So when I heard nothing, I assumed that she'd recovered."

Instead, Amy called a few days later, and by then it was far too late to do anything.

Notably, during Hurley's interview with Thompson, the doctor said she "called the acting medical examiner"—which would have been Dr. Howard King—"and he accepted my diagnosis of cholera morbus," and ultimately signed off on burial permissions.

No questions. No reports. No tests. No further explanation needed—just a phone call.

King's incompetence and ignorance, or culpability, was further exposed with each new death. Later, when asked about this, King said, "Why, in a majority of the cases, I say, they were old people, and the trouble was generally hardening of the arteries, or old age. It is absolutely impossible to state when hardening of the arteries begins. I don't know how you would state when old age begins . . . You cannot fill in the duration; it is impossible, according to the nature of the condition."

Thompson told Hurley that as time went on, she "began to wonder." The "coldness and rigidity in Mrs. Gowdy's extremities" were unusual symptoms.

"How unusual?" Hurley asked. He wanted the doctor's opinion.

"I'm certain Mrs. Gowdy was poisoned," Thompson told Hurley.

As Hurley began to interview others, including Nellie Pierce and relatives of Charles Smith, a man who had also died under similar circumstances that same year (1914), it became clear that he was going to have to get a court order and begin exhuming bodies for forensic testing.

Another fact Hurley considered was that Amy Archer had been purchasing large amounts of arsenic (even during the winter months), and several of her patients—if not dozens—had died of symptoms comparable, if not identical, to arsenical poisoning.

Chapter 29

THE FACTS

O NE OF THE MOST FAMOUS ARSENICAL POISONING cases on record (which could never be emphatically proven beyond a reasonable doubt) is, of course, that of Napoleon Bonaparte, who was said to have been poisoned to death with arsenic over a period of time by one (or several) of his own men. Regardless of the facilitator, the symptoms of death by arsenical poisoning cannot be confused with much else. According to the *Journal of the American Medical Association* (*JAMA*), "Toxic doses of the strongly ionizable inorganic compounds of arsenic cause gastro-enteritis with vomiting, diarrhea and abdominal pain." The symptoms, moreover, are not immediate; they are "commonly delayed for half an hour or more."

All of Amy's alleged victims complained of identical symptoms, including a delay in each illness, as if the pain was staggered. The first symptom, according to the doctors who wrote the study, "is a feeling of constriction in the throat with difficulty in swallowing." In addition, "The evacuations are normal in appearance at first but later become watery and contain shreds of desquamated intestinal epithelium closely resembling the 'rice-water' stools of Asiatic cholera."

In Franklin Andrews's case, Dr. Howard King described this same condition almost to the point where you'd think he'd written part of the study, saying that Franklin Andrews's "vomit was liquid, as I remember it, and contained mucus, some bile, and had a coffee-ground appearance." When asked if this seemed odd to the doctor, seeing that it was indeed rare for someone to expel this sort of regurgitation without being poisoned, King added, "Well, it did not indicate anything very much to me at the time. It seemed to me that he was just throwing off the contents of the stomach, on account of an acute indigestion."

And at one time, King had said none of Amy's inmates had ever shown signs of poisoning. By King's own observation, he said later that "the presence of blood in the stomach, acted upon by gastric juice, will most always produce a coffee-ground appearance."

Franklin Andrews was bleeding from the inside out.

"The fluid," *JAMA* reports, "unlike that of simple diarrhea induced by saline cathartics, consists of the serum of the blood, or it may also contain some blood, and this loss of serum results in a train of symptoms closely resembling those of actual hemorrhage."

Those poisoned by arsenic over a duration of time appear to suffer from "weakness, dizziness, headache, cold sweat and collapse." They look "pale and shrunken."

All of Amy's victims fell into this category.

Respiration is generally deep and depressed, which was what Dr. Emma Thompson reported during her second visit to Alice Gowdy. The symptoms intensify over a period of days, "until coma and death occur." Death results from "either circulatory or respiratory failure; that is, either the heart or the respiration may fail first, but when both are affected so profoundly each reacts upon the other, so that one cannot say that either alone is the cause of death." This would give good reason for the varying causes of death on the certificates, but all falling into the same heart/gastro realm of medicine.

Important to the current investigation by the state's attorney and the Connecticut State Police, facts both arms of law enforcement would not learn until years later, was that gastrointestinal symptoms of arsenical poisoning are, more than anything else, brought on by the effects of absorption into the system. *JAMA* explains this important piece of evidence, which in turn becomes utterly important when analyzing the Amy Archer-Gilligan case:

> *Arsenic causes paralysis of the walls of the capillaries, and later those of the arterioles . . . rendering them more permeable than normally, so that there is a copious effusion of serum or even of blood, into the tissues. After the administration of very large doses of arsenic to animals one may observe extravasations of blood beneath large areas of the*

peritoneum. The escape of serous fluid raises blisters beneath the gastro-intestinal mucous membrane, and this is soon desquamated with the escape of large amounts of serum into the stomach and intestine, causing the "rice-water" diarrhea. The diarrhea and its attendant pain and loss of water cause a great fall in the blood pressure, and this is later augmented by the direct action of the arsenic on the heart, should the patient survive long enough [Alice Gowdy]. . . . Such serious disturbances of the circulation are always attended with corresponding depression of the central nervous system; especially is this true when the circulatory changes are induced suddenly. One has only to recall the frequency of dizziness due to interference with the cerebral circulation when one rises suddenly from a sitting or recumbent position, to appreciate that the great loss of serum in arsenic poisoning and the resulting circulatory disturbance must cause a variety of secondary effects. If vomiting occurs early . . . much, or comparatively little, of the arsenic may be evacuated . . .

The key for Hurley, Alcorn, and any future prosecution, however, something these men may not have known at the time, was to get those bodies out of the ground as quickly as possible—because any scientist or forensic examiner a defense attorney was going to hire would argue that the ground where these bodies had been buried was loaded with metals and chemicals and compounds and organisms.

Chief among them, of course, arsenic.

Chapter 30

GRAVE ROBBERS

Z OLA BENNETT WAS ABLE TO GET ROBERT HURLEY the names of several relatives connected to those "suspicious" deaths inside the Archer Home. Hurley and Thomas Egan could now conduct several additional interviews. Primarily, the State Police focused on the siblings of Charles Smith, Maude Lynch (a thirty-three-year-old woman who was staying at the Home, placed there by family, who had died, according to Dr. Howard King, of epilepsy and pernicious anemia, a disease that occurs when the body refuses to absorb vitamin B12), and Michael Gilligan. This took time, however, mostly because the families lived in different parts of Massachusetts and Connecticut. Although the State Police had been an official arm of the state's attorney's office for over a decade by then, the use of motor vehicles was not something the department favored or allowed for in its budget. When conducting an investigation in his district, Hurley generally walked, took the trolley, or traveled by horse and buggy or taxi.

As the summer of 1915 faded into the winter and spring of 1916, Hugh Alcorn and Thomas Egan saw the significance of continuing and even stepping up the Archer Home investigation. Egan told Hurley there was a good chance he was going to be getting a motor vehicle to use for what had become the most sensational murder investigation the State Police had ever embarked on. Between the period of 1911 and 1916, Alcorn, Hurley, and Egan estimated, there had been forty-eight suspicious deaths at the Archer Home. If someone had killed that many people, not only was the State Police and state's attorney involved in the most prolific female serial killer case in history, but the media attention alone would be surpassed by no other murder. The Lizzie Borden fiasco of a murder trial had taken place in nearby Fall River, Massachusetts, twenty years prior.

Although sensational in every aspect of the word, Lizzie had only faced double murder charges.

The Archer case could tally ten times that amount.

♣ ♣ ♣

It was nearly two years to the day of Franklin Andrews's death that Dr. Arthur J. Wolff got a call from Hugh Alcorn indicating that his services were needed. Wolff was a highly qualified, highly sought-after physician, but also the chief state bacteriologist (pathologist) for Connecticut.

By the first week of May 1916, Alcorn and Egan had the paperwork in order to exhume Franklin Andrews's body. It was May 1 when Captain Hurley took a ride to the Cheshire cemetery where Franklin had been buried. Nellie Pierce had been asked to go along.

After a short walk from the dirt road, up a hill and over a bridge, Nellie pointed to Franklin's grave. She was solemn, scared. Yet, at the same time, relieved something was being done to stop that madwoman.

Hurley brought Nellie back to his car and found the undertaker, George Keeler. "We'll need to have that body taken up tomorrow night," Hurley explained.

Keeler said he would be prepared.

It was Dr. Arthur Wolff's job to lead the ghastly task of examining Franklin's two-year-old corpse.

Wolff was no homegrown, hired henchman for the state of Connecticut. He had trained as a physician in Germany and France after growing up in a strict household with a father who was also a doctor. In 1876, Wolff graduated from a university in Texas, and then spent four years in New York at Bellevue Hospital Medical College. He was a member of several medical societies and had worked at St. Francis Hospital in Hartford for twenty-one years.

The guy knew his stuff. No doubt about it.

More important to Hugh Alcorn, Dr. Wolff had over thirty-five years of courtroom experience, testifying for the prosecution in scores of cases, many of which were murder. In a sense, Wolff was the Henry Lee of his day. Even more impressive where the Archer Home case was concerned, Wolff had testified in no fewer than five high-profile poisoning cases by 1916. If there was a doctor alive to look into the deaths at the Archer Home, deaths allegedly caused by poisoning, there were few more qualified than Dr. Arthur Wolff.

On the afternoon of May 2, Alcorn called Wolff again and asked him to head out to Cheshire that night to conduct a "secret" autopsy on Franklin Andrews's body. Alcorn said Franklin's body would have to be exhumed after dark and Wolff was to tell no one about the job. He and Hurley, Alcorn stated, would arrive late in the night to meet the undertaker and a few grave hands.

The doctor said he could do it.

That night, near seven o'clock, Captain Hurley pulled up in a motor vehicle in front of Wolff's Hartford office. State Police officer Rowe Wheeler drove, while Hurley sat in the back with the doctor.

The bumpy, loud, and rather uncomfortable drive took two hours. Hurley and Wolff discussed what would go down when they arrived. Undertaker George Keeler was going to be waiting for them.

"I understand," said Wolff.

They went to Keeler's office. "I'll take you out to the tool house," Keeler said. "You'll set up there."

Wolff looked at Hurley. "Yes." He was going to perform the autopsy inside the tool house. It was the only way.

Wolff put his bag and tools inside the makeshift autopsy suite— a wide wooden board placed between two wooden barrels—and then lit the lanterns and asked Keeler where the body was.

"The grave," he said, nodding toward the rolling hill outside. Hurley had been there the day before with Nellie Pierce.

"Let's go."

Hurley followed, Rowe Wheeler behind him.

"From there," Wolff later described, "we went to the grave, some little distance." Franklin's grave was opened. "The outer box lid was taken off and laid upon the side of the grave while we were there."

Hurley shined his lantern, Keeler following.

The coffin was open.

Keeler and two of his men, there with Hurley's approval, carried the cobwebbed, dirty box with what was left of Franklin's flesh and bones back to the tool house.

Bending down before they left the gravesite, Wolff noticed immediately that there was little or no smell.

Odd. Someone buried in the ground for a few years would certainly emit an awful odor. But the doctor had a theory as to why—and would soon explain it to those assembled there.

Franklin's casket had cost the family a pretty penny; it was a "black-covered coffin," Wolff noted, "with silver trimmings and upon a plate there was engraved in scroll work, FRANKLIN R. ANDREWS, AGE [60]."

They placed the casket on the "improvised table," as Wolff called it. Then the doctor went in for his first good look. Franklin's face was "covered with a brownish-colored scale," Wolff noted, "and the forehead and neck with a whitish, soapy looking material that is called *adipocere*." The substance Wolff described was more familiarly known as "grave wax."* Another known substance that was patently prevalent was *aspergillus*, a common mold that generally forms over rotting flesh or meat (think of those blue and fuzzy spots covering an orange that has been left out on a counter for one too many days).

All of this decomposition, however, was something Dr. Wolff was more than pleased to see. It meant that Franklin Andrews's body, because he had been buried so close to a stream and moisture in the soil was present all around him, had been preserved by the same process which had started to decay it.

Franklin's clothing was intact, Wolff noted, staring down at the body and then backing away to take copious, detailed notes. Keeler and an associate had "lifted" the body from the casket by this point and placed it on the board. Hurley and Rowe Wheeler stood nearby, watching, waiting for Wolff's orders.

The eyes were shrunken, Wolff noted, but the cheeks were quite fresh looking.

---

* According to Merriam-Webster Online Dictionary 2008, adipocere is "a waxy substance consisting chiefly of fatty acids and calcium soaps that is formed during decomposition of dead body fat in moist or wet anaerobic conditions."

Here were several men and a two-year-old corpse stuffed into a small wooden tool house in the middle of a graveyard, and yet, Wolff realized, there was no "odor of decomposition." A two-year-old corpse, not yet fully decomposed, would certainly stink.

Strange. Why didn't Franklin Andrews's rotting corpse stink?

His hands and feet were also covered with *adipocere* underneath *aspergillus. A thick layer of this material.*

Wolff took out a pair of curved steel shears and cut off Franklin's clothing to expose what was left of his flesh. Peeling off the clothing, some of the skin "stuck" to the clothing and bits and pieces of decomposed flesh were peeled off with the clothes.

The first order of business Wolff attended to was a full examination of Franklin's body to figure out if there were any *distinguishing marks of injury or disease upon the surface of the body.*

Boils?

He stepped back after doing this and made note that there were, in fact, none.

Amy had told Alcorn in writing that Franklin Andrews's body was dotted considerably with boils for weeks leading up to his death.

She was wrong—or lying. Dr. Wolff found no such evidence to corroborate such a claim.

In fact, before he'd left for the autopsy, Wolff had been told by Alcorn that he should find abscesses and boils about the body, so Wolff turned Franklin's body on its side and, with a spyglass, made a careful inspection down the back of Franklin's neck, spine, and back, where a good part of his flesh was still intact.

"I found a body," Wolff said later, "of a moderately well-nourished man . . ." with no pockmarks on the skin.

Placing Franklin on his back once again, Wolff began the process of opening Franklin's chest cavity. He made an incision underneath the skin, right down to the bone, in front of the pelvis, including part of the neck and chest wall and the abdomen.

Wolff was stunned when he curled back the skin of Franklin's chest and it was pink, like chewed gum. Then he studied the muscle tissue, and that, too, he noticed, was as fresh-looking and pink in color as a man two days in the ground.

Noting this, Wolff later said, "It was very natural in its color"—meaning the skin was "a little lighter, and there was absolutely no odor of decomposition . . ." The skin, moreover, had a delicate, distinguishable odor, Wolff claimed. He compared the smell to "pickled herring."

Next, he used a *costatom*, a strong pair of plier-like shears, to cut through the breast bone and the ribs in order to expose the innards of Franklin's chest and *reflex the front of the chest as you would the lid of a box*.

Now both of Franklin's lungs were staring back at the doctor. He grabbed hold of them with his hands and squeezed gently, a common test pathologists used to see if the lungs felt like "hair being rubbed together in the hands," which would indicate "certain diseases."

Wolff found that Franklin's lungs felt spongy and soft. "They were of brown color and upon cutting into the surface . . . they seemed to be perfectly healthy."

A moment later Wolff reached into Franklin's chest cavity. He gingerly pushed the right lung aside and noticed some "adhesion of the lung to the chest wall." He checked the other side. Same thing.

This, he knew, proved that during Franklin's life for "many years before his death he had suffered an attack of pleurisy,* which had diminished his chest cavity in that way."

Lifting the lungs, Wolff saw that blood had *congested* in back of the lung cavities, as would be the case, he later said, with any dead body laid on its backside. What it meant was that Franklin Andrews had died a fairly normal death up to this point. There was nothing Wolff could see thus far that pointed to a direct cause of death.

Looking further down toward the pelvis area, Wolff noticed part of Franklin's diaphragm was covered with a thin layer of brownish-yellow material. The vessels connected to the organs in this area were *rather dry and parchmentlike; and upon viewing the surface of the heart itself, and the membrane that surrounds the heart, this membrane was stained here and there with spots of the yellowish deposit.*

---

* The Mayo Clinic reports that "pleurisy occurs when the double membrane (pleura) that lines the chest cavity and surrounds each of your lungs becomes inflamed. Also called *pleuritis*, pleurisy typically causes sharp pain, almost always during the act of breathing."

From there, Wolff turned his attention toward the heart, the one place where any sort of chronic injury would be centered, seeing that the man had supposedly died of "heart failure" brought on by indigestion.

After taking an initial look at the heart Wolff stepped back from his patient and jotted something down: *The surface of the heart muscle itself showed quite a diffused deposit of this material.*

Franklin's heart was *of normal size,* Wolff wrote. He lifted the heart in his hand and, with a scalpel, put a small slit in it, so he could look inside and have a quick study of the chambers. "It was very easy to examine the different valves of the heart."

According to Dr. Wolff, Franklin Andrews had a strong heart—there was nothing he could see that was wrong with it. No blockages. No tears. No trauma.

As Wolff studied the heart, admiring how healthy it was, a "peculiar and penetrating odor from the body diffused itself through the room."

It was as if something had popped open.

"You smell that?" Wolff asked Hurley after cutting open Franklin's heart.

He shrugged.

Once again, the smell reminded the doctor of pickled herring, he said. A distinctive, pungent, sharp smell, vinegary and unique.

"It became very apparent and very plain."

The smell was something Dr. Wolff had been in contact with in the past—something he could never forget.

> *Why, this led me to believe, or led me to think, that the deposit that I found in the upper part [of the body], in the chest and throughout the tissues of the neck, that it smelled very much like arsenic, and whether it was a combination or some decomposition of the formalin that was used in the embalming fluid. . . .*

The smell did not alarm Wolff as he stood over Franklin and continued dissecting the dead man's organs. It was no smoking gun, per se, no *aha!* moment. Wolff was well aware that many undertakers used an arsenic-based embalming fluid.

Thinking about it further, though, the question was, *Why would the odor be coming from* inside *the heart?* Why not as soon as Wolff opened Franklin up? If an undertaker had used arsenic to embalm the corpse, the smell would be prevalent the moment Wolff opened up Franklin's body—certainly not *after* an organ had been slit.

Wolff continued his incision down through the abdominal region, near the pelvis. Afterward, he made a general inspection of the abdominal cavity and the organs there, *without disturbing anything else*.

This was the area of Franklin's body that began to set off alarm bells for Wolff. Indeed, he was now beginning to feel that there was definitely some type of poison issued, at some point, into Franklin Andrews's body.

Staring at the stomach, Wolf found it to be *greatly distended*, as if blown up like a balloon. When he cut the membrane covering the abdominal cavity, the stomach popped out, as if it were a bubble being held down and released.

Franklin's Andrews's two-year-old rotting stomach was full of gas.

"The absence of decomposition of the tissues was quite remarkable," Wolff said later, "considering that the body had been dead and buried for [so long]."

Looking at this area of Franklin's innards, if he hadn't known better Wolff would have guessed the body had been buried only days before.

Digging further, Wolff found that the liver, the intestines, and the apron, or *omentum* (that section of the abdomen—the fat—underneath the skin that covers the stomach: the beer belly), were in faultless condition and *perfectly preserved*.

Wolff was interested in this discovery. It could only mean one thing.

Next, he cut the lungs out and put them on a table beside the body. Then he cut the lungs into several slices and fit them into jars and containers he had brought with him.

Hurley labeled each one as Wolff went back to dissecting the body.

The heart came out next and Hurley labeled the sections Wolff had cut it into and placed into jars.

Franklin Andrews, come to find out, had one clot inside his aorta, which Wolff noted. It was a blockage, however, that had grown throughout the years and had no bearing whatsoever on his death.

The liver was normal.

Before removing the stomach, Wolff said, he tied it off where food deposited, this so he could keep it distended. He did this carefully, so as not to puncture the organ and disrupt the gases inside.

Both of Franklin's kidneys looked as though they had been taken out of a living human being.

And so, piece by piece, organ by organ, muscle by muscle, Wolff, with Hurley, Rowe Wheeler, and Keeler by his side, spent the better part of the night cutting samples of Franklin Andrews's body apart and placing them in various jars.

When Wolff had finished taking all of the specimens he needed to determine the manner of death, he sewed Franklin's body back together and carefully placed it into its coffin for Keeler and his men to return to its resting place.

Hurley dropped Wolff off at his office just before sunup, the doctor armed with a good sampling of Franklin's tissue and organs.

Chapter 31

MOTIVE

SUPERINTENDENT THOMAS EGAN ASKED CLIFTON Sherman and Robert Thayer to meet with him and Hugh Alcorn. It was nothing more than a professional get-together to see if the *Courant* had come up with any additional evidence. The promise from Egan and Alcorn to Sherman stood: As long as the *Courant* didn't run any stories, Sherman and Thayer would be kept up to speed as to what was going on and given the opportunity to be there if and when an arrest was made.

It was clear during this meeting that a lot depended on Dr. Wolff's report. Still, there could be an arrest in the case any day now, Alcorn noted.

"We're sure of five murders so far," Egan added, according to George Vedder Jones. It was the first time the State Police had come out with such a harsh statement pertaining to Amy's guilt. Egan explained that he and the State Police had stayed away from the Archer Home as long as they could to avoid any suspicion by Amy, but, he added, "I've got to make an arrest soon to protect innocent people."

They were worried Amy would not stop killing, even though they were beginning to put pressure on her.

As the meeting continued, Thayer and Sherman asked what sort of proof the State Police had in its possession. Had something new turned up?

Egan said they had "no positive evidence" so far. In fact, they had gotten "nowhere" with Alcorn's homicidal-maniac-among-the-inmates theory.

"That leaves us with only two suspects," Egan said, "and it's difficult to believe that either is guilty. Yet one must be."

"The doctor [King] and Mrs. Archer," Sherman said.

There was a problem, though, with the idea that Amy Archer was behind the deaths. Egan admitted that after an intense and laborious study of all the "poison records" from W. H. Mason's Drugstore, it appeared Amy had not signed for any of the arsenic herself. Dr. King had signed, Egan noted, along with several of Amy's inmates.

King's name now became the focal point of the investigation. He was being looked at as the true perpetrator, seeing that he had attended to many of the inmates who had died and also signed their death certificates. But the question remained: What did King stand to gain by murdering Amy's inmates?

Egan made the point that King had had nothing whatsoever to do with treating Alice Gowdy, but had certified her death.

♠ ♠ ♠

After a much-needed rest, late into the morning of May 3, 1916, Dr. Arthur J. Wolff poured himself a cup of coffee and began the careful and tedious process of examining the specimens he had collected the night before from Franklin Andrews's corpse. It was a slow process. First, he took portions of Franklin's liver, along with one large piece, and ground that up into a fine paste. Then he placed the paste into a small glass dish and added equal parts hydrochloric acid and water.

"I was making a preliminary examination," Wolff said later, explaining why he did this.

He then put that slimy, emulsified mixture into a test tube and heated it. As the concoction began to boil, Wolff added "some strips of . . . chemically pure copper foil."

After a few moments, he removed the foil.

Bingo.

"It was found thickly covered with a metallic layer of purplish-blue color, and this was washed very thoroughly with water."

He took the contents from the tube and smeared them onto a slide, which he then put "red heat" to. The metallic deposits on the heated slides indicated, Wolff later testified, "[t]he presence of a metallic poison in the tissues."

No longer did they have mere circumstantial evidence of murder. Now there was science to back it all up.

It was important to find the poison *in the tissues* of the body—in this case, the liver—rather than just in the bloodstream. If the poison managed to get into Franklin's tissues, it could *not* have been from the embalming process, but rather only by an extended period of ingestion. During the embalming procedure the heart is obviously not pumping. No poison can end up in an organ without being injected into that particular organ (which is not part of the embalming procedure) or driven into the organ by blood flow.

When Wolff put the slide under his microscope and analyzed it, he knew exactly what type of poison he was looking at.

"When I examined it under a microscope, it absolutely defined the character of the metallic poison. . . . [and] that metallic poison was arsenious acid and nothing else."

It was clear to the pathologist that Franklin Andrews had been poisoned over a long duration of time with some form of arsenic. Enough, in fact, Wolff said later, "To kill several men."

The question now was: Who had given Franklin the poison, and how was the state's attorney going to prove it?

⚜ ⚜ ⚜

Alcorn and Egan decided that Amy's bedside presence with Alice Gowdy for the duration of her illness, or, as they had put it, "constantly," cast guilt on their suspect.

So Alice Gowdy's corpse was also exhumed and examined by Wolff.

Lo and behold, the doctor found the same results: death by arsenical poisoning.

Now the attorney had to prove his theory of motive, and exclude Dr. King from culpability.

Robert Thayer, listening to Egan and Alcorn discuss this dilemma, suggested the motive that had been bouncing around for quite some time and pointed out how it played a role in Amy's day-to-day business. "I can tell you that Mrs. Archer seldom took guests on a monthly basis because their relatives didn't keep up the payments. She took them for life care." Life care made sense as a motive for murder—or, more like it, turnover.

Alcorn said he had heard this before.

Part of what solidified Alcorn's notion that Amy was behind the murders came in the form of a phone call Thomas Egan had made a few days before. Egan had decided to head out to Windsor and check the records at W. H. Mason's himself. There had to be an answer in those records, the smart cop realized. There had to be some sort of red flag.

A smoking gun.

Sure enough, Egan found the information he was looking for and called Alcorn from a pay phone around the corner of the drugstore, reportedly saying, "There are four Archer inmates now dead whose names appear on the record here. They bought more than two pounds of arsenic."

Two pounds.

In all of her cold-bloodedness, Amy Archer had apparently sent her victims to the drugstore to purchase the arsenic that would eventually kill them.

Egan thought it was despicable.

And so, without telling Thayer or Sherman, a decision was made. Things needed to be done in a stealthy manner so that Amy wouldn't get word and burn documented evidence, or hide or dispose of any arsenic she had hanging around the house. The element of surprise was important, not only for her arrest and indictment, but later, her prosecution.

It was time to arrest Amy Archer-Gilligan.

Chapter 32

In the Dead of Night

H UGH ALCORN CALLED CARL GOSLEE ON MAY 8, 1916. The state's attorney explained that he had a job for the part-time reporter. Carl didn't know it, but he was about to play an essential role in the biggest arrest of the nascent century.

At work inside the offices of the Phoenix Insurance Company, just up the block from the state's attorney's office, Carl answered the call and asked how he could be of help. He had turned over everything he knew about the case to Clifton Sherman and was confident that Sherman had shared it with the State Police.

"Come over to my office right away," Alcorn said, ignoring Carl's confusion. Carl rushed right over and found Alcorn in an excited state. The state's attorney got right down to business.

"Hold up your right hand," Alcorn instructed Carl Goslee, "and swear that whatever happens in this office will be a strict secret."

"Indeed," Carl said. What in the Lord's name was going on here?

Alcorn placed a warrant before Carl.

"What's this?"

It was an arrest application for Amy Archer-Gilligan, signed by a judge. It charged Amy with the murder of Franklin Andrews. Alcorn had his proof. Dr. Wolff had come through, now entirely certain that Franklin had been poisoned.

"In his position as grand juror," *Courant* reporter Bob Zaiman wrote years later, "it was Goslee's duty to sign the warrant. . . ."

Carl Goslee was, apparently, the one and only grand juror indicting his former friend and neighbor on charges that could eventually send her to the gallows. By signing the warrant, which Carl did without hesitation, the part-time *Courant* and *Times* reporter was saying that he could not call on the one person he had been waiting to contact with this information since the ordeal had begun: Clifton Sherman. During the meeting Alcorn and Egan had had with Sherman and Thayer earlier that day, they failed to mention the possibility that a warrant for murder was going to be issued anytime soon. As far as the newspapermen knew, the state's attorney and State Police were still developing their case. But here it was—an ordinary day in May that had just turned extraordinary.

Alcorn confirmed to Carl that an arrest was going to be made within twenty-four hours. Carl needed to be there, Alcorn informed him.

What about the *Courant?*

The newspaper would get the scoop, Alcorn promised.

Carl would be allowed to report the arrest, but no other reporter should be called in, Alcorn insisted. This was Carl's story. He had initiated the investigation to begin with, almost two years prior. Alcorn trusted him.

Carl was thrilled by his new role and the facts he had just learned—which he excitedly wrote about later:

> *Enough circumstantial evidence had been accumulated and Alcorn obtained permission to exhume Andrews's body. An autopsy was performed. Dr. Arthur Wolff and assistants performed [it] by lantern light in the dead of the night . . . its finding found enough arsenic in the dead man's stomach to kill several men.*

Indeed. Upon further testing, Wolff had discovered that Franklin's stomach was saturated with arsenic, inside and out. There was only one way for that to have happened, and the doctor was willing to go on record with this evidence.

As Carl stood in Alcorn's County Building office downtown, likely stunned by this recent development, the state's attorney explained that "two cars were waiting downstairs." The time had come. Alcorn wasn't going to wait any longer; they were leaving at that very moment to arrest Amy.

Carl later said that "two large, black automobiles, one was a Pope Hartford," were parked in front of the County Building, their engines running. Thomas Egan and Robert Hurley were inside one vehicle. Additionally, Deputy Sheriff [Peter] Welch and Zola Bennett, who had since moved out of Amy's home, were waiting with State Police officers Walter Stiles and Rowe Wheeler in the other.

They would all travel together to Windsor, Alcorn explained, and serve the warrant.

Carl rode with Thomas Egan, who explained that there would come a point during the evening when they would need to make a show out of the arrest. It was Alcorn's call. The community needed to see how serious this was for Amy. The public end of any prosecution, Alcorn knew, began with the arrest. Make it a spectacle and you begin to speak to your jury.

The perp walk.

The fact that two Pope automobiles were issued and used to travel from Hartford to Windsor to transport Amy from her home to the Windsor Town Hall—the first automobile-aided arrest for the State Police—proved how historic this night was going to be. Once at Town Hall, a formal grand jury with a judge would commence amid community members.

So they piled into the two vehicles and started out from Hartford to Windsor somewhere shortly after 3:15 p.m. on May 8, 1916. Through the grapevine of reporters and his sources in Windsor, Aubrey Maddock, another *Courant* reporter, was soon tipped off that something "big" was going down: Carl Goslee, Hugh Alcorn, and the State Police were heading out of the city toward Windsor at that very moment.

Aubrey Maddock was a seasoned reporter. When he heard about the two cars heading toward Amy's, he grabbed his fedora and notebook and headed out the door to see what was going on.

Chapter 33

OH, WHAT A BEAUTIFUL "MOURNING"

THERE WAS ONE ROAD—A DIRECT ROUTE—LEADING from Windsor to Hartford. During the late-afternoon and early-evening hours of May 8, 1916, *Courant* reporter and "sub-editor" Aubrey Maddock was waiting along that road on the Hartford side with his colleagues, George Hamilton and Raymond Maplesden. They were sitting in a hired car driven by a chauffeur. Maddock had received a tip that something was about to go down at the Archer Home. He had been waiting for that one story that would launch his career. This could be it.

"The motor of the car was kept running," Maddock recalled years later, "[as] I watched the road from Hartford." Maddock soon spied a car coming down the road. It was a Pope, black in color, puttering its way down the road heading into Windsor. Behind it was another, just like it.

Maddock could see several people inside both vehicles. He recognized the men.

"Follow that car," Maddock shouted to the driver as the first auto passed. "Don't let them lose you!"

The chauffeur gunned the engine to keep up.

"Away we went at a rapid pace," said Maddock, "in the direction of Windsor." Once they got closer to Amy's, Maddock said, they went "through devious by-ways and side roads."

Alcorn did not want to bring any attention to the arresting party. The motorcade of law enforcement Aubrey Maddock and his colleagues were following worked its way north from Trumbull Street, down Main, and over the Windsor town line in the north end of Hartford, along the banks of the Connecticut River. The convoy then pulled down Prospect Street and turned into the Archer Home driveway. Maddock and his team waited behind, just down the block.

Sister Amy's only child, who had stood behind her mother throughout all of the rumors and accusations made by townsfolk and Hugh Alcorn, Carl Goslee, and others, was at home with Amy at 4:50 p.m. when the motorcade arrived. Mary was stunned.

"It took a long time for the two cars to reach the house at 37-39 Prospect Street, Windsor," Carl Goslee later wrote, "because a back road was used to avoid passing through the center of the village. It was 4:55 when [S]tate [P]olice entered the house."

Carl, with Hurley, Egan, Alcorn, and several State Police officers in tow, soon got out and approached Amy's front door. Only Carl noticed Maddock.

"When the State Police finally moved in to make an arrest, Goslee was the only newspaperman allowed inside the house with them," wrote *Courant* reporter Bob Zaiman.

Talking about this important moment, Carl later said, "Aubrey Maddock was mad as a hornet when I came out [of the car]. But I was still sworn to secrecy so I couldn't give him anything until Alcorn gave out the information."

Amy had a look of annoyance on her face when she confronted Egan, Alcorn, Hurley, Goslee, and the other officers waiting at her door. It was almost as if she had been expecting the visit, but wanted to act surprised by it at the same time.

"I am glad you have come," Amy said, opening the door, putting on her best game face. "I know of the gossip about me and of the Home that has been going around Windsor, and I am indeed glad you have come."

They were invited into the front room, the most spacious part of the house. Mary's piano stood in the corner with several chairs and stools flanking it like a lounge. Hurley, Goslee, and Alcorn stayed with Amy in the front room while the others searched the Home. Hurley took the lead, introducing everyone, and then got right down to business.

"We have come here to have a talk with you and look over your place."

Amy started to say something, but Hurley cut her off. "Before you say anything, I want to say to you that you do not have to say anything if you do not care to, and anything that you do say we may be called upon to use against you in court."

Amy thought about that. "All right," she said. Then she sat down on one of the piano stools and seemed ready to talk. She was dressed in a white nurse's uniform, her hair set back in a bun, and appeared to be in total control of her emotions.

"How long have you been here in Windsor?" Hurley asked. He paced in front of his suspect.

"Oh, eight years."

"How many inmates have you at the present time?"

Amy counted to herself. "Fifteen."

Hurley was a big man with a large belly. He wore a three-piece suit and had a long watch chain hanging from the front pocket of his vest, clipped on a belt loop. He had a habit of tucking his hand inside the pocket and playing with his watch.

"Are you a trained nurse?"

"Yes," Amy said without hesitation. It must have rattled her cage real good to see Carl Goslee standing there, taking notes. She knew he would soon write a story about this moment.

"Where did you graduate?"

Amy stumbled a bit with her words. She had a moment where "she hesitated," Hurley said later. Then, "No, I am not a trained nurse, but I used to work for Dr. Higgins [a local physician]."

"Have you got any arsenic around the place?" Hurley said, pointing to nowhere in particular. They would find it soon enough, he knew. But it was better if Amy just told them.

"We had some in the barn," Amy said without a quiver, "but we used it all up."

"Who used it?"

"I don't know."

"Then how do you know it has been used up?"

Good point.

Amy refused to answer that one. Hurley stood in front of Amy now as she sat there calmly, apparently having no trouble answering his questions without an attorney present.

"Did Franklin Andrews die here?"

"Yes," she said, offering no further explanation.

"Did he pay you a thousand dollars to keep him for the remainder of his life?"

"Yes."

"Would you let me see the contract?"

"I haven't it," Amy lied. "I always destroy the contracts when an inmate dies."

"Did Charles Smith die here?"

"Yes."

"Did he pay you a thousand dollars to keep him for the remainder of his life?"

"Yes."

"Did you later go to New York to draw some of Mr. Smith's money?"

After a long pause, "Yes."

"How much did you draw?"

"Oh, about thirteen hundred dollars."

"Did Mr. Smith pay your expenses when you went down?"

"No, my daughter, Mary, and I went down, and I paid the money out of my own pocket."

The others were poking around the bottom floor, keeping the inmates out of the front room. Word had spread throughout town that there was a get-together taking place at the Archer Home between Amy and law enforcement, and a crowd began to gather out in front of the Home. The local Windsor *Hartford Times* reporter walked up to Aubrey Maddock, who was waiting patiently by his car.

"What's going on in there?" the local asked.

"I'm sure I don't know," Maddock said. (Recounting this moment later, he added, "I lied without blinking.")

The *Times* reporter said he was going to phone the *Times* office and tell his editor that something was happening at the Archer Home. He might have a scoop for him later on that night.

Maddock talked him out of it, saying that he would miss anything that happened if he took off to make the call.

Inside the house, Hurley continued questioning Amy, asking, "What did you do with Mr. Smith's money?" He looked out the window at the swelling crowd.

"I gave it to Mr. Smith."

"Did he then pay you for your trouble of going down?" Hurley obviously had a point to make, but Amy did not pick up on it. He based his questioning on an interview he had conducted with Smith family members. He had looked over Smith's bank records. He knew Amy had stolen money from the man's account, same as she had done to Franklin Andrews.

"No," Amy responded, "he never paid me for going down."

"Have you any papers or contracts around the place that I could look at, or that we"—he pointed to Egan and Alcorn—"could look at?"

"Yes." Amy stood up and walked into the dining room nearby, returning with two large boxes. "Here," she said. "Have a look."

They took their time digging through the papers as Amy sat and watched. Mary would come into the room and then leave. She was disturbed by the interrogation and was often seen with tears streaming down her face. Amy would give her daughter a sullen hug and say, "Do not worry, child, everything will be okay."

It was pushing 6:00 p.m. It would take all night and possibly the following day, Hurley knew, to go through all of the paperwork the way he needed to. So Hurley turned to Amy, fixed his fedora, cleared his throat, and said, "Mrs. Archer-Gilligan, look, we have a warrant for your arrest charging you with causing the death of Franklin Andrews, and you will have to go to Town Hall."

At Town Hall Amy would be put in front of a group of her peers and formally charged. In effect, the Town Hall acted as an arraignment court. There was a judge waiting. Amy could make her plea there and the judge could decide what to do with her for the time being. There was a chance she could walk out of Town Hall on bond.

Amy's shoulders dropped. "Very well," she said. "I'll need to get my cape and hat." She mentioned that she wanted to change out of her nurse's uniform into a more fashionable dress.

Hurley told her to take her time.

Amy went upstairs by herself, locked the door behind her, got dressed, and then did something no one would find out about until months later. She reached inside her drawer and took out a small package, sat on the bed, took a few moments to complete the task, and then put the items back inside her drawer.

She waited a few minutes.

There it was—that burn, that numbing feeling.

She was ready.

Carl Goslee watched Amy as she returned from her room. She put on her cape and hat in the front parlor. She said nothing.

Carl later assessed what had happened thus far:

> *Mrs. Gilligan was arrested . . . after she had been closeted for about one hour with the [S]tate [P]olice. The talk resulted in the officers obtaining much information. Mrs. Gilligan maintained her innocence. When she was told that she was charged with murder of Franklin Andrews by poison, she calmly said, "I will prove my innocence if it takes my last will. I am not guilty and I will hang before they prove it."*

Mary Archer followed as the State Police led Amy out the door. Mary was "sobbing" by this point, said a report the following day. Before the group reached the front steps of the Home, Mary, in an "angry tone," called out, "Mother, is it all right that *those two men* should be going all over the house?"

"Yes, darling," Amy said. "Don't talk that way. They have a perfect right and we must let them."

Amy was ready to leave the house and go to court.

The crowds grew as the motorcade made its way from the Archer Home to Town Hall just a few blocks around the corner. Amy had changed into a plush white dress with a tight-fitting neckline that choked up underneath her chin. She wore a black veil over her head and face as she walked from the Home to the car. She had a look of both steadfast determination and fearful defeat about her.

A look of "mourning," the papers would call it the following day.

Captain Hurley held Amy by the hand and walked with her. As they exited the car near the front steps of Town Hall, she turned and asked him, "What is the best thing for me to do?"

Hurley shook his head. "I cannot advise you, Mrs. Gilligan, but there are three [options] for you to do. You can plead guilty, you can plead not guilty, or you can waive examination. I simply mention all this so you can use your own judgment."

Amy thought about it. "Which would be the best?" They were approaching the doors into Town Hall.

"I cannot say."

Amy wanted to understand the law. She needed to know what was going to happen after her plea. Hurley explained as best he could, telling her that a guilty plea meant she would be "bound over" without question, regardless; a not guilty plea would force the state's attorney to produce "sufficient evidence . . . to warrant the Court in binding" her over; and if she waived examination altogether (essentially not revealing whether she was guilty or not guilty), there was no question she would be jailed immediately following the proceeding.

"I think I'll waive examination."

As the crowds piled into Town Hall, Amy was brought into a small room and told to sit before Hugh Alcorn, assistant state's attorney William Maltbie, who Alcorn had summoned for the proceeding, Judge Ralph Grant, Carl Goslee, and Hurley. Amy reportedly never moved the black veil from her face. Save for the white dress, many said she had the look of a widow on funeral day: dark, solemn, stoic.

"Throughout the trial and the intervals which preceded and followed it," reported the *Hartford Courant*, "the prisoner maintained a remarkable degree of composure."

She sat and did not move—that is, until Mary charged into the room with "an older gentleman," an inmate from the Archer Home, disrupting the proceeding for a moment.

"What are you doing to my mother? You can't do this to her!" Mary yelled pleadingly. Amy was shocked by this behavior. Mary was "calmed after a moment and persuaded to leave."

In advising Amy to waive her rights, Hurley was trying to move things along. He wanted to get Amy out of the public spotlight and into an interrogation room as quickly as possible. She needed to be booked and questioned further—this, as Hurley's men spent the remainder of the night searching the Archer Home.

The crowd was wound up. Banging his gavel, Judge Grant quieted the gallery, then instructed Alcorn and Maltbie to read the charges.

Many winced at the part of the charge that said Amy had "willfully and with malice aforethought caused the death of Franklin Andrews . . ." When Maltbie said it, Amy grimaced and began to sink down in her chair, before realizing what she was doing and, quickly, collecting herself.

"[H]er eyes began to water," the *Courant* reported, "although her face remained set in the same expression and her head was held steadily erect."

When Maltbie mentioned *murder*, however, Amy couldn't control her emotions and dissolved into tears. Then she shook her head back and forth, some claimed, mumbling to herself, *No, no, no*.

"You have heard the reading of the complaint," Judge Grant said to the suspect. "What is your pleasure?"

The room went silent as Amy shifted in her chair without answering.

Judge Grant waited, but Amy did not speak.

"I understand that you have decided to waive examination," the judge said, perhaps speaking for her, "not pleading guilty or not guilty. Is that so?"

Amy answered at once, in a "clear voice and without a trace of worry," saying, "Yes! That's right. I want to waive examination. I don't want any trouble or notoriety if I can help it. Not that I care anything about it for myself, but for my daughter's sake."

The multitude stirred. The crowd began whispering.

"I proclaim that the prisoner be bound over to the June term of the Superior Court [in Hartford]," Judge Grant explained, making his ruling, "without bonds under a charge of murder in the first degree."

The judge had to use his gavel to calm everyone in the courtroom.

With that, Robert Hurley directed Amy to a waiting car outside the doors of Town Hall. Before getting in, Amy turned and said, "Thank you for the advice."

Amy then asked if she could speak with Mary, who was waiting in the crowd. Amy's daughter was visibly upset by what had just transpired.

Amy said her good-byes and assured Mary that all would be fine in due time.

"She was bound over," Hurley commented later, "and brought to the Hartford County Jail."

♣ ♣ ♣

As Amy Archer-Gilligan was processed at the Hartford County Jail and placed into a holding cell, the State Police continued searching the Archer Home.

Almost immediately, the search yielded several contracts, even though Amy had stated earlier that she had destroyed all contracts belonging to deceased inmates. Beyond that, various bottles of fluids with different labels, along with letters, notebooks, and bank records were collected. The locals, watching from outside on the street, saw case after case of bottles and box after box of documents carried out the front door and put into waiting cars.

Hugh Alcorn finally addressed the press. It was late, near eight o'clock. Alcorn admitted that he had been involved in the case against Amy for nearly a year and a half.

"After our general investigation of affairs at the Archer Home," the young, good-looking attorney said, "that included following many clues, we became certain that something was wrong. Then we exhumed the bodies and were convinced it was a case of cool, calculating, premeditated murder of inmates of the home."

In addition to that of Franklin Andrews, Michael Gilligan's corpse had been dug out of the earth. Wolff had found his stomach loaded with enough arsenic to kill five men of Gilligan's size. Alcorn was certain that Amy had not only murdered several inmates (upwards of twenty, he was saying behind closed doors), but that she'd also killed her second husband, and, as he would soon realize, her first husband, James Archer.

An Angel of Death and Black Widow combined.

Reporters pestered Alcorn for more information, but he wasn't going to say anything more at this point. The state's attorney and State Police were still building a case. It was imperative that the law be followed, so Mrs. Gilligan, obviously with the means to hire a credible attorney, would not get off on a technicality or error on the state's attorney's part. In due time all would be made public, he promised.

Captain Hurley had dropped Amy off at the jail and had driven back to Windsor to help with the search. After they uncovered a cache of arsenic (in powdered form) in the barn out in back of the property, Hurley drove back to the jail to speak with Amy. Amy had been acting bizarrely since being confined to her cell. She had been let out at times to roam the corridors of the jail, but was doing things that didn't seem to fit with the character she had revealed during her court appearance.

"She was wringing her hands," said one cellmate, who had watched Amy pace the hallways in front of the cells, "[and] saying things."

Interviewing Amy's cellmate later, Hurley wanted to know what she'd said.

" 'Why did I do it? What made me do it?'" the witness claimed Amy had muttered over and over, as loud as if she were talking to someone who wasn't there.

Hurley went in to see Amy. It was probably around ten p.m. He asked her if she wanted to talk. Amy seemed different—more subdued and remote than before, as though she'd had time to think things through and wanted to discuss certain issues.

"Tell me," Hurley said, "did you poison Mr. Andrews? We found arsenic in the barn."

"I did send some of my inmates to Mason's to purchase arsenic," Amy admitted.

"Yes, we know. But did you *poison* [emphasis added] Mr. Andrews? He died from arsenical poisoning."

Amy thought about it. "So far as Franklin R. Andrews dying from arsenic," Amy said rather stoically, "if I gave it to him, it was unintentional."

Unintentional? What was the woman trying to say?

Chapter 34

"Murder Factory"

Aubrey Maddock had telephoned Clifton Sherman from Windsor on the night Amy was arrested and arraigned at Town Hall. Recounting this moment later, Maddock explained how the massive coverage of the Archer case had come together for the *Courant*: "I had telephoned Mr. Sherman [and learned that . . .] the 'copy' which had been 'on ice' in the safe for a year was on the composing machines being put in type."

Sherman had the *Courant's* presses running nonstop.

Maddock returned to the office that night and got to work himself, along with several other reporters called in to assist.

"The *Courant* was required by its contract with the Associated Press," Maddock said later, "to put the story 'on the wire.'" But that didn't stop Sherman from holding back on releasing the most exclusive details so that the *Courant* could break them the next morning.

As soon as the story hit the wires, metropolitan dailies from all over began calling the *Courant* offices. Sherman and Maddock refused to give more than just the essential details.

While reporters and press people worked all night long, when the morning's edition hit the streets, it was obvious that a majority of the stories had been ready for press long before Amy's arrest. The space Clifton Sherman devoted to the Archer Home story was unprecedented for the *Courant*, and clearly showed how important a story this was going to be. The people of Connecticut awoke on May 9, 1916, a clear and cool Tuesday morning, to the most sensational headlines they had ever seen on the front page of their local papers.

"Newspapers throughout the East," wrote one reporter, "took up the case and it became an overnight sensation."

At a cost of three cents per copy, readers received an edition of the *Courant* that dedicated not just one or two pages (four columns wide, running the entire length of the page from top to bottom) of fine print to Amy's arrest, life, the charges against her, the exhumation of her alleged victims, and more, but *four and a half* pages of inked landscape, complete with photographs, headlines and sub-headings, quotes and statistics.

It was the story of a lifetime for any newspaperman. Clifton Sherman spared no expense to get the most out of the coverage, working his inside sources for everything they had. "Mr. Sherman's greatest coup . . . ," said Sherman's obituary in 1946, "came in 1916, when the *Courant*, under his direction, conducted an investigation which resulted in 'cracking' the Amy E. Archer-Gilligan murder case. . . ."

Newspapers during this period rarely printed articles with bylines, yet it was clear the lead article had been written by Carl Goslee, who had acted as both grand juror and the sole reporter allowed total access during Amy's arrest. The headline, which took up the entire top section of the *Courant*'s front page, from left to right, in large block-letter font, was three lines deep: POLICE BELIEVE ARCHER HOME FOR AGED A MURDER FACTORY; MRS. ARCHER-GILLIGAN ACCUSED OF MURDER OF INMATE; AUTOPSY SHOWS TWO WHO DIED WERE KILLED BY POISON.

In the article, Carl laid out the case against his former friend and neighbor, detail by painstaking detail. The story contained dialogue that had taken place between Captain Robert Hurley and Amy, during Hurley's questioning in the front room the previous night. It explained how the State Police had driven over to the Archer Home and surprised Amy with the warrant. It talked about the exhumations. Bank records. Poison purchases made by the Archer Home from W. H. Mason's. Franklin Andrews's untimely, strange death. This, along with every other aspect of the case Carl had been investigating since the day he'd first suspected there was malice going on inside the Home.

There was a booking photograph of Amy printed at the top center of the page, next to a subheading: MAY BE 20 WHO HAVE BEEN POISONED.

By page three it was clear who had sparked the finger-pointing and initial rumors against Amy so long ago. As it turned out, it wasn't Carl Goslee, Robert Hurley, Hugh Alcorn, Nellie Pierce, Clifton Sherman, or even the hot-and-cold community of Windsor. In the end, a strange woman Amy had taken into the Home, Lucy Durand, seemed to have been the first to point an angry, critical finger at the matron from Windsor.

A "*Courant* reporter," later identified as Aubrey Maddock, had tracked down Durand's former doctor and conducted an exclusive interview with him, before locating Durand herself. The story appeared under the following headline: [MRS. ARCHER] HAD MRS. DURAND TAKEN TO ASYLUM: INMATE VISITED NEIGHBORS, TOLD STORIES, CAUSED INVESTIGATION; WENT OUT FOR A RIDE, NEVER RETURNED.

Lucy Durand was admitted to the Archer Home in 1914 by family members who paid Amy $1,000 for life care. Although Durand was much younger than the average Archer Home inmate, somewhere near middle age, her family had needed help in caring for her. She was mentally challenged in some ways; manic and aggressive, she talked a lot. She scared people.

Nonetheless, things seemed to be going reasonably well for Durand as she acclimated herself to her new surroundings inside the Archer Home. Almost immediately, she made several friends inside the Home and also in and around the immediate neighborhood.

As the days went by, however, Durand began complaining to Amy's neighbors that she was being mistreated and abused by Amy. One thing led to another, and several neighbors sent word to state's attorney Hugh Alcorn that perhaps there was some sort of problem inside the Home. Alcorn began to take notice. At the same time, it just so happened that Carl Goslee was in the process of discovering an extraordinary increase in the amount of obituaries he was writing for the town of Windsor. It seemed that Divine Providence was working as one thing led to another, and the investigation all came together.

When Amy found out that Durand had been talking to the neighbors regarding what was going on inside her Home, she borrowed a motor vehicle and took Durand for a ride to Derby,

Durand's hometown. Once in Derby, Amy found a doctor to declare the woman insane and had her committed to an asylum in Middletown. And there she stayed, locked away, prevented from running her mouth any longer.

Amy had thought she had gotten rid of the woman.

Through his own investigation, however, under the careful direction of Clifton Sherman, Aubrey Maddock had tracked Durand down and sat with her. It was a few months before Amy's arrest. Maddock later said he had been working on the Archer story by then for thirteen months.

When Maddock arrived at the asylum, the attending doctor, Henry Noble, fetched Durand and brought her into a room where Maddock waited.

"Happiness and contentment were evident in her face," Maddock reported, "and an appreciation of kindness shone forth in her smile as she greeted [us]."

Durand was "short, with gray hair, neatly brushed back. She wore a gingham dress [o]ver which was an apron. Her face was wrinkled and drawn, her eyes faded and her lips almost without color." That aside, Durand appeared like any other woman her age. Furthermore, she was "quiet" and "calm," Maddock reported, and pleased to be able to sit and talk with him.

"I am a Hartford newspaperman," Maddock said, "and have come down here to see you for a few minutes."

As they talked about the town of Windsor and some of the people Durand had gotten to know during her short stay at the Archer Home, the reporter mentioned Amy and the Home, to which Durand said, "I used to live there."

"Did you?" Maddock asked ignorantly. He said he did not want to coerce Durand into going in any particular direction with her story, so he allowed her to control the topics and tempo of the interview.

"Yes," she replied, "and I wasn't treated very good."

"Tell me about it."

Durand put on a serious face. "She hit me once for going out—Mrs. Archer, I mean." Durand described how she "used to go out around the neighborhood and see the folks." Once Amy found out about it, however, she told Durand not to do it anymore. She was adamant; in the Archer Home, there was a price to pay for disobedience. "But I got a mind of my own," Durand said, "and the door was always open, so I went. When I got back one time, she . . . doubled up her fist and struck me."

This was the first time an inmate had reported any sort of physical abuse on Amy's part. Durand went on to explain that Amy had never intended to keep her for "life care," but instead took the $1,000 Durand's family had paid and, as soon as she could, got rid of the woman. The plan on Amy's part from the moment Durand had set foot inside the Home was to see how Amy could get rid of Durand and fill the bed with a new inmate.

Near the end of the interview, Durand leaned in toward the reporter and spoke in a hushed tone, looking around, making sure no one else was listening. "I am happy here . . . ," she said, meaning the insane asylum. "I couldn't ask for anything more. And I had rather go to hell than go back to Mrs. Archer's home."

Maddock saw this interview as one of the turning points in the Archer investigation by the *Courant*, later recounting, "The exclusive story which developed . . . was the greatest thrill of my whole newspaper career. . . . Probably one of the greatest news 'scoops' in the history of the *Courant* . . ."

▲ ▲ ▲

Captain Robert Hurley got a shock when he showed up at the Archer Home the morning after Amy's arrest. When he returned to the Home to help continue the search with the others, he was told that the barn in back had been locked the night before by police. Still, Seth Ramsey, an inmate who had taken over Franklin Andrews's role as Amy's "helper" around the house, had broken into the barn during the night. Even worse, Ramsey had apparently taken all of the papers and other "articles" from inside the barn and burned them in the incinerator.

When Hurley asked where Ramsey was, the other inmates—who were now being looked after by Amy's sister, Katherine Duggan; Alice Howland, Amy's niece; and Mary Archer—said he had taken off. And no one had seen him since.

Hurley met with Amy later that morning. There's no record to indicate that he mentioned the burning of the documents. In any case, Hurley had other business on his mind. He needed an official statement from Amy regarding the death of Franklin Andrews. She had said some rather peculiar things about Franklin's death the previous night, and Hurley wanted them down on paper.

Called a "defendant's declaration," Amy sat down and wrote:

> *I, Mrs. Amy E. Archer-Gilligan, do hereby state free and unsolicited without any threats or Promises and knowing what I say in Court can be used against me, that we did use arsenic around the home and so far as Franklin R. Andrews dying from arsenic, If I gave it to him it was unintentionally. I don't remember [. . .] ever giving him any medicine. I have sent some of my boarders to Mason's Drugstore a few times to get me arsenic. That is all I care to say for the Present.*

She signed it. Then State Police officer Rowe Wheeler and Captain Hurley witnessed her signature with theirs.

The document was official.

It was a firm statement, locking Amy down to a *story*, but in no way an admission of guilt on her part. Hugh Alcorn was not worried about keeping Amy in jail while he continued to build a case. Alcorn knew the law, and he knew that if Amy got herself a high-priced, high-profile lawyer who was in the mood to file motions for dismissal and bail, that he (Alcorn) could file other charges he was working on to keep Amy right where she was.

In removing Franklin Andrews's body in the middle of the night without the proper permits, Amy had violated the law. As it read, the state law was clear in this matter: Removing a dead body from any home—business or private residence—without a permit was in violation of the law. Transporting that body across town lines, moreover, was a second violation. Amy was guilty, admittedly, of both. Franklin Andrews had been driven to Hartford—Smith and Sons' Undertaking—immediately after his death.

Later that afternoon, and for the next several days, Amy spoke out. But not to Hurley or Alcorn. Instead, she began to plead her case to the press. Amy's supporters began to surface, too. Dr. Howard King was livid. He could not believe his friend and employer had been arrested and charged with murder—especially in the death of Franklin Andrews.

Dr. Howard King was concerned that someone in town had framed Amy, taking things as far as sabotaging Franklin Andrews's body. The doctor had a lot to lose in regard to the outcome of Amy's case. Not only a paycheck, but perhaps his freedom, too. After all, King had signed off on just about every death certificate the Archer Home had requested. And, according to the list the *Courant* printed on the morning of May 9, the number of dead was in the neighborhood of forty-eight in just over five years. Under a bold headline, STARTLING NUMBER OF DEATHS AT ARCHER HOME, the indication—or, maybe, *implication*—in the accompanying article was that the number of deaths inside the Archer Home was six times higher than that of any other home in Connecticut. The more flagrant charge was that Dr. King was not only employed as the Home's in-house physician, but was also the medical examiner for the town of Windsor (which, as it turned out, was not so much a strange coincidence as it might have seemed). This was not news to townspeople, of course. But as word spread around the state, residents were overwhelmed by the duration in which the killing had gone on. The evidence appeared to suggest that the same man who diagnosed and treated the inmates was the same man assigned to give a reason for their deaths.

King, the article continued, had failed to put the "duration of illness . . . on a majority of [the] returns."

The good doctor had not said anything for months. Reporters had tried to talk to King during those weeks and months leading up to Amy's arrest, but apart from that one brief interview he had given to Robert Thayer on King's doorstep, he had declined to comment. Now, however, as Amy sat in jail waiting for a visit from her attorney, King went on the offensive, lashing out at anyone who judged Amy before all of the facts had been presented.

Being a smart-aleck, and citing the "Show-Me" state's famous motto, King told the *Courant*, "I'm from Missouri. The woman may be innocent or she may be guilty, but they've got to show me—and until they have proved her guilty, I will believe she is innocent."

One theory King presented publicly was that Franklin Andrews's body "could have been twice exhumed."

It seemed to be a ridiculous statement and accusation—that someone had dug up the man and planted the arsenic in his system. Who would go to such lengths?

King went so far as to say that the arsenic found in Franklin's stomach, because it was so prominent, was probably placed there, either by police or an overzealous Windsor neighbor who had been fed up with Amy and rumors of the Home, so decided to take it upon him- or herself to get Amy kicked out of the community.

After thinking about it, however, the doctor reluctantly admitted that his theories were just that: hypothetical explanations. Another side of the story, if you will. He was in no position to "sponsor" such nonsense in a court of law, he explained further, or to back up the ideas with medical evidence. He had simply wanted to make the point that every avenue needed to be explored before a woman he had known for a decade could be condemned in his eyes.

Further along in the *Courant* interview, King questioned himself and his own judgment, saying that perhaps he should have paid closer attention, and that his diagnosis of "gastric ulcers" in relation to Franklin Andrews's death could be, in theory, changed to arsenical poisoning. The symptoms, when he thought about it, would appear similar.

"Maybe I ought to have analyzed the contents of the stomach," he said, "but I certainly did not suspect that there was anything wrong," adding that Franklin Andrews was, in fact, the one who had told him he suspected it was gastric ulcers causing the pain in his stomach.

"There [was] nothing suspicious to me about the death and no reason why I should have gone any further with the examination.... Did you ever hear of death by arsenic being discovered," King asked rhetorically, "as such immediately after death? I never did."

Finally, Mary Archer came out and defended her mother against what she perceived were outrageous claims. Mary was considered beautiful, with large round eyes, supple skin, soft to the touch, a perfect little actress's nose, and thin, feminine lips. At eighteen, the last thing Mary Archer wanted to do was spend her days visiting her mother in the Hartford jail. Yet, there was no way Mary was going to turn her back on her mother, run off to college, and act like nothing had happened. Mary had been inside the Home throughout it all. She knew her mother better than anyone. She had seen things. She could explain what had happened.

Mary first talked about Franklin's death, telling reporters that there was nothing out of the ordinary concerning how the man had died. He got sick after dinner one night. He retired to his room. He progressively got worse as the night went on. He died. How was that murder?

Regarding all those other deaths for which the state was accusing her mother of causing, Mary lashed out, stating emphatically, "They [those five deaths] were not queer in any way. But we have been the subject of gossip here, and people thought they were queer. . . . I know that Mother is innocent."

When asked to discuss the charges against her mother in more detail, Mary refused, saying, "You had better ask my mother's attorney."

By now Amy had lawyered up. She was being told to keep her mouth shut and to put a leash on her daughter.

PART THREE

TRIALS & TRIBULATIONS

Chapter 35

A CHANGING WORLD

To be at work was something defense attorney Benedict Holden looked forward to more than anything else in his life. He once said that he got up every morning and went to the office "not for compensation, but for the satisfaction derived from the work itself."

The guy loved what he did.

Good thing for Amy Archer-Gilligan. She was facing a possible death sentence if convicted of just *one* murder. To make matters worse, Hugh Alcorn was talking about exhuming more bodies.

Holden was forty-two when he got the call on May 8, 1916, that Amy Archer-Gilligan was in trouble and needed his help. Would Holden be willing to take the case? It was sure to be a media fiasco and the "trial of the century." Could Holden step in and take care of things as Amy prepared the best defense she could muster?

It would be a day or two, Holden said, before he could get away to represent her, but he was sending in a colleague, Fred Hungerford, an attorney Amy had used for civil matters. Hungerford was notified immediately and went in to see Amy.

Benedict Holden knew that a potential media-circus case like Amy's was going to be a watershed moment in a career that had already been highly respected and renowned. Win or lose, representing Amy could only help Holden. Not to mention he was never one to turn his back on a challenge. Law was Holden's life. Arguing the particulars of murder in a case like this was a DA's World Series. Holden knew Alcorn. They weren't buddies, but they got along. Facing off against the state's attorney would be fun, rewarding, exciting. How could any trial lawyer refuse?

As Amy prepared for her legal battles that May, what some called the "greatest naval battle of the First World War" took place.

The Battle of Jutland saw two fleets and no fewer than one-hundred-and-forty-nine British and ninety-nine German ships stage a colossal showdown. It was a remarkable display of naval ingenuity and force. This inconceivable event, showing how two sides could wage war in gargantuan proportions, served as a metaphor for what was a constantly changing world around Amy Archer.

Amy had one of the best attorneys money could buy fighting for her rights. Furthermore, the scientific community was breaking out one new resource after another, which, depending on how long it took for the trial to get under way, could possibly help Amy's cause.

Benedict Holden became a lawyer the old-fashioned way: earning the money for law school by working hard on his father's farm and, later, in a factory. He liked to say that he was in no way born with the "proverbial golden spoon," as he suggested that most lawyers of his era were. Instead, he had clawed his way up from poverty to Yale Law School's class of 1895 by getting his hands dirty. This gave Holden an inherent sense of the average man, John Doe, and the challenges and struggles normal Americans faced in the real world. More than that, perhaps, watching his mother work her fingers raw on the farm showed Holden how hard it was for a woman to succeed in what was certainly a man's world. He and Amy bonded almost immediately.

Holden had set up his first practice after graduation in Bristol, Connecticut, about a half hour's drive from Hartford. Holden's first law partner in Bristol was none other than Marcus Holcomb, who served as Connecticut's governor from 1915 through 1921. Both were up-and-coming attorneys, each showing great promise and skill. Their partnership broke up when, in 1898, the Spanish-American War began and Holden was called into military service. He leapt at the opportunity, ultimately becoming a sergeant-major in the Second Battalion, Twenty-seventh Regiment, United States Volunteer Infantry.

The man was a patriot of the highest order. Not to mention a fighter.

When Holden returned from the Philippines in 1901, he relocated to Hartford and resumed his law practice, perhaps with a new outlook on life and death.

"He is still a hard worker," writer Samuel Hart said of Holden in 1917, "is devoted to his profession, has had meted out of him a generous measure of success and approaches the future with confidence born of that spirit of self-reliance and independence developed in his youth."

Holden was a solidly built man with pudgy cheeks, brown eyes that could hold a stern gaze, and slicked-back hair, displaying an obvious receding hairline. He dressed like he believed a lawyer should: three-piece suit, the finest ties, and only the choicest pressed shirts. Married in 1902, Holden was the father of a daughter, Mary, and a son, Ben Jr.

One of the first things Holden did upon taking Amy's case was to retain the services of Dr. Otto Schultze, a noted bacteriologist. In his book, *Blood on the Table*, Colin Evans called Schultze "a fussy, self-important man with a knack for insinuating himself into high-profile cases . . ." Self-important or not, if there was one pathologist out there to dispute the venerable Dr. Arthur Wolff's claims of arsenical poisoning, Schultze was the man for the job.

Schultze was not only the medical assistant to the District Attorney of New York County, but also the Professor of Jurisprudence at Cornell University Medical College. Beyond that, the doctor had been involved in pathology on a scholarship level since 1898, and had the utmost respect and admiration of his colleagues and peers.

On May 15, 1916, Schultze took the train from his office in Manhattan to Hartford. The idea was to meet with Alcorn, Hurley, Holden, and Dr. Wolff. Schultze wanted to go over the evidence the State had against Amy. Check it out for himself. See where he and Holden stood.

Before meeting with Wolff at his downtown lab, Schultze stopped at a local drugstore with Holden and Alcorn to purchase several new glass jars and what he called a "cake of paraffin," that waxy red or black substance used to seal cheese. Schultze needed the jars and the wax so he could take his own specimens of the forensic evidence and fasten the jar lids with the wax in front of Alcorn and Hurley.

At Wolff's office some time later, "Dr. Wolff and Hurley produced a jar," Schultze explained later. Wolff opened the jar and removed a piece of an organ taken from Franklin Andrews's corpse. They weighed it, put it inside one of the jars Schultze had purchased, and then sealed it with paraffin.

Schultze did this with several additional pieces of organs and took the jars with him back to New York to be tested at Cornell University's chemistry lab. The results would tell Holden and Hungerford where their case was headed.

Chapter 36

THE GREATEST SUCCESS

FORTY-FOUR-YEAR-OLD HUGH ALCORN HAD a promising political career ahead of him if he could stave off any major pockmarks to his clean-cut image and law record. He had been a member of the Connecticut State House of Representatives from 1903 to 1905, delegate from Connecticut to the Republican National Convention in 1912, and was slated to return under the same title during the next major election. Alcorn was a freemason, and some said that if he played his cards right, there was a nomination for Connecticut governor waiting for him at some point down the road.

First, Alcorn had to get past this unfolding drama of Amy Archer-Gilligan. No sooner had Amy lawyered up than she stopped talking to Captain Hurley and the state's attorney's office. Yet she continued to fight for her innocence in the press. In one interview, Amy attacked Alcorn's theories of arsenic poisoning, saying, "Shortly after Mr. Andrews's death, I received information that the authorities were trying to connect his death with [a] criminal act on the part of somebody in the home." She suggested that Hurley and his team of investigators went into her home without probable cause and "found" the evidence they needed once inside.

Amy was promoting the idea that the State Police had planted evidence. It was a setup—all of it.

"Some of the neighbors in Windsor distorted the facts," Amy added, "and invented stories to keep the agitation alive." Then she started in on the notion that her rights had been violated.

"When I was arrested, I asked the police officers if it would not be better for me to consult an attorney, and they told me to follow their advice—that they were friendly to me and wanted to carry the thing through without notoriety. I followed their advice. And now I am in jail without a hearing."

She went on to say that Captain Hurley was the true criminal, the man behind a scam on the state's attorney's part to get her to admit to the murders. She said Hurley had promised that if she signed a statement, admitting to one charge, all of the other charges would be dropped. What was a judge going to say about that!

"Thank God I did not follow his advice. Because my counsel informed me that if I had, this so-called 'friend' would have rounded out his friendly advice with a conviction on the awful crime of murder . . . and I am innocent of wrongdoing against any person who has ever been an inmate in my house."

Amy mentioned how destitute she was at the time of her arrest. She was a Christian helping the community, which needed her. How dare anyone accuse a woman of God of such horrific crimes? She was appalled that the community of Windsor had banded together to crucify her. They were jealous and bitter people.

Hugh Alcorn kept his comments centered on the facts of the case. He had a formal grand jury in session, weighing evidence, hearing testimony, as his experts continued to exhume more bodies and conduct additional tests for arsenic poisoning.

All did not go well for the state's attorney, however. He quickly realized his case was anything but open and shut. Alcorn's first problem came in the form of testimony from Frank Smith, who had embalmed many of the bodies. Smith told the grand jury that he had purchased the embalming fluid he used on the bodies from New York, but did not know of the "formula," as he described it. Smith testified that the Red Falcon embalming fluid he used could have contained arsenic, and that he would not have known the difference. He also said that all of the permits required to remove a body from a home in the middle of the night had been secured— that is, with the exception of permits for Franklin Andrews and Alice Gowdy.

Spinning this, Alcorn did his best to defend the evidence he had, telling the press on May 17, 1916, "We have had the greatest success with the case today. In fact, it has taken definite shape."

According to what Alcorn believed, it was likely Amy would face a judge by the end of September 1916, three months away. He said he'd be ready for trial by then.

Benedict Holden countered by indicating that he was ready now. What was the holdup?

A few days before this latest development, Alcorn had called the case against Amy one of the strongest he had seen in all his years as a trial lawyer, adding, "This has developed in evidence in my possession into one of the biggest poisoning cases in the history of our country. There were a number of murders. And I repeat: they were cool and calculated."

Any momentum that might have been thrown Amy's way was quickly halted by a story about her family that soon surfaced. It appeared that Amy's oldest brother, John Francis Duggan, had been committed to an insane asylum back in the late 1890s. The elder Duggan had apparently been born with a rare, incurable mental condition.

"He is suffering from a peculiar form of insanity," said one report, "known medically as dementia praecox."

Dementia praecox was, essentially, schizophrenia. One of John Francis's more bizarre behaviors was to stand "in front of a mirror all day, playing the violin." There can be little doubt that the inspiration for the "crazy nephew" role in *Arsenic and Old Lace*, Teddy, who liked to announce visitors to the home by blowing his trumpet, was inspired by John Francis.

Moreover, it was then reported that one of Amy's sisters had become an invalid by jumping off the roof of the house when she was a child.

Another lunatic, some suggested.

With news of the "crazy Duggan family" now out in the media, some asked if Amy was also mentally unstable, or if she had suffered from mental illness herself. Maybe she could plead her way out of it all? If the woman was mad from the get-go, she had every reason to plead insanity. But the idea that several of her family members were mentally ill made an easy sell of the claim that Amy could have murdered inmates in her home. One of those "the apple doesn't fall far from the tree" insinuations that a prosecutor doesn't even need to respond to. All Alcorn had to do was allow the information to trickle out into the community.

Holden kept quiet on this issue of insanity for as long as he could. No defense attorney wanted to give up on any one particular position. It was always best to leave every option open. But it seemed that as much as he wanted to, Benedict Holden couldn't let a wayward comment go without having a reaction to it.

"There will be no insanity plea," Holden snapped at newspaper reporters while leaving his office one afternoon. "We are now in the ring and the capital charge against my client will be fairly met in court. In fact, though it may sound like braggadocio, I am willing to turn the case over to my office boy and go on to other cases until the trial."

Holden was confident that the State had been bluffing all along—even more so now that he'd had a good look at the evidence. Alcorn had absolutely nothing on his client that the State could prove beyond a reasonable doubt. When Holden looked at all the evidence, none of it, he was certain, would hold up.

♠ ♠ ♠

One indication that Hugh Alcorn was perhaps not as confident as he had led the press to believe came on June 20. Captain Hurley was called into Alcorn's office and told that he would be traveling to Waterbury.

Gas up that motor vehicle. Get the shovels ready. It was time to exhume another body.

Two days later, Hurley grabbed Thomas Egan and Rowe Wheeler. They drove to North Main Street in Waterbury to meet with Ida Warner, Charles Smith's sister. From there they made their way to Riverside Cemetery.

When they arrived, "The grave had been opened and the box and casket taken out and set beside the grave," Hurley commented later.

Ida bent over and took a look inside the casket to confirm that it was the body of her brother. Cemetery officials took the body to the undertaker, who had been waiting.

Hurley, Egan, and Wheeler stood and watched as Dr. Phillip Bunce removed several organs from Smith's corpse. Hours later, he gave the organs, which had been jarred and sealed, to Hurley and his men, who drove them to Hartford.

Alcorn felt that he needed more evidence to seal Amy's fate. Within a few days, he had it.

Dr. Wolff declared that Smith had also been poisoned by arsenic.

▲ ▲ ▲

On the third Tuesday of September 1916, a Hartford grand jury handed down a formal indictment, charging Amy with five counts of first-degree murder in the deaths of Franklin Andrews, Alice Gowdy, Michael Gilligan, Charles Smith, and Maude Lynch.

No one could believe it. A female serial murderer in Hartford.

Word traveled fast throughout the country. By the following day, newspapers in all major cities were reporting the story.

Amy pleaded not guilty. She said she would fight until the end to clear her name and restore her tarnished reputation. This was an outrage, Benedict Holden proclaimed. No matter what happened, the woman had lost her business for sure. A mere circumstantial case with no substantive evidence to speak of had come down to five charges of murder? Preposterous! Holden was certain the case would be thrown out of court once he was given the opportunity to argue the evidence.

Hugh Alcorn remained confident that the evidence would speak for itself. "This is the biggest crime that ever shocked New England," he said.

Get ready.

Chapter 37

WITCH OF WINDSOR

IN THE WAKE OF AMY'S ARREST, formal indictment, and the sensational news coverage of her life and alleged crimes, the Connecticut state legislature got to work on passing a bill to regulate invalid homes such as Amy's throughout the state. Until then, private-sector homes for the aged had no governmental hand watching over their daily operations, either on a local, district, or state level. It was only when an inmate or an inmate's family member hired an attorney and made a complaint that local or state law enforcement got involved. There needed to be some sort of accountability, managed and supervised by the government. The mere fact that there were unanswered questions regarding the deaths of inmates inside the Archer Home proved at least *that* much, no matter how Amy's court case would eventually turn out.

The bill mandated supervision by the State Board of Charities and required all homes for the aged to provide the board with annual reports. "Legislation intended to make impossible a repetition of events such as the state charges transpired at the Archer Home . . . ," the newspapers reported on January 26, 1917, calling to mind the theory by Benedict Holden that Amy had been found guilty in the court of public opinion before she had even had a chance to face a jury and explain her side of things.

The bill—introduced and developed in the lower house of the Connecticut Legislature by Representative Samuel Russell Jr., from Middletown—was rather extensive and detailed. Among the many other numbered sections was a line pertaining to how the State Board of Charities would continuously monitor homes and conduct both covert and open investigations anytime it wanted.

No old people's home or similar institution, unless specifically chartered by the state, and no person or group of persons, whether incorporated for the purpose or not, shall make a business of caring for or boarding persons over 60 years of age not related to them in any number exceeding two at the same time in the same place, without a license obtained from the state board of charities; provided, however, that certain boards of charity, selectmen of towns and similar official bodies shall not be subject to the provisions of this act.

There were time limits during which a home's proprietor had to answer charges lodged against a home by the Board of Charities. In the shadow of Amy's alleged crimes, Section 4 stood out the most. It detailed how each home was now responsible for filing a report explaining the number of inmates received and removed during the year, along with the number of deaths. This would certainly make every homeowner responsible for answering to any suspicious rise in deaths during a specific period of time.

Without being found guilty of any crime, Amy Archer-Gilligan and her business had single-handedly inspired a change in the law. It was three years before the 19th Amendment to the Constitution would be signed into law, giving women in the United States the right to vote, and here was this strange little woman with large ears and a boxer's pushed-in nose—now frail and beaten down by jail time, surely on the verge of mental collapse, accused of being a serial murderer—inspiring change in the laws of Connecticut.

Events taking place around the alleged—and now infamous—killer, who could easily be called the Witch of Windsor, were changing. It wasn't just the women's suffrage movement pushing for the right to vote and other civil liberties. The headline everyone was talking about on June 7, 1917, as both sides continued to prepare for a trial that was slated to begin on June 18, said it all: MRS. GILLIGAN INSANE. The story that followed was brief, yet the subheading seemed to sum up what many had been betting on all along: WOMAN HELD IN POISONING CASE MAY NEVER BE TRIED.

Was Amy Archer-Gilligan ready to plead insanity on the eve of trial? Was she prepared to admit her role in the murders and give up her fight?

"Mrs. Amy Archer-Gilligan," the *New York Times* detailed, "was today reported violently insane in her cell in the Hartford County Jail, and the alleged murderess may never face a jury . . ."*

As it turned out, the *Times* story was folly. Nothing more than incompetent reporting. Come to find out, the delay in the court case wasn't based on Amy's mental condition, her capacity to understand what was going on, or anything having to do with Benedict Holden's pretrial, eleventh-hour antics. Instead, Hugh Alcorn had told the court he was not yet ready to present his case. Alcorn had enlisted the services of Dr. Victor Vaughan, who was considered an expert in the field of toxicology. Vaughan was going to verify Dr. Wolff's argument regarding how the poison was administered into the bodies of the victims. Alcorn knew the case was going to come down to the jury not only understanding, but also *believing* that the arsenic was introduced into the systems of the dead not by natural occurrence, but by a woman—namely, Amy Archer—looking to murder these people so she could make room for new inmates (which meant more money in her pocket), and embezzle any funds she could from their bank accounts.

This was not going to be an easy task for Hugh Alcorn, and he knew it. Benedict Holden would argue that the arsenic could have been administered into their bodies any number of natural ways, none of which included Amy giving it to them.

Thus, Alcorn enlisted the expertise of Vaughan all the way from Ann Arbor, Michigan, where he had reigned as dean of the University of Michigan's Medical School for the past twenty-six years. Vaughn could counter any expert Holden might produce. In addition to his studies in Michigan, Vaughan had been tutored in Berlin, Vienna, Paris, and London by some of the more renowned doctors of the world. One of the most famous trials he had been involved

---

* *Violently insane* was a common euphemism near the turn of the twentieth century for a raging maniac—someone who was considered to be stark raving mad, acting manic, and, perhaps, in need of a straitjacket and "rubber room."

in was *State of Michigan v. Matthew Miller*, in 1882. Vaughan later explained the particulars of the Miller case, noting that it "was a question of the postmortem diffusion of arsenic. It was claimed that arsenic was injected into the body *after* death, and that the arsenic found in various organs was diffused through the body *after* death [emphasis added]."

This was the driving force behind Amy's defense: Could arsenic be introduced into the body's organs after a person died? Not the bloodstream or muscle tissue or even the lining of the stomach, but the kidneys, spleen, liver, inner stomach wall. If so, Hugh Alcorn had better pack it in now, because, scientifically speaking, he had no case.

Vaughan was there to say that arsenic could only get into the body's organs two ways: ingestion or injection, through the mouth or the vein—neither of which occurs during embalming. If Amy fed the arsenic to her victims, the proof was in the autopsy reports and scientific examinations of the organs.

With Vaughan now in Alcorn's camp, the court ordered that "the expenses of Dr. Otto Schultze," Amy's expert, be paid by the State. A small victory for Amy, who was broke by this point, and was considering selling her Home.

Benedict Holden had filed for a change of venue. In his view (which was probably a good judgment, considering), Amy could not get a fair trial in Hartford. Surely not with the Windsor community constantly bad-mouthing the woman, and word quickly spreading throughout the state and country that she was probably guilty as charged. It seemed that no one was behind Amy any longer. Of course, Mary Archer claimed that her mother was being railroaded, but who was going to listen to the daughter of a murderer?

As a formality, in those days leading up to the proposed start of trial, Benedict Holden asked that the grand jury indictment be tossed out. Secondly, that Amy be granted separate trials on all five counts. And, finally, at the State's expense, Holden said he wanted some much-needed legal help.

Within ten days all of the motions filed by Holden were denied, with the exception of the State providing Amy with an additional lawyer.

Jury selection, the judge informed both sides, was set to begin on June 18, initiating the start of the *State of Connecticut v. Amy Archer-Gilligan*. There would be no more delays. No more surprise motions. And no more quarreling by either side. The woman had a right to a fair and balanced trial, and it was high time she was given her day in court.

Chapter 38

VICTORY FOR THE VANQUISHED

MANY DECADES AFTER AMY ARCHER-GILLIGAN'S case was adjudicated, noted trial attorney F. Lee Bailey explained the importance of jury selection to *Time* magazine. "*Voir dire* is really the start of a criminal trial. If you do it carelessly, you can lose a case by the time you get a jury together."

Indeed, a defendant's freedom, or, in Amy's case, her life, hung in that strange, uneasy balance of human opinion and emotion a jury was going to bring to her trial. Amy had better hope that no one on the jury had a relative or friend or neighbor sitting in an elderly care home somewhere. Relationships between attorneys, defendants, and juries, furthermore, were made during that crucial *voir dire* process. Jurors began to like or dislike lawyers, judges, and defendants almost immediately, forming opinions about them as they sat and listened and waited. Regardless of how *objective* people claim they are, when it comes to weighing justice, a verdict depends on what takes place behind closed doors during deliberations and what sort of opinions and ideas those jurors take into the room with them.

Edward Stevens, an employee of the Connecticut State Highway Department, was the first to undergo *voir dire* questioning. Stevens was a "family man," he said. He wasn't opposed to the death penalty "in a proper case." Alcorn was smooth with his approach, both he and Holden eliciting answers to their questions from the witness that would send attorneys running for the door in today's legal world.

At one point, Alcorn asked Stevens, "Would you, under the charge of the Court and upon evidence in this case—would you be satisfied with circumstantial evidence as to guilt of a person, provided that evidence was strong enough to satisfy you?"

"I would have to be satisfied beyond a doubt," Stevens answered.

This sort of finger-wagging, are-you-this-or-are-you-that type of questioning went on as each prospective juror walked in and took the stand.

Holden asked Stevens, "Have you read an account of these incidents in the newspapers?"

"Yes," Steven said.

"What papers did you read?"

"The *Hartford Courant.*"

"At the time you read the *Courant*, did you form an opinion as to the guilt or innocence of the accused?"

Stevens thought about it. "No. I did not."

"Did what you read in the papers have any impression on you?"

"I didn't understand."

Holden asked the question again.

"I don't think so. I read it as any other news."

Amy lived in a tight-knit community of people, many of whom were said to be out for her head on a platter; as such, it was important to weed out those who might be seeking revenge disguised as justice. Through questioning, it was clear how small-town Hartford and Windsor were. "Do you know [Alcorn's co-counsel,] Mr. Maltbie?"

"Yes. I know Mr. Maltbie."

"Do you know him intimately?"

"Why, I should not."

"Do you know Chief Egan of the State Police?"

"Why, I know him when I see him."

Despite these connections, Stevens was still chosen for the jury!

Next was a man named Henry Hart, who worked for the local Water Works. He lived in Plantsville, south of Hartford. Then Roland A. Barnes, a civil engineer from Bristol. Frederick Griswold from Wethersfield, an insurance agent. Each man, along with eight others, answered questions and were "accepted" by both Holden and Alcorn.

As Amy prepared for trial, the year 1917 was quickly shaping up to be one of the most crucial periods in American history. That January, President Woodrow Wilson gave an address before the Senate that conveyed a personal belief that peace and harmony throughout the world could be achieved if the United States stood up and led the way. Wilson was optimistic. He felt America should show her superior leadership skills during such a volatile time in world politics. Moreover, the global harmony Wilson trumpeted needed to be "peace without victory," as opposed to "peace forced upon the loser." If the "victor's terms" were somehow "imposed upon the vanquished," Wilson added, any peace achieved would be "accepted in humiliation, under duress, at an intolerable sacrifice, and would leave a sting, a resentment, a bitter memory upon which the terms of peace would rest, not permanently, but only as upon quicksand."

Nevertheless, a mere three months later, on April 7, 1917, Wilson signed a Declaration of War with Germany, sending troops overseas to engage militarily in the First World War. Connecticut ended up sending some 67,000 men to the cause, an astounding number for such a small state.

Though the world seemed to be in disarray, the streets of Hartford were bustling with talk of Amy's trial as the first tulips of spring poked their heads out of the cold earth. Little Katharine Hepburn, who had just turned ten on May 12 of that year, was born on Hudson Street, a mere three blocks from the courthouse, and later moved to Hawthorn Street, north of Capitol Avenue. The talk around the city was that the most prolific and infamous serial killer in history—and a female, at that!—was about to meet her fate. If Amy was found guilty, she would hang.

Could real-life drama get any more compelling? A female serial murderer caught and hanged would be unprecedented in the U.S. by any means. People could not believe the stakes. It made the trial of a woman who had supposedly killed her parents with an ax in nearby Fall River look like child's play.

Amy had a chance to stave off death by hanging if she pleaded her case at the last minute and Hugh Alcorn accepted the plea. An insanity plea was the only way out for Amy at this pivotal moment.

While an insanity plea could save her life, such a plea this late in the proceedings was difficult for a defendant to pull off. It bodes well, of course, if the defendant has had a history of mental problems—i.e., arrests, crazy behavior that has been documented, a history of stays in mental institutions—none of which Amy could stake claim to.

An admission of guilt would be paired with the premeditated and "coldly" planned nature of the crimes. Whatever her plea, Amy had little hope of shedding the image of a calculated killer. An insane person snaps, kills in a methodical and fantastical manner; one could not carefully plan and carry out the murders Amy had allegedly committed without some sort of rational thinking. Logically speaking, the plea would not make sense.

By June 21, Alcorn had agreed to "proceed on the first count (Franklin Andrews) of the indictment . . ."—that is, only after the judge made the decision that the state's attorney could not present evidence for any of the additional four victims named in the indictment. The judge had warned Alcorn to focus his case on Franklin Andrews's death and his death alone. Bark up any other tree and there would be grounds for an appeal. The reason the judge made such a decision was to keep the case focused on the evidence the State Police had uncovered, which centered on Franklin Andrews's death. To bring in other deaths would invite speculation. Alcorn didn't have much evidence to support a murder charge for any of the other deaths, apart from a few anecdotal testimonies.

Carl Goslee was in the front row, reporting for the *Hartford Courant*. In one of his first dispatches from the trial, Carl sounded as though he was in his element, seeing the murder case of his career through until the end as it unfolded before him:

> . . . *Gardiner Greene is the judge on this case and he ordered that Mrs. Gilligan be tried only for the murder of Franklin Andrews, even though the police believe she killed at least 22 of her patients in the six years she operated the Archer Home. Hugh Alcorn, state's attorney, called the home a "slaughterhouse." Mrs. Gilligan was a polite, "bible-toting" nurse.*

William Maltbie ended up stepping in to assist Alcorn, and Holden was able to get himself an attorney by the name of William Mulligan, a smart, cogent, respectable lawyer with experience. Although Alcorn himself was young, he was known as a venerable, thorough prosecutor, a lawyer who liked to work alone. Once he'd set his mind to a cause, he would see it through until the end. Alcorn never considered losing this case, which was certainly evident in the way he handled the investigation. Alcorn hadn't jumped to conclusions, or flown off the handle, making erroneous accusations against Amy. Hugh Meade Alcorn had been appointed state's attorney in 1908. He would hold the office for an unprecedented thirty-four years, until 1942. According to the attorney general's office, Alcorn "came to symbolize Connecticut's tough, yet fair, approach to criminal justice."

The courtroom was packed—SRO. Many of the family members of Amy's victims sat in stoic shock, unable to wrap their minds around the fact that murder had come to those who had paid a woman to care for them. It seemed so senseless, and doubly tragic. A cloud of melancholy hung over everyone as both sides readied for round one of the trial.

As the testimony portion of the trial got under way, Alcorn called a series of witnesses to paint a picture of Franklin Andrews's health throughout his life, leading up to his stay in the Archer Home. The testimony made it clear that while Franklin may not have been as healthy as an ox, he was certainly more or less a normally aging American male who had battled the same illnesses many others of his era had.

Normal health became the battle cry for Alcorn throughout the morning of June 21, as Holden did his best to counter each witness by focusing on Franklin's obvious problems with rheumatism and lameness—neither of which, of course, had any bearing whatsoever on his death.

Alcorn put Franklin's banker from Cheshire on the stand to explain how Franklin had deposited money into his account at various intervals throughout his later years. This gave Alcorn the opportunity to introduce Franklin's bank records into the record as evidence, the banker verifying all of them.

After that, the first major witness of the case sauntered into the packed room to whispers and critical stares. Dr. Howard King appeared sheepish and malnourished, as if he hadn't slept much lately. He was filling two roles in the trial: one, as medical examiner for the Town of Windsor, and the other as the Archer Home's personal physician. His name had been associated with Amy's case for years, even before her arrest. King had been the subject of vicious accusations and rumors, and was probably going to be a hostile witness seeing that he wasn't all that thrilled to be taking the stand against his former employer and good friend.

For her part, Amy sat composed, listening, watching intently, with little reaction. Behind Amy sat her daughter, Mary; her sister, Katherine Duggan; and several of Holden's experts, including Dr. Otto Schultze.

Miss Emily Smith, Charles Smith's sister, sat on the opposite side of the room. She wore a large round hat and stared gravely at Amy with a look of continuous disbelief and disgust on her face.

The jury, made up of all men (women could not sit on juries in most states until late in the year 1917), sized the doctor up, no doubt eagerly awaiting his testimony.

A well-educated professional, King could hold his own in a room full of legal eagles. He started out by listing his rather extensive credentials. He talked about his children, and then merged into how he had become acquainted with Amy.

Alcorn managed to get the doctor into a discussion regarding how Amy had paid him. There was a sense in the room that Alcorn was holding off on the hardball questions because at 4:40 p.m., it was getting close to the end of the day. Alcorn paused; then, knowing full well it was probably going to be his final question of the day, he asked, "Now, Dr. King, do you remember being called to attend to Mr. Franklin R. Andrews, or to see Franklin R. Andrews before his death?"

"Yes," King said softly.

Displaying a bit of dramatics, Alcorn said, "Speak up now so the jury can hear you."

"Yes!"

"Mr. Alcorn," Benedict Holden said, interrupting Alcorn's questioning, "if Your Honor please, it is so near to a quarter of five, and that is so important a subject, I don't know as it would pay to get into it."

The judge thought about it. "Perhaps we should suspend here?"

Whispers and movement.

"Court adjourned until tomorrow morning, ten o'clock."

Gavel.

▲ ▲ ▲

Without a clear explanation, yet assuming the state's attorney's office had additional cases of importance going on, Alcorn's assistant, William Maltbie, "retired from the case" the following morning, leaving Hugh Alcorn, for the time being, to continue his quest against New England's most famous murder suspect by himself.

At ten o'clock the next morning, June 22, 1917, the courtroom was once again bustling as Alcorn resumed his questioning of Dr. King. Amy had been brought in by a jailhouse guard. After Amy sat down, Mary leaned over the railing and kissed her mother on the cheek, giving her a soothing glance of support.

Dr. King went through his version of the events on the night Franklin died. He was straightforward and direct with his explanations; there were no histrionics or earth-shattering revelations—perhaps only that King had shown up to tend to Franklin when it was too late—that is, not by his own choice, but at the beck and call of his boss, Amy.

Be that as it may, King had made a diagnosis—"severe indigestion and gastric ulcers"—based on his conversations with Franklin. He had prescribed some pills and left the Archer Home under the impression that Franklin would be just fine in a day or two.

Over and over again, Alcorn asked King to explain himself in more detail. The doctor tried as best he could to tell the jury what was said, by whom, and what it all meant to him as a physician. None of it mattered much. The more King said, the less he added to Alcorn's case.

From there, Alcorn had King go through the ailments Franklin had suffered throughout his stay at the Home.

After they finished, Alcorn went on to note for the jury that Dr. King was not the most cooperative witness at the beginning of the investigation, and would have rather been left alone. Nor did he feel all that good about taking the stand against his former employer.

Surprisingly, King agreed with the prosecutor.

So Alcorn asked what had changed his mind and led him to cooperate with the court now.

"I think I followed my own judgment in that matter," King answered, to several hems and haws from the gallery.

Benedict Holden was watching carefully from his seat near Amy, listening, taking notes, waiting for the appropriate moment to object. Shortly before Holden was asked to cross-examine King, as Alcorn and King got into a little discussion over King's new line of thinking that Amy could be guilty, Holden shouted in a snappish tone to Dr. Otto Schultze, who was sitting nearby, "That's a . . . damned lie!"

Holden made sure everyone heard.

Alcorn was incensed. "I ask that Mr. Holden be disciplined by the court, Your Honor."

"I did not hear it," the judge said after Alcorn explained.

"I would suggest that Your Honor ask the jurymen if they . . . heard it."

"I would sooner ask Mr. Holden," Judge Greene intoned.

Benedict Holden approached the bench after being summoned.

"Did you make the remark, Mr. Holden?" the judge asked.

Holden looked down. Paused. "I believe I did, Your Honor."

"Well, I would ask that you be careful of your expressions, Mr. Holden."

Chapter 39

THE EXPERTS

Benedict Holden announced on June 23rd that his client was going to take the stand in her own defense. It was the only way to rectify a terrible wrong that had been done to Amy, Holden suggested. He blamed an overzealous press and "newspaper persecution" that had been looking to hang the poor woman ever since members of her community decided they wanted her run out of town.

The question most asked afterward centered on whether Holden was merely blowing smoke—stirring up the court of public opinion, hoping to sway the pendulum in favor of Amy—or was he actually telling the truth?

Either way, everyone was going to have to wait. No matter what Holden said, if one had been keeping a scorecard, by this point in the trial Hugh Alcorn would have had the advantage. It seemed that every witness Alcorn called over the first few days of the trial helped piece together what was turning into a circumstantially guilty picture, one that was going to send Amy Archer to the gallows.

By June 27, a beautiful Monday, the trial had endured its first weekend recess. Dr. Arthur Wolff came in and testified as to his findings; Captain Hurley explained his role in the investigation and arrest; and Nellie Pierce sat on the witness stand and discussed how she had suspected wrongdoing on Amy's part after uncovering letters between Amy and Franklin, and how she'd taken her accusations of murder to the *Courant*.

Then Frank Smith talked about his skills as an embalmer and how he was certain that his company did not use embalming fluid that contained arsenic.

Dr. Wolff spent two full days explaining every single nuance and detail of his investigation: the lab results from the organs of the victims; how he had drawn his conclusions; and why he believed the victims had been murdered by arsenical poisoning.

Benedict Holden did his best to poke holes in Wolff's testimony, but his questioning provoked answers that at best bored the jury with technical mumbo jumbo. For example, for nearly an hour Holden and Wolff discussed the topic of ulcers and how the doctor could discern through a simple autopsy that a particular victim had suffered from the awful condition but did not die from it.

In the end, Dr. Wolff would not be undone. The guy stuck to the science he had relied on for the past two decades.

Breaking off from Wolff, Alcorn called Dr. Emma Thompson, who had treated Alice Gowdy. But by the following morning, June 28, at 10:00 a.m., Dr. Wolff was back on the stand, recalled for what turned into a second marathon session of tedious medical and scientific Q&A.

Here, though, the talk centered on the stomach contents and condition of Franklin Andrews's heart on the day he died—two important issues Alcorn needed to put before the jury.

During the next several days, Dr. Emma Thompson was recalled, as was Frank Smith, the now infamous undertaker.

Benedict Holden was indeed a smart lawyer, perhaps more seasoned and trial-experienced than his counterpart. What Holden had been doing all along was trying his best to force Alcorn to drag into the trial inadmissible information about the deaths of Michael Gilligan, Alice Gowdy, Maude Lynch,* and Charles Smith. It was strategy on his part all the way. The doctors could not talk at length about their findings without mentioning the other victims in the indictment—something the judge had earlier been firm about not discussing.

It got to the point where the judge had to make a special ruling in Alcorn's favor, allowing him to bring in information about Michael Gilligan, Charles Smith, and Alice Gowdy. It was impossible

---

* The circumstances of Maude Lynch's death were strangely similar to the deaths of Franklin Andrews and Alice Gowdy. However, when Lynch's body was exhumed and examined, forensic scientist Dr. Arthur Wolff found strychnine in her stomach. To avoid confusion, the judge wanted to keep the trial focused on arsenic.

for the expert witnesses to discuss the case of Franklin Andrews without talking about their findings in the other cases. Maude Lynch, however, was off the table, Judge Greene warned. The State had claimed Amy used strychnine to kill Lynch. The judge wanted the trial focused on arsenic. Bringing strychnine into an already-confusing situation would only complicate matters further.

With this new decision came scores of additional witnesses.

Amy sat throughout most of the testimony not saying much of anything. "She rarely moves a muscle," wrote one reporter. "[M]ost of the time her eyes are closed and [she] speaks only in answer to her daughter's words."

There were mild theatrics throughout the first ten days of testimony, consisting mostly of verbal sparring between Alcorn and Holden. As Alcorn moved away from his expert witnesses for the time being, Lizzie Sullivan was brought in to talk about what she had witnessed at the jail on the day Amy arrived. Lizzie was key to Alcorn's case. She was going to put inculpatory words in the defendant's mouth.

Lizzie had a hard look to her, the rough street vibe of a transient or prostitute. It came through in the way she expressed herself. Sitting uncomfortably, shifting and moving in her chair, Lizzie testified that Amy had been uneasy when she arrived at the jail, at one point shouting to herself, "Why did I do it?" This comment, reverberating throughout the courtroom with the punch of a racial slur, brought gasps and disbelief from the gallery. Here was a witness attributing a breath of guilt—even remorse!—to Amy. It was as close to an admission or confession as Hugh Alcorn was going to get.

All seemed to be going well for Alcorn until Benedict Holden got a chance to question Lizzie. Holden's cross-examination was thorough and eye-opening, without the experienced trial attorney coming across as overpowering or unsympathetic. After a few inconsequential questions, Holden casually asked, "Lizzie, how many times [have] you been put in that jail in the last five years?"

"I haven't been up there [in] five years."

It seemed that Lizzie didn't understand the question. So Holden reframed it. "There has been an interval, but how many times have you been there in the last five years?" He was a bit more firm. It was obvious he thought Lizzie was trying to dance around the issue of her credibility.

"Well," Lizzie said, "I couldn't tell that."

"Too many to count up here for this jury?"

"I didn't keep track of how many times—a good many."

"You don't keep track of how many times you [have] been sent up to the jail by the police court?" Holden said, hoping to hammer home his point.

"No."

"You don't care?"

"No; it don't bother me."

"It is all the same in your young life whether you are in jail or [not], Lizzie," Holden said, more as a statement, not giving Lizzie a chance to reply, adding, "Where did you get that shirtwaist?"

"I don't know."

"What?" Holden barked. Now he was loud. The courtroom was silent.

"I don't know," she said again.

"And you don't care, do you, Lizzie?"

"No!"

"It was given to you, wasn't it?"

"I guess so."

"They dressed you up pretty nice to bring you down here, didn't they?" Holden asked with a sarcastic ring.

"They are good to me up there."

With no objection, Holden took it a step further. "They are pretty good to you now while this case is going on?"

"They have always been good to me."

"So you want to be good to them!" Holden answered.

"Yes."

Where was the objection?

"Any little thing you can do to help out you want to do. When you saw this woman [Amy] . . . ," Holden said, pointing at his client, "she was in the hospital as a patient, wasn't she?"

Lizzie was confused. "As a patient?"

"In the jail hospital, yes?"

"Yes, sir."

A few questions later, Holden asked, "Lizzie, this whole thing is a joke to you, isn't it?"

"It ain't much of a joke to me."

"It is a joke to the state's attorney," Holden snapped, hoping to get a rise out of Alcorn, "who is forced to make good."

"We are not forced to do anything except offer the truth," Hugh Alcorn stood and shouted, finally objecting in his own dramatic way.

"Offer the truth from the mouth of a woman who lives in that jail," Holden shouted back, "at a time when the state was paying [three people] to take care of this woman," meaning Amy Archer, "when she couldn't be brought to trial because of her condition. That is a noble thing to do!" It was clear that Benedict Holden was disgusted by a witness who could not be trusted—or one who *should not* be trusted.

Lizzie was told she could leave the stand.

At a time when it seemed the trial could not get any more complicated, Dr. Howard King was recalled to the stand and asked to talk about Michael Gilligan, Alice Gowdy, and Charles Smith. It was Friday afternoon, June 29, before King's second round of testimony concluded, and additional witnesses were brought in to discuss the deaths of Charles Smith and Michael Gilligan.

The trial broke for the weekend and resumed on July 3. On this day, witnesses were asked questions based on the State's theory of Amy's proposed motive—how she had bilked her inmates out of their money and then callously murdered them to cover up her greed. If there was anything more mind-numbing and boring for jurors than inflexible testimony regarding pathology and medicine, it had to be finance and bank records.

Late into the day, Holden and Alcorn got into a bit of a spat over the fact that Alcorn had somehow gotten testimony into the record having to do with Maude Lynch's death. The court, Holden had said, was clear on this matter.

The judge listened to both sides of the argument by the lawyers as the jury was told to sit out the afternoon session.

In the end, the judge agreed, but warned Alcorn to watch his step.

Over the next several days, save for a recess here and there, Alcorn brought in a long line of witnesses to explain what amounted to dozens of jars of organ samples from various victims. It was back to the pathology portion of his case and more monotonous testimony regarding enzymes and the average weight of the body's organs. It seemed at one point that the courtroom had been turned into a science lab, as livers and spleens and hearts and lungs sat in glass jars for everyone to gawk at. Witness after witness, cops and doctors alike, all said the same thing: It was arsenical poisoning. The victims had died from ingesting arsenic. There was no other scientific or medical explanation for their deaths.

As July 9 rolled in, Alcorn closed his case with more of the same: Dr. Arthur Wolff, State Police superintendent Thomas Egan, and more from Captain Robert Hurley.

Benedict Holden began presenting his case on the same day. Since it was still fresh in the jury's mind, Holden brought in several witnesses to prove that Lizzie Sullivan was nothing more than a street urchin and alcoholic who had spent much of her adult life in jail. Her testimony should be tossed out. It meant nothing.

Then Holden brought in his group of medical experts, who countered Alcorn's scientific case by saying that the arsenic could have gotten into the victims' systems by any number of means, none of which included the hand of his client. It was a stretch, they collectively suggested, to make the leap that Amy had administered the poison.

Where was the proof? Where was the State's eyewitness?

It got to the point where Hugh Alcorn waived the right to cross-examine many of Holden's witnesses. Why? Well, by Hugh Alcorn's estimation, none of Holden's witnesses had much to offer in the form of countering *evidence*. Their testimony was based on *opinion*.

At 10:00 a.m. on Wednesday, July 11, Benedict Holden bent down and whispered something into Amy's ear, then stood and announced confidently, "The defense rests, Your Honor."

Everyone took a deep breath.

Hugh Alcorn had called fifty-five witnesses over a period of three weeks, as opposed to Holden's fourteen witnesses over two days. Lopsided didn't even begin to express how most people in the courtroom felt about the two opposing sides.

Several rebuttal witnesses were recalled.

Amy Archer-Gilligan, contrary to what Benedict Holden had promised, was never called to the stand.

Chapter 40

"Dark Murder Hole"

J ULY 13, 1917 WAS SET TO BE A SPECTACULAR MOMENT in the life and times of Amy Archer-Gilligan. The courthouse was bustling with people from all walks of life, many of whom had expected to hear an enraged Hugh Alcorn give his final thoughts in the form of a summation on the most sensational murder trial ever staged in Hartford, Connecticut. In terms of theatrics, many believed that this was going to go down as the most fantastic closing argument in Hartford legal history.

Alcorn had been state's attorney for the past eight years. It was no secret that he was about to embark on a closing argument that would come back to haunt him for the remainder of his career if it failed to meet the standards of such a judgmental community.

"The most amazing statement I ever heard from this side of the table," Alcorn said, referring to Benedict Holden, "was the statement I heard yesterday from a lawyer of experience. It was that you [the jury] could report but one of two verdicts, that of murder in the first degree or not guilty." He took a respectful pause. "Why was that statement made, I wonder? He knows. And I know. He believed I would refer to it and ask for a verdict of murder in the second degree. I'm not asking for that, but for a verdict that she is guilty of murder in the first degree! There is nothing in this case but sweeping condemnation of everyone connected with it, the state's attorney and State Police, the sheriff, Lizzie Sullivan, and even Reverend Roscoe Nelson of Windsor didn't escape it!"

There was standing room only in the courthouse as Alcorn spoke of a woman who had murdered not one or two old men, but dozens of healthy, aging tenants who had paid her a generous sum to care for them.

Extra chairs had been brought in to accommodate the crowd. People stood elbow to elbow wearing their Sunday best. A second judge sat next to Judge Greene in case pandemonium erupted.

Alcorn talked about how Amy had purchased arsenic one day from Mason's store and on that same day wrote a letter to a potential inmate, and then, *how coincidental*, that Franklin Andrews just happened to suddenly die on that same night.

It all fit, the state's attorney suggested. When you added up all of the evidence, the circumstantial along with the scientific, you could only come to one conclusion.

Further along, the sharp prosecutor sat on the edge of the table which had been his desk throughout the trial, as if to seem pleasantly confident and at ease with his case. "Talk about the defense in this case," he said casually, "with his experts at his side. The lawyer for the woman constructs his case as he goes. The first we heard was 'conspiracy' and the '*Hartford Courant,*' the newspaper that the state of Connecticut owes a debt of everlasting gratitude for the assistance it has rendered the state . . . But the several defenses that have been suggested have fallen by the way."

After Alcorn closed with some sort of bizarre rant about God and "the Great Temple on High," a place where he hoped "the children of Man will meet" one day and the "members of the jury would be counted" as saintly and blessed for their great work, and all will rejoice in the name of justice, he asked jurors to come in with a verdict of murder in the first degree.

"He followed close to the evidence," the *Courant* said of Holden's closing the following morning, "and the opinion of many in the courtroom who have attended important criminal trials was that a more able presentation of a case had never been made in court."

Carl Goslee was one of the first to exit the courtroom and wander the halls, working his sources in hopes of finding out what was going on, and in which direction, perhaps, the jury was leaning.

After wading through an afternoon of rumors and gossip, Carl wrote, "This has been a long day and the courthouse is filling up quickly," describing this intense moment when he believed that the jury was coming back with a verdict, "but it is a very subdued group."

According to Carl, there was a strong sense of sadness in the air, along with the belief that Amy was going to be found guilty.

"What will it be?" Carl asked during a report he gave that afternoon. "I have interviewed several persons and they all say 'guilty.'"

Near five o'clock that afternoon, Carl wrote, "There is some activity in the courthouse." He ran inside the building at that moment. He heard the jury had concluded its deliberations after just four hours and was ready to return to the courtroom. There was a scramble outside the courthouse, people running into the building, shouting, insisting that a verdict was about to be read.

Judge Greene, Carl noticed when he entered the room, had returned to the bench. Everyone was respectfully quiet, anticipating what would happen next.

Carl captured this moment perfectly in his reporting:

> *There is a hush in the courthouse and all rise. Now the judge is sitting and so do the spectators. The jury is returning. The foreman is standing and Judge Greene is asking him if the jury has come to a unanimous decision.*

After being asked if the jury had reached a verdict, the jury foreman, Samuel L. Williams, looked toward the judge with a somber flush rising in his face. "Yes," he said in almost a whisper. The rest of the jury refused to look at the judge, Amy, or the attorneys; they found a spot on the floor and stared, knowing what their verdict would ultimately mean for the defendant.

Silence.

The judge waited.

"The verdict is murder in the first degree as charged in the first count of the indictment."

The gallery began whispering and jostling about. Judge Greene demanded order. He asked the sheriff in the room to "make a proclamation of silence and to have order preserved."

At Hugh Alcorn's request, the judge needed to propose a sentence on Amy immediately. It was the right of the state's attorney to make such a demand.

As a formality, Benedict Holden asked that the case be tossed and the verdict set aside.

Denied.

Amy shook her head, saying, "No . . . no . . ."

There was a moment of confusion, some rustling, then silence, save for the hysterical crying of Mary Archer, now a nineteen-year-old woman.

"Amy Archer-Gilligan is guilty of the crime of murder in the first degree . . . ," the judge said without emotion. "[S]he is remanded to the custody of the Sheriff of Hartford County . . . and that she be conveyed by him . . . to the Connecticut State Prison at Wethersfield . . . and that upon said sixth day of November, 1917, before the hour of sunrise, within the walls of said prison, by warden of said prison, she be hung by the neck until she is dead."

In four short months, the woman her neighbors had once called Sister Amy would swing from the gallows in Wethersfield. Courtroom spectators were made speechless by this reality. It had come down to this: The matron of Windsor everyone had been pointing their fingers at for years would finally pay for her crimes.

Hung by the neck until she is dead . . .

Amy started to hyperventilate and cry uncontrollably, unable to contain what little emotion she had left.

"Never before in the history of this country," wrote one reporter, "has the superior courtroom beheld such a sense as when the jury came in to report the result of its deliberations."

Chapter 41

DRUG ADDICT

AMY ARCHER-GILLIGAN'S LIFE AS THE PROPRIETOR of the Archer Home had routinely revolved around remarkable twists and turns. Ever since she had murdered her second husband, Michael Gilligan, and become a target of Windsor townsfolk, not a day had gone by without some sort of problem, accusation, or explanation on her part driving the day. It was as if once a guilty sign had been tacked to Amy's back, she couldn't shake off the notoriety it had brought her, no matter what she said or did.

Amy's shameless tenacity in presenting herself as an innocent, Bible-carrying member of Windsor's pious elite, coupled with a sure case of extreme narcissism, finally paid off for the incomparable Witch of Windsor. Not three days after Amy was found guilty and sentenced to hang did the governor of Connecticut step in and make what could only be perceived as an extraordinary, unprecedented announcement. Governor Marcus Holcomb told reporters he was ready to grant Amy a stay from her execution until her case was heard by the Court of Errors, which was said to be holding its next session by the end of December. Holcomb made it clear he would see to it himself that Amy's appeal was presented before the State Board of Pardons in due time—there would be no delays.

A woman's life was at stake.

The governor was asked if he would exercise an executive order.

There would be "no need" for that, he explained, "until after the October session of the Supreme Court of Errors."

One had to wonder if Benedict Holden's previous friendship and partnership with the governor had impacted this decision.

Either way, Amy could not lose. If the Supreme Court of Errors rejected the appeal Benedict Holden was in the process of filing, refusing what were, according to Holden, 200 "exceptions and objections" he planned on citing, the governor would step in and save Amy from the gallows himself, ultimately exercising his executive power.

A short time after this decision was made public, Hugh Alcorn's office released the cost of prosecuting Amy. Connecticut had spent roughly $30,000, an enormous sum of money then, which translates into approximately $600,000–$700,000 in terms of inflation. Out of that, the two experts—Dr. Arthur Wolff and Dr. Victor Vaughan—had walked away with the bulk of it: $10,000 each.

▲ ▲ ▲

As it turned out, Governor Holcomb did not need to step in and save Amy Archer-Gilligan from a date with a rope and a trapdoor. The Supreme Court of Errors found that Hugh Alcorn had terribly disobeyed the judge's ruling not to include details of Maude Lynch's death in the State's case against Amy. When the decision came in that fall, the court ruled in Amy's favor, granting the convicted serial murderer a second trial.

The official ruling was posted several months later, in March 1918, just as Benedict Holden and his new team of two additional lawyers suddenly withdrew from Amy's case. Apparently, just as Holden was getting ready for the start of Amy's second trial, he (or someone from his office) had tried to interview Amy on numerous occasions, telling her that she would have to take the stand in this next go-round. There was no way they could win without the jury hearing from Amy herself.

But Amy refused to talk. Not only to the jurors in her next trial, but to anyone at all; she even refused to speak with Holden.

Holden was frustrated: How could he represent a client who literally would not speak to him? Furthermore, neither side really wanted to go through what had been four weeks of tedious medical and forensic testimony all over again. Was there some sort of plea everyone could agree upon?

Hugh Alcorn said no. He wanted a conviction of first-degree murder. Nothing else would suffice.

A public defender was appointed to represent Amy, and pretrial hearings began in June of 1919. It was likely that Amy had planned all along to form the basis of an insanity plea. By not talking to her attorneys, she was underhandedly trying to secure a place for herself at the table of the mentally unhinged.

Then Benedict Holden astonished everyone and stepped back into the ring, agreeing to act as Amy's defense counsel once again. Amy had decided to begin talking—yet what she said wasn't about her guilt or innocence. Instead, Amy was now prepared to make an admission of her own—something she had been wanting to say for many years.

Amy now claimed to be a drug addict. She said—and records backed her up—that she had purchased 20,500 morphine tablets from W. H. Mason's Drugstore over a three-year period, beginning back in 1912.

Amy Archer-Gilligan was a morphine junkie. She had been addicted to the drug at the time of Franklin Andrews's death.

Holden went to Alcorn with an insanity plea from Amy based on this new notion that she was a drug addict.

Alcorn said no way.

Game on.

In Middletown Superior Court, on June 19, 1919, Benedict Holden presented witnesses who testified as to the nature of Amy's sanity and her former drug addiction. Her case had been transferred to Middletown, about twenty miles south of Hartford, because of all the pretrial publicity and the fact that the woman had been tried in Hartford once already.

The most surprising witness to testify on that first day of hearings was a woman referred to as the "matron of the Hartford county jail." Louise Cowles was reluctant and a bit standoffish as she began to speak. Benedict Holden started to pry into the way in which she had cared for Amy at the jail. For many months prior to the hearing, Amy had been acting "insane," talking to invisible people as well as breaking into annoying crying spells for no apparent reason. This bothered the other inmates, Cowles said. So prison officials had to "put Amy in the dungeon."*

---

* The prison "dungeon" was what we would call solitary confinement today.

After being pressed, Cowles explained that Amy was famous in the jail for crying out the same sentence, over and over: "I want to go home! I want to go home!" Cowles couldn't recall exactly how many times Amy had been put in the dungeon since her arrest, but it had happened quite often, the guard said.

When pressed about Amy's condition and the constant visits Amy had received from doctors, Cowles added, "I think she is simulating insanity."

This sudden craziness on Amy's part was a ruse, Cowles was certain of it. She had been around Amy for years. She knew when the woman was lying. The insane condition, Cowles insinuated, was something Amy had made up. In fact, the entire time Amy had refused to talk to Benedict Holden was nothing more than subterfuge, Cowles said, so that Amy could come across as some sort of poor, mentally challenged woman who needed to spend her days in an institution. Amy knew she would never see freedom again, so why not spend the rest of her life in a hospital, as opposed to a dirty prison?

W. H. Mason took the stand and told the court that he had always believed the morphine Amy had purchased from his drugstore was for "her inmates." He never once believed that Amy was a "drug fiend." She had carried herself off so professionally and properly. How could a drug addict have so much control over herself? Mason had no record of the purchases, he said, but considered that Amy bought the morphine once a month and generally bought enough of the drug to last for that same period.

Holden called another Windsor druggist, Robert Barnes, to the stand. Barnes had a store across town, and did keep records. He presented to the court "eight double-columned pages" of morphine purchases made by either Amy or someone from the Archer Home on her behalf. On average, Amy had purchased 250 tablets of morphine per month from Barnes. This was a stunning amount, an incredible piece of evidence. There were some months when Amy had bought four times that amount, or 1,000 tablets. On the day Michael Gilligan died, for example, Amy had purchased 250 tablets. On the day before what amounted to a federal Drug Act became law—more formally called the Harrison Act, which made it illegal to sell or distribute these types of powerful narcotics without a prescription—Amy walked out of Barnes's store with 5,000 tablets. Apparently she wanted to stock up before it became illegal to purchase the drug.

The question was, however, were the tablets for Amy?

At one point Holden asked Barnes if during the murder investigation, State Police captain Robert Hurley had ever interviewed him or asked him any questions regarding such large amounts of morphine being purchased from his store.

"No," Barnes said, "he just took my poison records."

Tunnel vision.

Just in case Alcorn had wanted to drag Dr. Howard King back into this mess again, Holden had each of his pharmaceutical witnesses testify that Amy had never once bought morphine with a prescription.

Then Holden had Barnes tell the judge what he thought about Amy.

"As good a businesswoman as the average woman," Barnes said with a sarcastic tone. Those in the courtroom, many of whom were women, busted out in laughter in light of the fact that Barnes had said such a thing about a woman already convicted of serial murder.

A childhood neighbor and classmate of Amy's from Milton, who had lived near the Duggan family for forty years, took the stand to talk about Amy's family life in her hometown. At one point, the man said, "One [of Amy's] sisters was born an idiot, and died when she was ten."

As the pretrial hearings continued several days later, it didn't take long for Hugh Alcorn to figure out the new direction Amy was taking her case. Amy's sister Katherine Duggan—who had taken control of the Archer Home after Amy's arrest, but had ended up selling the house shortly thereafter because business had dropped off considerably—also testified that Amy was a morphine addict at the time of her arrest. Even more important, Duggan said, her sister had been doped up on the heroin-like drug during the month that Franklin Andrews died. Duggan said she had seen it herself. For that reason alone, she suggested, her sister could not be held responsible or accountable for her crimes. It was a terrible addiction over which Amy had had no control.

And so, a parade of Benedict Holden's witnesses walked in and out of the Middletown Superior Court over a period of a week, describing a woman who had been out of her mind on drugs during those years she had been accused of murdering her patients. One witness testified that beginning in 1904, and leading up to the opening of the Archer Home, Amy had done so many crazy and bizarre things in her hometown of Litchfield (Milton), it was a miracle she was ever able to function as a normal human being, let alone find the sanity to open and then run a business.

According to another family friend and neighbor, Amy's madness came to a head on the day she married James Archer. Amy had hired "ten hacks"* to wait outside the church and deliver her guests to the reception, the witness testified.

The only problem? There were no guests.

Amy's sister talked about how Amy had started to sleep more peacefully once John Duggan, their out-of-control, mentally unhinged brother, had been sent away to an insane asylum. Up until the day John had left the family home, Amy had been terrified of the boy and his crazy deeds and could never get a moment's rest. But on the day he left, Amy's sister said, "Amy went to bed and slept more soundly than is normal."

Katherine Duggan stated next that a similar event to that of Amy's wedding day had occurred at Michael Gilligan's funeral. Amy had invited six Catholic priests (which was strange in itself, seeing that only one priest is generally asked to say a funeral mass and he, then, invites whom he chooses to help) to the funeral, and had also arranged for several hacks to transport people to and from the cemetery and church. Testimony implied that Amy insisted Michael's body be stored in a vault until she could build a mausoleum and give him a proper place to rest in peace.

This, however, went against the truth of the matter: The law at the time had prohibited bodies from being buried during winter months (Amy murdered Michael Gilligan in February). Amy needed to wait because the ground was frozen solid. Moreover,

---

* Near the turn of the twentieth century, a "hack" was common slang for "a coach or carriage kept for hire," according to Dictionary.com.

what none of Benedict Holden's witnesses revealed as they continued to discuss Michael Gilligan's funeral was the fact that a Solemn High Mass (in the Latin form) had been celebrated as a memorial to Michael. In fact, most businesses in Windsor had closed for the day because of his funeral. Despite his drinking, Michael had been viewed as a "prominent citizen of the town, having been a member of the Windsor Fire Company for many years," his obituary stated. He had even served as the fire department's chief for twenty-four months. Men from Michael's parish, the Holy Name Society of St. Gabriel's Church, had met at a local store downtown on the day of his funeral and marched in a formal procession to Amy's Prospect Street home so they could honor and pay tribute to Gilligan and his memory. In truth, Amy had had nothing to do with any of it. Now, however, her family was trying to say that Amy had taken charge of Michael's funeral and burial and had played the part of grieving widow.

Hugh Alcorn could only listen, and, when it came time to cross-examine each witness, ask direct questions, hoping the judge would see through what was obviously a posse of Amy's supporters banding together to paint Amy as the poor victim of an overzealous prosecution.

The question none of Amy's supporters could answer, however, was why hadn't any of these facts come out during her first trial?

◆ ◆ ◆

Mary Archer wore a skullcap-tight toque hat. Her large round eyes were what most everyone talked about when describing the young beauty. Mary had a look of defeat about her as she walked into the courtroom. Dread shadowed her modest figure. It was June 25, 1919, when Mary took her seat on the stand and began speaking of a mother who, according to Mary, had been in a constant morphine-induced "stupor," living in some sort of dreamlike, hallucinogenic state for many years. Mary explained how she'd walk in the door from school and find her mother talking on the telephone—but no one was on the other end of the line. There were times, Mary suggested, when her mother would say things that didn't make any sense. It was almost as if Amy was speaking in tongues. When the people of Windsor began to accuse Amy of having played a role in several deaths inside the Archer Home, that was when, Mary said, her mother went off the deep end and started using more morphine than she ever had before. What's more, Amy continuously thought someone was watching her. She was paranoid. Always on edge. Constantly looking out the windows, asking questions about the neighbors.

When asked by Benedict Holden to explain further, Mary talked about waking her mother up one day from what was, she later learned, a drug haze. "Mother?" Mary had said. "Mother? Wake up!" Amy was out cold.

Mary began to panic. "Mother!" Mary cried.

"It's you—you—you!" Amy snapped as she came to. She had no idea, Mary said, who she was talking to, or where she was.

Mary said next that on the day of her mother's arrest, Amy not only went upstairs to change her clothes before being brought to Town Hall for arraignment, but also to pop several morphine pills she had hidden in her bureau.

Other witnesses, including friends and neighbors and the Duggan family doctor, had already testified that Amy had been insane all her life, but had not been committed to an asylum because she went off and got married to James Archer instead. If it wasn't for her husbands, said one of her childhood schoolteachers, Amy would have been put away like her brother long ago, adding that even as a child, Amy had routinely been prone to "crying spells."

How convenient, Hugh Alcorn seemed to suggest as he cross-examined Mary Archer.

Judge John Keeler decided he needed to have a few of his own questions answered. The judge was confused about a few key issues. While Mary was on the stand, the judge asked, "When was it that you discussed your mother's use of morphine with Dr. King?" This had been a sticking point for Alcorn, who had asked Mary several times why she had never gone to Dr. King and talked to him about getting her mother committed, or, at the least, to ask him to help her mother to stop using the drug. Mary had even suggested at one point that King had become involved, prescribing the morphine for her mother in hopes that he could control how much she took. It apparently made no difference that Amy was buying the drug from another druggist across town.

"In the spring of 1914," Mary answered the judge.

"That was when Dr. King was prescribing for your mother and trying to reduce the quantity of drug she was using?"

"Yes."

The timing of this was an issue for the judge. If King had prescribed morphine to a known addict *after* December 1914, well, he would lose his license and possibly be brought up on criminal charges himself.

"I shall take juridical notice," the judge explained, "that the Harrison Act [also called the Drug Act] for the regulation of sale of narcotic drugs was not approved until December 1914."

The doctor and his waning reputation were safe.

The Harrison Act, established on December 17, 1914, as one of the first drug laws in the country, was clear in its explanation regarding the distribution of prescription drugs:

> *Sec. 2: That it shall be unlawful for any person to sell, barter, exchange, or give away any of the aforesaid drugs except in pursuance of a written order of the person to whom such article is sold, bartered, exchanged, or given, on a form to be issued in blank for that purpose by the Commissioner of Internal Revenue. . . . b) To the sale, dispensing, or distributing of any of the aforesaid drugs by a dealer to a consumer under and in pursuance of a written prescription issued by a physician, dentist, or veterinary surgeon registered under this Act.*

Mary Archer had certainly cast a spell over the proceedings with the many new and different versions of her mother. There was yet another shocking revelation of what had become a day filled with wild speculation regarding Amy and her drug habit, one that no one could have expected: Mary claimed that back on May 30, 1914, the day Franklin Andrews had become sick and died, her mother was in such a morphine-crazed stupor that she could not take care of Franklin herself. So she had demanded that Mary do it for her.

The reason why Dr. King had not been called to look in on Franklin until later that night, Mary said to a packed courtroom, when Franklin was arguably too far gone to receive the benefits of medical treatment, was not because her mother was a vicious sociopath and wanted the man to suffer and die.

No.

According to Mary Archer, it was Franklin himself who had requested that Mary watch over him and not call on a doctor.

Chapter 42

ONE LAST TRICK

ONSIDERING ALL THE EFFORT SHE HAD PUT INTO IT, not to mention the fact that for every question asked, Amy Archer-Gilligan seemed to have the answer, when it was all over Amy could certainly call herself a fighter, if nothing else. As soon as the governor became involved after her conviction in 1917, Amy realized she had a chance to survive the gallows, and she made the best of the opportunity. Understanding that all she had to do was act a bit abnormally and make up a few stories, and she could possibly spend the rest of her life in a hospital, Amy went for it.

The judge accepted Amy's guilty plea (to second-degree murder) and found that Amy should receive a life sentence. That being said, the judge was clear: Amy Archer-Gilligan, convicted serial murderer, would not get her way this time around. The judge remanded Amy to the state prison in Wethersfield for the rest of her natural life. The plea agreement saved everyone involved the hassle of another tedious trial with likely the same outcome. No matter what he did, Hugh Alcorn must have known by now, he was not going to see Amy swing for her crimes. With a life sentence, at least he could feel good knowing that she was going to spend the rest of her days in prison.

Or was she?

As Amy served her time in Wethersfield, it became clear that she was not finished fighting.

For nearly five years she kept her mouth shut and acted like a "model prisoner," prison officials said in July 1924.

But one day everything changed.

Reports began to file in. Amy Archer-Gilligan was up to her old tricks again. She was apparently beginning to show signs of a meltdown. At one point, unable to put up with complaints any longer, Wethersfield State Prison warden W. H. K. Scott asked the governor of Connecticut for the "temporary commitment" of Amy to the state hospital for the insane in Middletown.

"Her mental trouble is of a peculiar nature," the warden said. He wanted the woman evaluated after hearing stories from other inmates about Amy acting strangely. The warden summoned two doctors affiliated with the prison to examine her. After spending a few days with Amy, Dr. Percy Battey and Dr. Frederick Thompson both agreed with the warden: The woman was off her rocker.

It had started in early July 1924, when Amy began refusing to do anything asked of her. She acted, both doctors reported, as if she could not understand anyone. Inmates and prison officials would go to Amy and say something, but Amy acted as though they were speaking a foreign language.

Whatever she did had worked, because Amy was shipped to Connecticut Valley Hospital in Middletown for a full-scale mental assessment.

And never left.

"She was . . . declared insane . . . ," one report noted. "She had previously been in the habit of talking at length on the [prison] telephone to herself and of playing funeral music on the [prison] piano when on those rare occasions nobody had died recently . . ."

♠ ♠ ♠

In the years to come, Amy's case would take on a life of its own. To those who were deeply involved, it was an open-and-shut serial murder case that not only stunned and scared the community, but also pointed out how vulnerable people are in their aging years.

Meade Alcorn was ten years old when Amy was tried in Hartford, and watched his father stress over the case day in and day out. As with most people who knew Hugh Alcorn and his opinions of the Archer case, Meade recalled years later that for his father, it was never about whether Amy Archer-Gilligan was insane or guilty. "The only controversy," Meade said in a 1986 interview, recalling what his father truly thought of the case, "wasn't whether she did it—it was whether she should [have been] executed or not."

Chapter 43

ARSENIC AND OLD LACE

THE THEATER WAS PACKED TO CAPACITY ON OPENING NIGHT.
Word had spread quickly: Joseph Kesselring, a churlish, thirty-eight-year-old playwright, had written a smart comedy so funny that theatergoers were holding their bellies a few minutes into the first act, laughing out loud, applauding Kesselring's larger-than-life, amusing, but also macabre characters.

"For Joseph Kesselring has written one so funny," *New York Times* theater critic Brooks Atkinson wrote, "that none of us will ever forget it. . . . It may not seem hilarious to report that thirteen men succumb to one of the blandest murder games ever played . . . [b]ut Mr. Kesselring has a light style, an original approach to an old subject, and he manages to dispense with all the hocus-pocus of the crime trade."

It was January 1941. Laughter was indeed a comforting presence, as the United States was preparing to enter into World War II. Americans, particularly, were desperate for anything that might take their minds off the reality of more violence and bloodshed on the battlefield.

Amy Archer-Gilligan was somewhere in her late sixties, happily tucked away in the Connecticut Valley Hospital, living out her life in an atmosphere unlike any prison, unaware at this time that her life had been distilled into entertainment.

With each day that passed, the world around Amy looked as though it was involved in a rapid decline. But the bright lights and overall festive atmosphere of Broadway had helped many forget about the fear of war, the certainty of once again losing thousands of young American soldiers. Theaters were selling out. The economy was experiencing a steady upswing in direct relation to world events. When a play like Kesselring's debuted to laughs, word of

239

mouth was a guarantee that sellout crowds and favorable reviews would soon follow.

Within days of opening night, critics weren't so much applauding the humor in Kesselring's strangely entertaining play; instead, they were cheering for the absolutely inane premise on which it had been built—that murder could be amusing.

The play was *Arsenic and Old Lace,* a clever mix of ridiculous and gruesome drama. The idea focuses on two elderly sisters, the fabulously colorful Brewsters, who, because of their numerous acts of charity, have become quite celebrated in the Brooklyn neighborhood where they live. Part of their charitable temperament, however, includes secretly poisoning lonely old men who have sought solace (and shelter) in their spacious home. Much of the humor comes in the form of the Brewsters' "mentally challenged nephew," who thinks he's Teddy Roosevelt. Bringing down the house several times throughout the play, young "Teddy" stands center stage (the Brewsters' living room), blasting a bugle, announcing his arrival, screaming "charge"—no doubt Kesselring's ode to Amy's violin-playing brother who was institutionalized. Part of the nephew's role in the Brewster household is to bury the dead in the basement.

In his review, Brooks Atkinson went on to note that:

> . . . *the Brewsters of Brooklyn are homicidal maniacs. But Aunt Abby and Aunt Martha are, on the surface, two of the nicest maiden ladies who ever baked biscuits, rushed hot soup to ailing neighbors and invited the minister to tea. Part of their charitable work consists in poisoning homeless old men who have no families to look after them. Their lunatic brother, who, for no apparent reason, imagines that he is Theodore Roosevelt, buries the bodies in the cellar with military and presidential flourishes.*

The conflict (and humor) in the play reaches a crescendo when, midway through, a second nephew, who happens to be a theater critic and writer, discovers that the Brewster sisters are, in fact, serial murderers.

One writer said, "In his adroit mixture of comedy and mayhem, [Kesselring] satirizes the charitable impulse as he pokes fun at the conventions of the theater."

Whatever Kesselring had managed to accomplish, politically correct or not, had worked. *Arsenic and Old Lace* ran in New York for 1,444 performances and an additional 1,337 in London, which turned out to be the longest run for an American play in the British capital. In 1944, Hollywood caught the wave and made a successful adaptation out of Kesselring's script. Praised director Frank Capra directed a cast that included Cary Grant and, reprising their roles on Broadway, Josephine Hull and Jean Adair as the lovely and lethal Brewster sisters—and it, too, brought in impressive box office receipts.

Nevertheless, as with any winning endeavor, controversy soon followed. For Kesselring it started with who actually wrote the play. Renowned playwrights Howard Lindsay and Russel Crouse came forward and claimed *Arsenic and Old Lace* had been a collaboration between the two of them and Kesselring. And who might question one of the most successful playwright teams in history? Lindsay and Crouse had written the *Sound of Music, Anything Goes*, and *Red Hot and Blue*, worldly bodies of work scored by the likes of Hammerstein and Cole Porter.

But it was *Arsenic and Old Lace*, Lindsay and Crouse maintained, that they wanted their names attached to. "Legend has it that the play," the *Oxford Companion to American Theatre* reported, "originally called *Bodies in Our Cellar*, was conceived as a serious thriller and that producers Howard Lindsay and Russel Crouse were responsible for turning it into a comedy."

New York Sun drama critic Richard Lockridge described the play as "noisy" and "preposterous," while admitting that it was also an "incoherent joy," writing, "You wouldn't believe that homicidal mania could be such great fun."

Joseph Kesselring had not invented the story entirely; in other words, the play wasn't entirely a work of fiction. In fact, one could say Kesselring had done years of research. Born in 1902 in New York City, as a young man Kesselring had traveled the country, teaching and studying the art of acting. When he returned to New York to start penning short stories and plays, he picked up on the Amy

Archer-Gilligan true-crime drama unfolding in nearby Hartford. "[Kesselring] came to Hartford," Carl Goslee wrote, "and asked Hugh Alcorn to help him turn a real-life drama and Connecticut's most heinous crime into a stage play."

Alcorn wouldn't help, but, according to Goslee, the prosecutor gave Kesselring access to court documents. The dramatist went to work studying every nuance and detail of the Archer Home murders.

The controversy surrounding who actually wrote *Arsenic and Old Lace* would shadow Kesselring and his career for fifty years. But what theatergoers couldn't get over, regardless of who wrote it, was the moral dilemma that stemmed from sitting and laughing at what were, essentially, gags and jokes based on actual murders. The comedy in the production sneaks up on you, most agree, as you sit and slowly become enthralled by what amounts to a pair of sisters—modeled after Amy—who openly and pleasantly kill men by serving them elderberry wine and arsenic (as opposed to arsenic-laced lemonade).

"Hardly knowing that it is happening and certainly not knowing how it happens," said a wireless telegram written by W. A. Arlington from London and sent to the *New York Times* after the opening performance of *Arsenic and Old Lace* in England, "we find our old scale of moral values dissolving into something new and strange and are ready to laugh in the right tone when the exact nature of the philanthropy practiced by Miss Abby and Miss Martha unfolds itself."

Arlington had put his finger on an important aspect of the play that would interject itself into popular culture as the role of the media grew in America and murder became a form of entertainment in the decades following the play's debut. Continuing in his review, Arlington noted, "If the author had put so much as a foot in the wrong place, he might have had the audience coldly refusing to agree there was anything funny about an old gentleman's corpse. . . . The Brewster household is not one of those in which the lack of an American accent is a worry, for Miss Abby and Miss Martha might as easily have been aunts of ours or aunts of yours."

And that was just it! The proverbial nail. The attraction—as American popular culture would prove in the decades to come—of the *true* murder story as a form of entertainment had come full circle. The idea that your friendly next-door neighbor, that man in the Bermuda shorts and T-shirt you wave to each morning and talk to over the fence each evening, or the woman sitting next to you in church, kneeling, praying, giving of herself at countless community charity events—that same individual could turn out to be a serial murderer of the most horrendous type, and it fascinated people. It is that dynamic, where good and evil seem to commingle and live so close together, that keep people tuned in.

Epilogue

WHATEVER HAPPENED TO AMY?

E VIL IN SUBURBAN AMERICA. Like many killers before her, and certainly many after, Amy Archer-Gilligan played a cruel, deadly game with the innocent and naive, the vulnerable, using the pious mask of Christianity, her role as a caretaker, and her standing in the community as a veil to disguise a dark and brutal nature. It would seem on the factual surface that Amy was a callous serial murderer who killed out of greed—and that is likely true. But when you dig deep into her psyche and analyze her behavior, why she did it, and the fact that she refused to take responsibility, the evidence implies that Amy was also a narcissistic sociopath, with a discernible grandiosity, who enjoyed the process, methodology, and comfort that murder provided her soul. Morphine wasn't Amy's drug of choice; it was murder.

"When a man contemplates evil as expressive of power . . . ," noted member of the Christian Science Board of Lectureship William McKenzie said during an address he gave "under the auspices of Mother Church" at Symphony Hall in Boston on November 2, 1905, "he tries to satisfy himself that this is in line with the inscrutable plan of God, and that somehow the rampant evil is to be a schoolmaster for his virtue."

Without knowing it, McKenzie was describing Amy. She used the Bible as a cover, and her belief in Jesus Christ as the sharp point of a jagged sword. Amy fed her evil soul with the pleasure she took from committing murder.

On the flip side, however, McKenzie said, "The philosophy of contrast is also urged. . . . How are we to value honesty if thieves do not help us; how [are we to] appreciate truth if no liars abound; how [are we to] be grateful for the ease of health if it be not offset by disease."

Good exists, in other words, because there is evil sitting next to it at the table of moral virtue. This sums up Amy's story better than any quotation available: There was a sardonic, ethical struggle between good and evil in Windsor as Amy's crimes were slowly exposed. Think of the moral dilemma the people in her community faced as they questioned themselves and their judgments; and consider the evil Amy continued to perpetrate as the investigation began. She used her social standing as a mask. While most killers would have stopped the moment a finger was pointed, Amy picked up her pace.

Following McKenzie's logic, Amy certainly understood this rather cogent and profound philosophical catch-22, the same way she understood who she was in relation to it, thus acting on what she heartily believed was her righteous place in society. There was a sense of hubris about Amy, sure, both as she murdered and got away with it, and even after she was caught: *How dare you accuse me of such heinous crimes against humanity?* And that excessive pride and arrogance on her part was what shocked many after they realized the true horror of her crimes.

I have written several books about serial killers, eight books about female murderers. They all seem to fall into this category of existing in a world that is built around their own set of values and rules; and they all believe that the world they live in is a stage, the people around them actors in a play centered on a sick and twisted amusement provided by their vanity and self-reliance, which they feel is crucial to their survival. You see, when the rules changed for Amy Archer, she changed along with them. She saw once again how she could exploit the moral goodness of honorable men and women and, in the end, we can say she accomplished that task with a wide margin of success.

▲ ▲ ▲

For all of his stubbornness and skill in the courtroom, along with the professional fear his adversaries displayed when facing him, Benedict Holden built a reputation as one of the most respected and esteemed trial attorneys in Connecticut's legal history. It was a shock to everyone, not to mention a great loss, when, in 1937, Holden dropped dead unexpectedly one night.

"Benedict M. Holden," the *Courant* reported the following morning, "one of the State's most prominent lawyers, died suddenly about 9:30 o'clock Friday night in the Hotel Roosevelt, New York City, where he had stopped off on his way to Florida for a vacation. He was sixty-three years old."

It was a "heart ailment" that got Holden.

Hartford Courant editor Clifton Sherman retired in the 1930s and moved to Florida, where he died in February 1946 at the age of seventy-nine. In his obituary, the newspaper Sherman had helped to put on the map with his editorial proficiency called the Archer story Sherman's "greatest coup." After being billed a "yellow journalist" by Holden and being accused of wading in the waters of what was the sensational journalism of the time, Sherman would not back down in his belief that he had played the Archer story by the book, waiting until he had solid evidence before publishing an incriminating story about the woman.

Sherman had asked to be cremated, and his ashes placed in a vault in the family plot at the Prospect Hill Cemetery in Brattleboro, Vermont.

Hugh Alcorn died in 1955, at the mighty age of eighty-two. As it turned out, Alcorn stayed on as Connecticut's state's attorney for thirty-four years, making a name for himself by prosecuting death penalty cases, confidently walking into court with the grim-reaper-like nickname "the Hanging Prosecutor" following him. He made a Republican run for the governor's seat in 1934, but lost by a slim margin of 8,000 votes to Wilbur Cross, who now has a highway named after him. As Alcorn's obituary put it quite perfectly, referring to his desire to run for office but also summing up what could be a slogan for his life, "He was not a baby kisser."

On March 14, 1962, "eighty-seven-year-old" Amy Archer-Gilligan was rushed to the infirmary inside the Connecticut Valley Hospital in Middletown, where she had been institutionalized by that point for nearly forty years. What Amy suffered from was never released, but one would have to assume it was old age that finally began to work on Connecticut's most prolific serial murderer.

Amy never left the infirmary. A little over a month later, on a clear and cool Monday, April 23, 1962, she died in her hospital bed. As though she were just an afterthought, not worthy of fact-checking, the *Hartford Courant*—the same newspaper that had claimed she was "eighty-seven" just six weeks prior—now published her age at death as "eighty-nine."

No longer was the Witch of Windsor front-page news in Connecticut. Amy's obituary appeared on page six.

Amy spent her latter years working in Connecticut Valley Hospital's cafeteria. She had been at the hospital for thirty-eight years. Officials quoted in her obituary said Amy had always been "a quiet, cooperative patient," adding, "Mostly she sat in a chair, dressed in a black dress trimmed with lace, Bible in her lap, and prayed."

Well into her late sixties, when her mother died, Amy's only child, Mary Archer, was living in New Haven—perhaps ironically, as a patient herself in a convalescent home.

The only one involved in Amy's story who outlived the matron (and everyone else) was, appropriately, Carlan Goslee, who died on August 3, 1970, at eighty-four years of age. Despite what other *Courant* reporters would lay claim to in the years following Amy's second trial, Carl Goslee was the hero of this story. Because Carl noticed an increase in the obituaries he was writing for the town of Windsor and brought that information to Clifton Sherman, the ball, so to speak, began rolling toward justice. Without Carl's astute awareness and objectivity, one wonders how long Amy would have gone on killing.

Totals are a guess, but there were sixty-four deaths at the Archer Home that one could look at queasily and raise a suspicious eyebrow. It's likely Amy killed no fewer than forty. Yet there's a good indication that had Amy been tried, say, eighty to eighty-five years later, when DNA and forensic medicine and science began to play a pivotal and deciding role in many murder trials, she would have had a far better chance at being found innocent. Today, juries expect "smoking gun" evidence before they are willing to drop the gavel on a case where a woman's life hangs in the balance, on the words of a few generously paid experts.

▲ ▲ ▲

After her arrest, Amy quit-claimed the house to her sister, Katherine Duggan. Thus began a sort of musical-chairs game with the property. Two days later, Katherine quit-claimed the house to Benedict Holden. Amy's former attorney then quickly quit-claimed the house to Windsor resident Frederick Kirkbride. Sometime later, Kirkbride quit-claimed the house to Timothy Driscoll, who kept it for quite some time. Under Driscoll's ownership, the Murder Factory was referred to in news reports and paperwork as the "Gilligan House," which had a softer, gentler tone.

From approximately 1923 onward, the house went through several more ownerships.

Today, the Archer Home is a residential dwelling. In 2004, on a clear but cool day, I showed up at the house with a crew from Beyond Productions, an Australian documentary company. We were in town to film a segment for a Discovery Channel show called *Deadly Women* (Amy's story is included in the "Greedy Killer" episode).

We knocked on the door. A nice woman, who looked to be in her early fifties, answered. She looked at us. Nodded. Smiled. "Can I help you?"

She and I spoke briefly. Within a few moments it was clear to me that this kind woman had no idea she was living in a former slaughterhouse. Nor did she know anything about the morbid history surrounding this brick home that has stood up surprisingly well to the test of time.

"I'm a renter," she said.

We wanted to go inside, take a look around. Maybe film an interview upstairs or in the kitchen.

"I'm on my way to work," she said.

"Got it."

I told her to have a great day. We were going to do some filming in the front yard, if that was okay.

She said, "No problem."

I did not have the heart to tell the woman she was living in a house known at one time as a Murder Factory, and that perhaps dozens of people had been killed inside the four walls she now called home.

▲ ▲ ▲

What follows is a list of the "reported" dead. It is based on the vital statistics from the Town of Windsor as published by the *Hartford Courant* on May 9, 1916. Following the name of the deceased is the cause of death listed on the death certificate, and each person's age as given by the Archer Home. The average "duration of illness" for each death was between hours and days—not, as one would expect, months and years. This is a staggering number of deaths, considering the time each person spent at the Archer Home, which, in many instances, was months or weeks, even days in some instances. As the data seems to prove—perhaps by mere happenstance—the number of dead increased dramatically after Amy's first husband was murdered, and then decreased sharply as the investigation and finger-pointing in town began. Out of the sixty-six recorded deaths listed here, Amy Archer was responsible for witnessing and "reporting" twenty-nine.

Do the math. That's almost half.

Numbers do not lie.

With respect . . .

1908–1911

Jane Heald, *cerebral hemorrhage, 80*

Josephine Graley, *creeping paralysis, 62*

Fanny Fayne Fuller, *cerebral hemorrhage, 82*

James Archer, *Bright's disease, 50*

Seth E. Andrews, *old age, 78*

Janet Wilson, *blood poisoning, 68*

George Donal, *apoplexy, 72*

Jay Stone, *Euclo carctutis, no age available*

George Frank Skinner, *locomotor ataxia (Syphilis of the
    spinal cord), 58*

Celia Smith, *cerebral apoplexy (stroke), 66*

Philip Bacon, *rheumatoid arthritis, 84*

Elizabeth Burbank, *locomotor ataxia (syphilis of the spinal cord)*, 41
Hilton Griffin, *old age*, 81
Charles Hess, *cerebral apoplexy*, 70

1912
Abraham Soper, *arteriosclerosis (basically, hardening of the arteries)*, 71
Charles Hyneck, *old age*, 85
John Beach, *cerebral apoplexy*, 85
Everett Learned, *pneumonia*, 70
Henry Clemons, *arteriosclerosis*, 71
Eugene Cushman, *arteriosclerosis*, 71
Bridget Lynch, *old age*, 93
Rosa Lynch, *arteriosclerosis*, 62
Matilda Shields, *old age*, 77
Charles Humeson, *old age*, 86
Susan Sperry, *senile decay*, 89
Riensi Clarke, *cerebral apoplexy*, 71
Jennie Beckwith, *arteriosclerosis*, 78
Jeremiah Rockett, *arteriosclerosis*, 74
Louise Teft, *apoplexy*, 79

1913
William Churchill, *valvular heart disease*, 65
John Latimer, *diabetes militias, arteriosclerosis, no age available*
Abram Smith, *arteriosclerosis*, 87
Caroline Post, *pulmonary tuberculosis*, 59
Charles Miller, *old age*, 94
Mary E. Rockett, *valvular heart disease*, 64
Virginia Lee Bezanson, *epilepsy*, 26
Franklin Jones, *arteriosclerosis*, 83
Julia August Beckwith Goodrich, *diabetes*, 88
James Adamson, *cerebral apoplexy*, 58
Julia Teresa Duggan (Amy's sister), *cirrhosis of the liver, valvular heart disease*, 35

Herbert Baldwin, *apoplexy, 76*
Lydia Sherman, *old age, 92*

1914
Elizabeth Hubbard, *capillary bronchitis, old age, 82*
Augusta Kimball, *infirmities of old age, 90*
Michael Gilligan, *valvular heart disease, 56*
Charles Smith, *epilepsy, 89*
Urban Dunaway, *arteriosclerosis, 71*
Mary Lonsbury, *old age, 78*
Harriet Matthewson, *old age, 84*
Franklin Andrews, *gastric ulcers, 61*
Amy Hosme, *apoplexy, 85*
Alice Gowdy, *cholera morbus, 69*
Elizabeth Brown, *cerebral apoplexy, 56*

1915
Eliza Ann Squires, *old age, 94*
Charles Galgut, *pulmonary tuberculosis, 20*
Matilda Doolittle, *cerebral apoplexy, 73*
Nathan Fish, *pneumonia, 87*
Margaret Chamberlain Reynolds, *cerebral apoplexy, 73*
Richard Herridge, *crystilis, enlarged prostrate, 76*
Judson Munger, *arteriosclerosis, 75*

1916
James Norris, *valvular heart disease, 81*
Maude Lynch, *epilepsy perniscrom anemia, 33*
Fidella Joyce, *organic heart disease, 74*
Albert Robinson, *arteriosclerosis, 78*
Anna Donovan, *arteriosclerosis, 73*
Burton Lewis, *cerebral apoplexy, 78*

Acknowledgments

This project has been years in the making, and has seen various forms. I need to first offer my utmost gratitude to anyone who has listened to me talk about this case over the years, and understood my relentless desire to publish it. Peter Miller, my consummate, hardworking business manager, and Adrienne Rosado, Peter's conscientious and tirelessly working assistant at PMA Literary & Film Management, have been supporting my quest to publish this book for no fewer than four years. I greatly appreciate their passion, motivation, and determination to see this project through until the end. Sometimes, when it seems like maybe there's good reason to let go of a project, an author should step aside and allow those people around him to dictate his next move. In this case, Peter Miller stealthily—and quite doggedly, I should add—worked behind the scenes, unbeknownst to me, to see that this book found the right publisher. Peter Miller is a true Literary Lion.

My editor at Globe Pequot/Lyons Press, Keith Wallman, who expressed a desire to work on this project with me many years before we actually rolled up our sleeves, was instrumental in seeing that the book became what it is. I could never say enough about Keith and his desire to see Amy's story in print. Without Keith's excitement and direction, I believe the manuscript would still be sitting on my desk(top) collecting (electronic) dust. Keith is a remarkable person, an astute editor, and a true friend, who helped me contain what might have been, under different circumstances, a monster of a book. His editing skills and suggestions truly shaped the final product.

In addition, I'd like to point out that copy editor Melissa Hayes did a wonderful job, catching what would have been several mistakes, typos and errors, not to mention shaping some of the language into an easier read. Likewise, Globe Pequot project manager Jennifer Taber was very helpful. I also want to take this opportunity to give a huge shout out to the art department at Globe Pequot for working so hard on the cover, and marketing and sales for putting so much thought into a side of the book business—making the entire package appealing—many take for granted.

The *Hartford Courant* was an important part of this story on many different levels. Of course, without the newspaper's prodigious and sensational reporting, there would have been no book; of that much I am certain. But more than that, I have to acknowledge the professionalism of Clifton Sherman and Carlan Goslee, two *Courant* journalists who controlled the output of the reporting and made sure it was the best the newspaper could produce at the time.

Kaelyn Moore and her father, Spencer, along with the entire Moore family, came through with some great resource material. Kaelyn's good friend, Abriana Tasillo, was equally helpful, especially in deciphering two of Amy's letters and clarifying who they were written to. Pete Dowd, from the Law Library in Middletown Superior Court, was courteous and obliging, even though our harvest yielded no new fruit.

The Windsor Historical Society was supportive as well, along with the Hartford Public Library, and the State Library and the State Archives, including State Archivist Mark Jones. Of course, I could never write a book about a piece of Connecticut history without thanking those hardworking, great people at the Connecticut Historical Society in Hartford: Ben Gammell, Rich Malley, and Nancy Finlay, in particular.

Rosa Ciccio at the *Courant* was equally gracious with her time.

I know there are people I've forgotten, and I apologize for that. I'm no good at keeping lists, and even worse at remembering names. I lose things. I write names on scraps of paper with notes to myself (*I need to thank this person . . .*) and they mysteriously disappear, only to show up years later (when it's too late).

In any event, my family—Mathew, Jordon, April, and Regina— are an important part of every book I write. Without their continued support and interest in my career, I could not do this. As always, my biggest fan has been my mother, Florence Borelli, along with her late husband, Thomas Borelli, my stepfather—as well as Mary and Frank Phelps, my pops and stepmom. Equally important to me is the support and friendship I get from my Wednesday-morning coffee group ("the Donut Munchers") at St. Luke's: Louise and Ron, Terry, Jane, Bob, Fr. Tom and Fr. George, Midge, Daphne, Lisa G., Carol, Kathy, Stan and Ann, and Sister Theresa, along with anyone else who happens to join us from time to time, not to mention all my fellow parishoners at St. Luke's Church in Ellington. And everyone at Hall Memorial Library (in Ellington) who continues to support my career.

Finally, a note of special thanks to everyone at Globe Pequot Press. Editor-in-chief Eugene "Gene" Brissie is one of those wild-about-books people this business needs today. While at Globe, Gene kept an honorable balance of quality books in the marketplace. I appreciate the interest all of you at Globe have shown for this project. I could not have considered a better combination: Connecticut author, Connecticut story, Connecticut publisher.

Endnotes

A BRIEF NOTE ABOUT MY RESEARCH

Writing a book of nonfiction is, at times, similar to gathering the pieces of a puzzle and, without a model picture to work from, creating some sort of a perfect image. The idea is to present a cohesive narrative that, hopefully, tells a story. You realize at some point during this process that you have likely not found every piece of that puzzle (and probably never will), but you have a well-rounded view of what that picture looks like, nonetheless. Thus, with confidence, you proceed.

In the case of Amy Archer-Gilligan's life, I spent years gathering documents and newspaper articles, photographs and diaries, journals, letters, and other primary source material. In sifting through all of this research, I came to the realization that Amy Archer-Gilligan's life was as much a mystery to her contemporaries as it has been to me a century or so later. Amy was an enigma. Every one of her peers would have agreed with this statement. Take, for example, Amy's supposed addiction to morphine. There is very little evidence—save for anecdotal hearsay—to back up this claim. It seemed to me this "addiction" was pulled out of a hat when Amy needed it most, making liars out of four of her closest relatives and friends, turning them into perjurers.

For the sake of what, I had to ask myself?

To protect a serial murderer.

I searched for years to find a descendant of Carlan Goslee who had actual papers and research from Carl's past. I had finally given up after almost four years. I figured the family had moved, had different names; maybe married, died, and would never be found. Even a genealogical study didn't do me much good.

But then an e-mail arrived one day as I was in the middle of finishing my book. It was from a third-generation Goslee descendant working on a "History Day" project for school. She had read an article I'd written about this case for Amazon.com's "Shorts" program years before.

From: Kaelyn Moore
To: M. William Phelps
Sent: Friday, October 10, 2008 3:42 PM
Subject: Amy Archer-Gilligan

Dear Mr. Phelps:

Hello, my name is Kaelyn, and I recently read your short story about Amy Archer-Gilligan. I just wanted to let you know that I found it very helpful in my research (I am doing a project about her for school). It was actually my great-grandfather that wrote the first article about her in 1916, Carlan Goslee. Anyways, I just wanted to tell you that I liked your [article], and a full-length biography would be super-cool and helpful.

If you know of any other people or places I could go to get more information, that would be awesome.

Thanks!

Spencer Moore is Kaelyn's father—and Carlan Goslee's grandson.

Go figure. The Moores lived in a neighboring town not fifteen minutes away from my office.

So you see, this is how researching history unfolds when you're working on a long-term project: Things can change in an instant. One new piece of information can break down a wall you had considered giving up trying to climb over.

I say all of this because in addition to the notes you are about to read, there is an enormous amount of additional legwork and source material that is just too bulky and abundant to include here. I stuck to noting, mainly, the quotations I used in the book. But I want to be clear that in creating every word of this book, I used resource material from a variety of sources, both primary and secondary.

This book was a joy and honor to write, as well as a frustrating journey for me. There were times when I thought it would never end. Coming to an understanding of all this material took years.

The trial transcripts alone—1,200 pages of single-spaced text—were a disjointed, tangled mesh of words. Testimony bounced from year to year, case to case. There was no linear, unified narrative structure to the state's attorney's case. This made it extremely difficult to understand the State's case from beginning to end.

The letter excerpts I used in the text were left as they were written nearly a century ago, except where I thought they were impossible to read and thus slightly tweaked the grammar or punctuation to create an understandable structure of words, without changing the content or context. The same can be said for adding and/or omitting unneeded punctuation, etc. Beyond that, I've added nothing to these letters, except where duly noted in the text.

PROLOGUE / SIMMERING DEATH

x.   "Whisper," he told the doctor: (in addition to the dialogue following this paragraph) "Doctor King Indicates Possible Line of Defense in Archer Home Poisoning Case," *Hartford Courant*, May 9, 1916, p. 10; and *State of Connecticut v. Amy E. Archer Gilligan*, Trial Transcripts, including letters and evidence, No. 667, Supreme Court of Errors, Hartford County, First Judicial District, October Term, 1917, Hartford Public Library, pp. 1083–1125 (Trial Transcripts).

xi.   "Mr. Matthewson," the doctor recalled later, "told me": Ibid.

xi.   "I want you to take that," Matthewson explained: Ibid.

xii.   "He loved . . . everywhere nature beckoned him passionately": "Lyman Dudley Smith," *Hartford Courant*, (Obituary in the form of a Letter to the Editor), August 1, 1911, p. 16.

xiii.   "His fine face," said a letter written about him . . . : Ibid.

xiii.   "All right," the doctor said, obliging Mr. Matthewson . . . : "Doctor King Indicates Possible Line of Defense in Archer Home Poisoning Case," *Hartford Courant*, May 9, 1916, p. 10.

xiv.   "If I am alive the next day . . .": Ibid.

xiv.   "He was a natural scholar and applied himself to his studies . . .": "Lyman Dudley Smith," *Hartford Courant* (Obituary in the form of a Letter to the Editor), August 1, 1911, p. 16.

xv.   "I'm still alive," the doctor said later . . . : "Doctor King Indicates Possible Line of Defense in Archer Home Poisoning Case," *Hartford Courant*, May 9, 1916, p. 10.

xv.   "Do you think I would have drunk that lemonade," the doctor said: Ibid.

Also helpful to me in creating the profile of Lyman Dudley Smith and his last days, along with the many additional suicides on that dreadful day, was, "Inferno Becomes a Survival Test," *Hartford Courant*, by Jim Shea, July 22, 2003, p. 1; and the scores of newspaper accounts of the heat wave I read over a period of years.

PART ONE

SILENT KILLERS

CHAPTER 1 / THE MATRON AND THE REPORTER

3.   It was a plan of the Archer Home to take . . . : "Archer-Gilligan Murder Case," Transcribed from Carlan Hollister Goslee's handwritten notes, *Windsor Storytellers: A Chronicle of 20th-Century Life in Windsor* (privately published by the Town of Windsor; 1999), p. 96. (From this point on, I will refer to this document as the "Goslee report.")

3.   " 'There was a minor lawsuit brought against Mrs. Archer . . . ,' " "Carlan H. Goslee Took Dual Role in Murder Probe," *Hartford Courant*, January 4, 1953, p. 1.

3.   The information about Carlan Goslee's life in general is from many different sources, including interviews with Spencer Moore, Carlan's grandson, and various family documents, journals, photographs, and other materials Spencer provided me with; I'll refer to my interviews with Spencer and these materials from this point forward as IA-FD (Interview with Author, Family Documents).

4.   Everyone knew him . . . : Ibid; Goslee report, p. 97.

5.   Looking deeper into the Home's affairs . . . : "Archer Home in Windsor Attached," *Hartford Courant*, December 1, 1909, p. 7.

6.   At first, Narcissa felt her mother was being ungrateful and encouraged . . . : These paragraphs (including the quotations) about the

Narcissa McClintock lawsuit incident were constructed with the help of several sources: "Faked Letter to Quiet Inmate, Is Nurse's Charge," *Hartford Courant*, May 9, 1916, p. 1; several letters written by Narcissa McClintock, which can be found in Trial Transcripts.

8. The Archers purchased the colonial . . . : Photograph of Archer home, circa 1920; "Archer Home on the Market Again," *Hartford Courant*, September, 1982; Trial Transcripts.

9. Amy called her residents 'inmates'. . . : Merriam-Webster's Medical Dictionary (Merriam-Webster, Inc.; 2002); "Have to Like Home, Says Aged Inmate," *Hartford Courant*, May 9, 1916, p. 1; "Often Dined at Home as Guest," *Hartford Courant*, May 9, 1916, p. 1.

9. For the most part, the ebb and flow . . . : Trial Transcripts, p. 1.

9. With his waxy, walrus mustache, fat cheeks . . . : "Doctor King Indicates Possible Line of Defence in Archer Home Poisoning Case," *Hartford Courant*, May 9–10, 1916, p. 1; Trial Transcripts, pp. 237, 262–263, 672, 687, 737.

10. Any information and quotes beginning with Amy and Dr. King's relationship . . . until . . . many would soon begin to question, was not necessarily a medical explanation of death, are from: "Startling Number of Deaths at Archer Home," *Hartford Courant*, May 9, 1916, p. 1; "Doctor King Indicates Possible Line of Defence in Archer Home Poisoning Case," *Hartford Courant*, May 9, 1916, p. 1; and Trial Transcripts, pp. 237, 262–263, 672, 687, 737.

11. " 'I thought she was a wonderful person,'" Carl said years later . . . : "Carlan H. Goslee Took Dual Role in Murder Probe," *Hartford Courant*, January 4, 1953, p. 1.

CHAPTER 2 / QUIET MENACE

12. As New Englanders eased themselves into bed on Friday, June 30, 1911: "A Blast from Hell," *Hartford Courant*, July 20, 2003, p. 1; *Violent Weather: Hurricanes, Tornadoes & Storms*, Stan Gibilsco (Tab Books, 1985), general reading of text; *Encyclopedia Britannica* (state of Maine entry); Baughan's *Guide to the Six States of New England*, general reading.

12. As this happened . . . : Goslee report, p. 97.

12. " 'The death rate is too high . . .' ": Ibid.
13. "Many people in town thought that Amy was a wonderful person . . .": "A Reporter Named Carlan Goslee," by Barbara Goslee Sargent, *Windsor Storytellers: A Chronicle of 20th-Century Life in Windsor*, p. 204.
13. " 'Because of this investigation . . .' ": Goslee report, p. 97.
13. Carl was a patient man, however: Ibid.
14. " 'She sent flowers to her victims . . .' ": Ibid.
14. " 'Miss [Amy Archer],' Carl added": Ibid.
15. Saturday, July 1, 1911, dawned as a rather . . . : A variety of sources were used to construct this paragraph, and much of the relevant information in this chapter regarding weather patterns and conditions. Among them: "A Blast from Hell" by Jim Shea, *Hartford Courant*, July 20, 2003, p. 1; a general reading of: *The Children's Blizzard*, by David Laskin (HarperCollins, 2004); *Storm Watchers: The Turbulent History of Weather Prediction from Franklin's Kite to El Nino*, by John D. Cox, (Wiley, 2002); *Heat Wave: A Social Autopsy of Disaster in Chicago* (University of Chicago Press, 2003), by Eric Klinenberg; *Encyclopedia Britannica* (state of Maine entry); Baughan's *Guide to the Six States of New England*; "A Return to Comfort," by Jim Shea, *Hartford Courant*, July 22, 2003, p.1.

   In addition, I also want to point out that other parts of this opening narrative were constructed with the help of: "The Weather," *New York Times*, July 2, 1911, p. 10; "The American Scientists," *New York Times*, August 17, 1884; "A Civilian in Charge of the Weather," *New York Times*, March 10, 1888; "The Signal Office," December 2, 1872; "Taft Sees His First Baseball Game of the Season," *New York Times*, April 8, 1911; general reading, *Skylark: The Life, Lies and Inventions of Harry Atwood*, by Howard Mansfield (University Press of New England; 2001).

15. Out of its Washington, D.C., office . . . : general weather data and entries, *New York Times*, July 2, 1911, p. 1; *New York Times*, July 2, 1911, p. 1; *New York Times*, March 10, 1888, p. 6.
16. For Connecticut residents . . . : "The Weather," *New York Times*, July 2, 1911, 1; NOAA History: Weather Bureau Topics (February 1950), essay, "Professor Abbe's Stories & Tales of the Weather Service."
16. Hot or cool . . . : General news, *New York Times*, July 2, 1911, p. 1.

17. From the sentence "Positioned in the center of the state ..." until the end of this section " ... newly formed Connecticut State Police would see in some seventy-five years, detailing the wonderfully rich history of Hartford," several sources were very helpful. Among them were: *A Century in Hartford: The Hartford County Mutual Life Insurance Company*, by Charles W. Burpee (Case, Lockwood & Brainard Company, 1931); *Lost Hartford* (Images of America series) by Wilson H. Faude (Arcadia Publishing, 2000); *Stone by Stone: The Magnificent History in New England's Stone Walls*, by Robert M. Thorson (Walker & Co., 2004); and "Touring Historic Hartford, Connecticut," by Tom Ross (*Travel America* magazine, September 2001), general reading.

18. Hartford bustled on July 1 ...: *Hartford Courant*, July 1, 1911, p. 1; *New York Times*, July 1, 1911, p. 1; *Extreme Weather: A Guide and Record Book*, by Christopher C. Burt and Mark Stroud (W. W. Norton & Company, October 30, 2004), general reading; "A Blast From Hell," *Hartford Courant*, July 20, 2003, p. 1.

19. Saturday nights in Windsor homes were spent ...: "Windsor and the Panic of '93," by Carlan H. Goslee; *Windsor: An Early Portrait*, by Ronald Milkie and Gary Null (Nebko Press, Tuckahoe, NY, no date), middle of book (no page numbers in book).

19. Sundays, most families were on hand for the church ...: Ibid.

20. "After I brought many obituary notices to the attention ...": Goslee report, p. 98.

20. As she often did when attacked ...: Letter, Amy Archer to Carlan Goslee, May 22, 1911 (Windsor Historical Society).

21. Carl was not one to let things go ...: Goslee report, p. 98.

CHAPTER 3 / SILENT KILLERS

22. As a young boy during the early 1850s ...: Trial Transcripts, pp. 647–649.

22. Growing up on a farm, Franklin ...: Ibid.

22. On the morning of July 2, 1911, Franklin ...: Trial Transcripts, pp. 274–284, 647, 658–662.

23. As the sun burned the morning sky ...: "Official Record Is 100 Degrees," *Hartford Courant*, July 3, 1911, p. 1.

23. Two young women drowned . . . : "Boat Capsizes; Three Drowned," *Hartford Courant*, July 3, 1911, p. 1; "Crazed by the Heat," *Hartford Courant*, July 3, 1911, p. 1.

24. Weather Bureau officials remained confident . . . : Forecast, *Hartford Courant*, July 3, 1911, p. 1.

24. From the sentence "This was great news for municipal . . ." until the paragraph ending "And then, as everyone settled in for the night, the pickpockets and thieves came out in droves," I relied on the "Throng of 400,000 at Coney Island," *New York Times*, July 3, 1911, p. 2; and "Hottest Day Here in Twelve Years," *New York Times*, July 3, 1911, p. 1.

25. Beginning with "In Philadelphia, a dozen people were" until the end of this chapter, see "Philadelphia Dead, 12: Two Suicides There on Account of the Intense Heat," Special to the *New York Times*, July 3, 1911, p. 2.

CHAPTER 4 / HUMBLE BEGINNINGS

26. When the Archer Home opened . . . : "Analysis Finds Clusters of Nursing Home Violations by State, Ownership," by Larry Wheeler and Robert Benincasa (Gannett News Service, 2003); National Registry of Nursing Homes; Trial Transcripts, p. 1084; "A History of the Offices, Agencies, and the Institutions of the Archdiocese of Chicago," Polish Genealogical Society of America (Chicago Archdiocese, 1981); and "The Franciscan Commitment," University Place of Franciscan Communities, Purdue University.

26. "I have a splendid home for my lifetime": Trial Transcripts, p. 1084.

27. The Archer Home was located . . . : To construct this description I relied on my many visits to the Archer Home in Windsor. Additionally, growing up on the Connecticut River has given me a wide base of knowledge regarding its ebb and flow and different characteristics throughout the seasons. The quote ". . . uninterrupted access to the channels of commerce along the way . . ." can be found in *The Connecticut River: New England's Historic Waterway*, by Edmund Delaney (Globe Pequot Press, July 1, 1983), introduction.

28. The first time I ran across this little-known fact detailing the "first execution in the New World of a witch in 1647" was in my home-town newspaper, "Author Tells Historical Tales in New Book," the *North Central News*, by Margo Van Kuren, October 2004, p.1. I then referred to an essay by Bruce Stark, "Witchcraft in Connecticut." The Society of Colonial Wars in the State of Connecticut and the Windsor Historical Society were both helpful resources in helping me locate oral histories and diaries regarding Windsor's economic and social history.

28. For Amy Archer, whose business . . . : "Archer Home in Windsor Attached," *Hartford Courant*, December 1, 1909, p. 7.

28. "She has applications . . .": Trial Transcripts, p. 1083.

CHAPTER 5 / DEVOUT CHRISTIAN

30. On the Fourth of July . . . : "The Weather," *New York Times*, June 30, 1911, p. 1. The photographs I've seen of Amy, along with the dozens of articles written about her, and the Trial Transcripts, all helped me to describe Amy Archer's appearance.

30. I have had hundreds . . . : *New York Times*, May 11, 1916, p. 4.

31. "I have been in this work for many years," she wrote . . . : Trial Transcripts, p. 1124.

31. From "I know it is hard for you to pack up . . ." until the end of this section, all quotes were excerpted from: Ibid.

31. What Carl found as he began to look into Amy's . . . : Goslee report, p. 98.

32. "I presume it is unnecessary for me to tell you of the *Courant* report-ers' . . .": Letter, Amy Archer to Carlan Goslee, May 22, 1911, Windsor Historical Society.

32. "[Written] up a book of falsehoods": Ibid.

32. "This man inhales chloroform for Asthma of the Heart . . .": Trial Transcripts, p. 1124.

33. "I have always done everything possible for me to comfort . . .": Ibid., p. 1120.

33. Even as Carl was now openly accusing . . . : Several books were help-ful to me in painting a portrait of the world in which Amy Archer lived. Among them, I'd like to cite: *Hetty: The Genius and Madness of America's First Female Tycoon*, by Charles Slack (Ecco, 2005), general reading; *America in the Gilded Age: From the Death of Lincoln to the Rise of Theodore Roosevelt*, 3rd ed., by Sean Cashman (New York University Press, October 1, 1993), general reading; *The Gilded Age: A Tale of Today*, by Mark Twain (Penguin's New Edition, 2001), gen-eral reading; and Charles Calhoun's *The Gilded Age: Essays on the Origins of Modern America* (SR Books; October 28, 1995), general reading. But there were some in town . . . : Several articles published in the *Hartford Courant* between May 1916 and July 1916, which referred to a "growing concern" among several of Amy's neighbors who were beginning to become suspicious about things going on inside the Archer Home, were helpful to me—all of which I have cited throughout my notes.

33. "I have always done everything possible . . .": "Faked Letter to Quiet Inmate, Is Nurse's Charge," *Hartford Courant*, May 9, 1916, p. 1.

33. "A life of this kind is trying . . .": Trial Transcripts, p. 1124.

CHAPTER 6 / LEFT BEHIND

34. "Great suffering and many prostrations in the large cities," read . . . : "Hot Wave Claims More Victims," *Hartford Courant*, July 5, 1911, p. 1.

34. Early that morning . . . : "New York Has Safe and Sane Fourth," *Hartford Courant*, July 5, 1911, p. 1.

34. The next several paragraphs pertaining to the Hannah Cavanaugh narrative, beginning with "That evening, Hartford resident Hannah Cavanaugh . . ." were constructed with the help of "Two Deaths and 3 Prostrations," *Hartford Courant*, July 5, 1911, p. 1.

36. In one instance, the famed actress . . . : "Miss Marlowe Overcome by Heat in Theatre," *Hartford Courant*, July 5, 1911, p. 1.

36. "While Miss Marlowe . . .": Ibid.

CHAPTER 7 / THE BIBLE THUMPER

37. The opening paragraphs of this chapter were constructed with the help of the many letters Amy's victims had written to her over the course of several years; please see Trial Transcripts, pp. 1083–1142. Moreover, the dozens of newspaper articles associated with Amy's case that I read over the course of my research were invaluable to me in terms of understanding Amy and the way she ran her Home. Several photographs of Amy also helped me understand that she was a nondescript woman who looked a lot older than she was.

37. Amy and James had one child . . . : Little is known about Amy Archer's only child, Mary. But Mary gave one interview, describing her determination to defend her mother at any cost: " 'We'll Fight for Mother,'" *Hartford Courant*, May 10, 1916, p. 1.

38. "It seems as if all the world has turned against me," she said . . . : "Mrs. Gilligan Says She Is Persecuted," *New York Times*, May 11, 1916, p. 4.

39. "I am told . . .": "Mrs. Gilligan Says She Is Persecuted," *New York Times*, May 11, 1916, p. 4.

39. By this point, Amy was taking in about $500 profit each month: This information was spread out through the Trial Transcripts, and was also part of the "evidence" portion of the trial.

39. "It has taken nearly every cent . . .": "Mrs. Gilligan on the Grill," *Hartford Courant*, May 9, 1916, p. 1.

CHAPTER 8 / THOUSANDS OVERCOME

40. Despite a strong public sentiment that the country was heading . . . : Helpful to me in getting to the core of how America was faring during this incredibly transitional period of technology and social change, Stephen Ambrose's *Nothing Like It in the World: The Men Who Built the Transcontinental Railroad 1863–1869* (Simon & Schuster, 2000) was extremely helpful, as were several books I have mentioned already: *Hetty: The Genius and Madness of America's First Female Tycoon*, by Charles Slack; *America in the Gilded Age: From the Death of Lincoln*

to the Rise of Theodore Roosevelt, by Sean Cashman; *The Gilded Age: A Tale of Today*, by Mark Twain; and Charles Calhoun's *The Gilded Age: Essays on the Origins of Modern America*.

40. Part of the narrative in the early part of this chapter was constructed with the help of many resources. Among them are: "Taft Caught in Storm; Senate Forced to Adjourn," *Hartford Courant*, June 28, 1911; "Taft in Two New England Cities," *Hartford Courant*, June 24, 1911; "Taft on His Way to New England," *Hartford Courant*, June 21, 1911; "Mrs. Taft Suffers Nervous Attack," *Hartford Courant*, May 15, 1911; "Taft Speaks Plainly to Railroad Men," *New York Times*, May 15, 1911; "Sunday Schools Have Taft in Tow," *Hartford Courant*, June 8, 1911; "President Taft in Cap and Gown," *Hartford Courant*, June 21, 1911; "Taft and Party Arrive at Beverly," *New York Times*, July 2, 1911; "World Peace Rests Upon Us, Says Taft," *New York Times*, September 8, 1911; and "Taft Not Likely to Drop Wiley," *New York Times*, June 14, 1911.

40. By July 6, 1911, the newspapers . . . : "31 Dead Here; Relief in Sight," *New York Times*, July 6, 1911, p. 1; "Over 500 Dead from Hot Wave," *Hartford Courant*, July 6, 1911, p. 1.

41. On hot days wear thin clothing . . . : Ibid.

41. The Town Manager of Windsor once called Carl Goslee a "symbol of good": "Carlan Hollister Goslee, Windsor Correspondent," *Hartford Times*, Tuesday, August 4, 1970, p. 4.

41. "I didn't have the money when I was raising a family of six children": "Bike-Riding Writer, 77," *Hartford Times*, June 1970, p. 10.

41. "Though most of his newspaper work was part-time": "Carlan Hollister Goslee, Windsor Correspondent," *Hartford Times*, Tuesday, August 4, 1970, p. 4.

42. That reputation, along with his keen news sense . . . : Goslee report, p. 99.

43. Also defending Amy, Dr. Howard King . . . : Trial Transcripts, p. 237, 262–263, 672, 687, 737.

CHAPTER 9 / FORECASTING THE WEATHER IS NO SCIENCE

44. Guglielmo Marconi was vacationing in the Swiss Alps . . . : The book *Guglielmo Marconi and Radio Waves (Uncharted, Unexplored, and Unexplained)* by Susan Zannus (Mitchell Lane Publishers, September 2004) helped me write this paragraph, as did *High Frequency Techniques: An Introduction to RF and Microwave Engineering*, by Joseph F. White (Wiley–IEEE Press, December 19, 2003).

44. By July 1911 . . . : "An Economic History of Weather Forecasting," by Erik D. Craft; Papers of Increase, A. Lapham's report "Disaster on the Lakes"; *A History of the United States Weather Bureau* by Don Whitnah (University of Illinois Press, 1961); Report of Willis L. Moore, Chief of the Weather Bureau, October 15, 1902.

44. . . . the technology behind weather forecasting . . . : "New Light on the Beginnings of the Weather Bureau from the Papers of Increase A. Lapham," an article by Eric Miller in the *Monthly Weather Review* (1931); *The Weather Bureau: Its History, Activities and Organization*, by Gustavus Weber (D. Appleton and Company, 1922); *A Century of Weather Service: A History of the Birth and Growth of the National Weather Service*, 1870–1970, by Patrick Hughes (Gordon and Breach, Science Publishers, Inc., 1970).

44. With the heat and chance of thunder showers . . . : "Storms Lower Heat in Many Sections: But in Philadelphia the Hot Wave Was Unabated, Causing Sixteen More Deaths," *New York Times*, July 7, 1911, p. 2.

44. By 1900 weather forecasting still suffered . . . : "Evolution to the Signal Service Years" (1600–1891), a National Weather Service article by the Department of Commerce; "An Economic History of Weather Forecasting," by Erik D. Craft.

45. English meteorologist . . . : *Scientific America*, April 1898; Sir Napier Shaw, entry in *Encyclopedia Britannica*; "A Short Account of the Circumstances Attending the Inception of Weather Forecast Work by the United States," an essay prepared by Professor Cleveland Abbe (Weather Bureau Topics and Personnel; April 17, 1916).

45. In the region of Hartford and Windsor . . . : *Brewer's Famous Quotations: 5,000 Quotations and the Stories Behind Them*, by Nigel Rees (Sterling Publishing Company, Inc., 2006), p. 470.

46. Even Carl Goslee, in his earliest . . . : Goslee report, p. 97.

46. If there were problems for Amy and James . . . : Several sources were helpful in re-creating Amy and James's life in Newington, Connecticut. Among them, "Brief Life Story of Mrs. Gilligan," *Hartford Courant*, May 9, 1916, p. 1.

46. "Mrs. Gilligan was a church-going woman . . .": "Mrs. Gilligan Says She Is Persecuted," *New York Times*, May 11, 1916, p. 4.

46. Soon after the Archers moved . . . : "Mrs. Gilligan Is Bound Over" and "Mrs. Gilligan on the Grill," *Hartford Courant*, May 9, 1916, p. 1.

47. "We have been fairly. . .": Ibid.

47. During that first week . . . : Ibid. While studying the Trial Transcripts and all the quotations Amy gave to the press, it became clear to me that Amy went to great lengths to conceal her crimes. I based this series of paragraphs on the theory that premeditated murder is not something sociopaths decide on at the last minute; rather, they plot and they plan. More important, they use the environment around them to their advantage.

48. "At a certain point . . .": Trial Transcripts, pp. 205–207.

48. Franklin liked that idea: "Mrs. Gilligan Is Bound Over" and "Mrs. Gilligan on the Grill," *Hartford Courant*, May 9, 1916, p. 1.

CHAPTER 10 / THE BIGGEST BOARDINGHOUSE IN NEW ENGLAND

49. The Federal Express was running an hour . . . : The paragraphs and quotations I used here regarding the Federal Express tragedy were drawn from "12 Killed, 44 Injured, in Bad Wreck at Bridgeport," *Hartford Courant*, July 12, 1911, p. 1.

51. "Washington Has Heat Monopoly . . .": "Washington Has Heat Monopoly," *Hartford Courant*, July 7, 1911, p. 1.

51. In certain cities the price . . . : "Iceman Protect Buffalo," *New York Times*, July 9, 1911, p. 7.

51. "We are way short": Ibid.

51. In what can only be described . . . : "Inferno Becomes a Survival Test," by Jim Shea, *Hartford Courant*, July 22, 2003, p. D1.

52. On Monday, July 10, in Hartford and . . . : Ibid.

52. Boston reported temps in the mid-80s . . . : Ibid.

52. For an aging Franklin Andrews, leaving . . . : Trial Transcripts, pp. 205–207.

53. "Dear Gramps and Gramma," he . . . : Letter, Franklin Andrews to W. F. Andrews, April 20, 1914 (Hartford Public Library).

53. Quiet and unassuming, Franklin Andrews . . . : Trial Transcripts, pp. 205–207.

54. At the Archer Home Amy was in dire . . . : Ibid.

54. From time to time . . . : Ibid., p. 207.

Chapter 11 / Cold Storage

56. They stood over one hundred strong: "Ice Riots in New York as a Result of High Prices," *Hartford Courant*, July 13, 1911, p. 1. (The quotations in this section are from the same article.)

57. Heat as a ferocious killer . . . : "Heat Waves and Heat Mortality in the United States During the Twentieth Century," Essay by Karl K. Leiker, Westfield State College, Westfield, Massachusetts.

58. A single wave of heat . . . : "Explains Heat Wave," *New York Times*, July 13, 1911, p. 3.

58. "For a prolonged period the barometric pressure has . . .": Ibid.

58. "The international weather map," Moore explained . . . : Ibid.

59. The temperature has gone so high that the self-recording . . . : Ibid.

Chapter 12 / Red Skies at Night

61. "The storm," the *Courant* reported . . . : "Hot Wave Busted, Smashing Storm, Lightning, Rain," *Hartford Courant*, July 13, 1911, p. 1.

61. For fifteen minutes, it rained so hard in downtown . . . : Ibid.

62. Although there was no danger of a frost anytime yesterday . . . : "The Day's Temperature," *Hartford Courant*, July 13, 1911, p. 1.

62. The day had started out at 75 . . . : "A Return to Comfort," by Jim Shea, *Hartford Courant*, July 23, 2003, p. D1; "The Worst Weather Disaster in New England History," *Yankee* magazine (1997).

CHAPTER 13 / THE BEGINNING OF FRANKLIN'S END

64. Franklin Andrews stayed three weeks in Meriden Hospital ... : Trial Transcripts, pp. 205–207.
64. Franklin spent an additional three weeks at Grace while doctors ... : Ibid.
64. "Well," Nellie Pierce said: Ibid., pp. 274–283.
65. "[Under] what conditions . . ." and the following quotations from Nellie Pierce are from: Ibid.

PART TWO

INVESTIGATION & INNOVATION

CHAPTER 14 / THEY COME AND THEY GO

68. The *Titanic* tragedy was such an overwhelming, loss-of-life story ... : "Duluth Woman Tells Story," *Chicago Tribune*, April 21, 1912, p. 1.
68. As the *Titanic* story faded and the leaves rotted into the ground ... : Goslee report, p. 98.
70. She is said to pay Mrs. Archer the sum of $700 cash ... : Trial Transcripts, p. 1101.
71. "Poor soul!" said one supporter. "It breaks my heart every time one of . . .": "You Can't Expect Them to Live Forever," *New York Daily News* (*Parade* magazine section), *The Justice Story*, by Joseph McNamara, March 11, 1990.
72. In early November, Franklin wrote to his brother, Wesley ... : Letter, Franklin Andrews to Mr. J. W. Andrews, November 13, 1913.
72. "He was getting into his years . . .": Trial Transcripts, pp. 226–230.
73. "Got Home Tuesday night Safe and Sound": Letter, Franklin Andrews to Mrs. J. Bennett, December 15, 1913 (Hartford Public Library).
73. "Fun-loving Andrews," reporter Joseph McNamara wrote, "considered . . .": "You Can't Expect Them to Live Forever," by Joseph McNamara, *New York Daily News* (*Parade* magazine section), *The Justice Story*, March 11, 1990.

CHAPTER 15 / DEATH AT FIRST SIGHT

74. Margaret Egan and Patrick Gilligan were born in Galway, Ireland, migrating to Connecticut . . . : State of Connecticut, Medical Certificate of Death (Michael Gilligan), February 20, 1914, Bureau of Vital Statistics, Hartford Public Library.

74. "Why, he was a man, I should say, in the neighborhood . . .": Trial Transcripts, pp. 647–651.

75. "They were sweet as pudding and twice as soft . . .": " 'Rat Poison' Bought by Mrs. Gilligan Just Before Second Husband's Death," *Hartford Courant*, May 14, 1916, p. 1.

75. "He was an agreeable man and always spoke . . .": Trial Transcripts, pp. 647–651.

75. "Full-blooded . . .": Ibid.

76. "He dropped over to the Windsor Hotel, on and off," Amy's attorney added . . . : Ibid.

76. Beginning with "Amy paid close attention to how much money her inmates had stowed away in the bank" and ending with the excerpted portion of the letter, these paragraphs were constructed with: Letter, Amy Archer Gilligan to Franklin Andrews, January 6, 1914.

CHAPTER 16 / THE LAST GOOD-BYE

78. The day after he'd received that rather strange letter from Amy, Franklin Andrews . . . : Trial Transcripts, pp. 226–231.

78. "You look good," Julia said at some point that night . . . : Trial Transcripts, pp. 226–231.

79. "Glad to Hear from You" (and the following quotations in this section): Letter, Franklin Andrews to Mr. George R. Johnson, January 19, 1914.

79. "Glad to Hear from You. Hope you are well. . . .": Trial Transcripts, pp. 226–231.

79. Before Michael married Amy, he had lived with Frank. . . . : Ibid., pp. 636–637.

80. All subsequent quotes and information regarding the meeting Michael Gilligan had with his son, see Trial Transcripts, pp. 636–638.

CHAPTER 17 / DEATH BY MARRIAGE

81. Near the turn of the twentieth century, the common household concoction . . . : *The American Journal of the Medical Sciences* (Philadelphia, PA: Carey, Lea and Carey, 1827, p 392); Dictionary.com. Unabridged (v 1.1). Random House, Inc. http://dictionary.reference .com/ browse/Purpura.

82. "Some of the inmates . . .": "Mrs. Gilligan Says She Is Persecuted," *New York Times*, May 11, 1916, p. 4.

82. On February 15, 1914, Roscoe Nelson, the respected pastor . . . : Trial Transcripts, pp. 647–649.

83. "He looked good," Filkins reported later: Ibid., pp. 650–651.

83. Michael Gilligan did not look so well: " 'Rat Poison' Bought by Mrs. Gilligan Just Before Second Husband's Death," *Hartford Courant*, May 14, 1916, p. 1.

84. Michael Gilligan's good friend Ralph Frost worked at the . . . : Trial Transcripts, pp. 658–662. [Please note: This entire scene, told from Ralph Frost's point of view, was constructed with the help of Mr. Frost's very detailed testimony.]

CHAPTER 18 / SWEET LITTLE AMY

87. "She was well respected and very highly thought of": "Windsor Murders Live on in History," *Hartford Courant*, September 21, 1986, p. H4.

87. A nurse who later took care of Amy . . . : Ibid.

87. Although she had a frequently changing . . . : "Police Believe Archer Home for the Aged a Murder Factory," *Hartford Courant*, May 9, 1916, p. 1.

88. "Please, Doctor, he's very sick. You must step over to the house at once": Trial Transcripts, p. 676.

88. "The doctor didn't get there until he passed away": Ibid., pp. 663–665.

88. The doctor was surprised: Ibid., p. 678.

89.   After King left and Michael's body . . . : Ibid., p. 1097.

89.   "Dear Brother . . .": Ibid., p. 1086.

90.   Later, when Dr. King's . . . "in generally . . .": Ibid., p. 673.

90.   "Why, he was complaining of extreme nausea and pain, burning . . .": Ibid., p. 674.

91.   Checking Michael over . . . : Ibid., p. 675.

91.   Word of Michael Gilligan's death shocked the small community: Ibid., pp. 1118–1119.

91.   Jack, Mr. Gilligan died last Thursday morning with indigestion: Ibid.

92.   "So they go one after another—that makes 21 that's died since I came here": Ibid.

92.   "This was done . . .": Trial Transcripts, p. 39.

92.   "[Michael] was a big, strong, healthy fellow up to the night he died": Ibid., p. 41.

93.   "My husband was practically no good to me": Ibid.

93.   With negative public sentiment building against her as February turned into March . . . : " 'Rat Poison' Bought by Mrs. Gilligan Just Before Second Husband's Death," *Hartford Courant*, May 14, 1916, p. 1; Trial Transcripts, pp. 1119–1120.

94.   On the front side of the postcard . . . : Ibid. (Trial Transcripts), p. 1119.

94.   Dear Mr. Alcorn: Ibid., p. 1120.

95.   "Windsor is a very Pleasant Town. Is 6 miles above Hartford" and the Franklin Andrews letter excerpt following it: Ibid., pp. 1093–1094.

95.   Mr. Archer died 4 years . . . : Ibid., p. 1085.

95.   "I am quite well," Franklin said: Ibid., p. 1085.

95.   Amy wasted little time in filing a petition with the Probate Court . . . : Ibid., pp. 1144–1148.

96.   "For a period [of time] . . . I was constantly informed . . .": "Mrs. Gilligan Says She Is Persecuted," *New York Times*, May 11, 1916, p. 4.

Chapter 19 / The Con

97. "He was a close friend of Michael Gilligan": "Carlan H. Goslee Took Dual Role in Murder Probe," by Bob Zaiman, *Hartford Courant*, January 4, 1953, p. A1.
97. "Sherman had me check the vital statistics at Town Hall . . .": Ibid.
98. "Why, yes, I've heard rumors about the Windsor Home for two years": "Governor Heard Rumors," *New York Times*, May 14, 1916, p. 9.
98. If not for his wife's sudden illness "of the mind . . .": This quote and the subsequent narrative told from Emily Smith's point of view, which encompasses the remainder of this section, was constructed with the help of Trial Transcripts, pp. 690–720. (Emily Smith gave incredibly detailed descriptions of the conversations she had with Amy and her brother, Charles. There were several instances of third-party hearsay thrown in for good measure that would have riled the most inexperienced trial defense attorney today. It is quite a direct examination by Hugh Alcorn and describes for jurors perfectly, without question, how Amy lied to potential inmates in order to attract them into her web, so she could manipulate and then ultimately steal from them.)
103. "[He] was there in the Home apparently satisfied": Ibid., p. 703.

Chapter 20 / Red Falcon

104. Franklin Andrews had all his senses firing . . . : Ibid., p. 1084.
104. Dear Cousin: I am Getting along nicely for me: Ibid.
105. I am Getting along quite well now [but] have had a hard . . . : Ibid., p. 1095.
105. "He had failed very much": Ibid., p. 706.
106. I am quite well. An old Ladie died Sunday night: Ibid., p. 1096.
106. Beginning at "Oh, he was far gone . . ." and ending with "shock": Ibid., pp. 690, 706, 711, 714.
107. This had turned into a common practice . . . : Ibid., p. 42.
107. For more information and the final quotation by Alcorn, see: Ibid., pp. 20–30.

CHAPTER 21 / "I CAN FIX THAT ALL RIGHT"

108. First they draw out the brains through the nostrils . . . : *The Histories of Herodotus*, by Herodotus and Henry Cary (New York: D. Appleton & Co., 1904), p. 114.

109. "I have advocated for years," said one prominent coroner: "Poison in Mrs. Todd's Body: But Embalming Fluid Contained Chloroform and Arsenic," *New York Times*, December 23, 1905, p. 1.

109. The ground was soft enough by April 18, 1914 . . . : " 'Rat Poison' Bought by Mrs. Gilligan Just Before Second Husband's Death," *Hartford Courant*, May 14, 1916, p. 1.

110. "He [never] complained of any trouble" . . . Nellie later said: Trial Transcripts, p. 276.

110. . . . glad to hear from you: Ibid., p. 1093.

110. On May 18, Amy received more frustrating news . . . : Ibid., p. 1150.

111. "Hope this finds you all well . . .": Ibid., p. 1099.

111. Shortly after inquiring about a room . . . : Ibid., pp. 346–350.

112. "Your kind note is before me," Amy wrote: Ibid., p. 1122.

112. "Try not to worry . . .": Ibid.

112. "I can fix that all right," Amy said smugly (and the remainder of these scenes in which the Gowdys visit the Archer Home): Ibid., pp. 346–350.

113. In her May 26 letter, after she'd made a point . . . : Ibid., p. 1122.

113. I wrote this so that it will . . . : Ibid.

113. "I know you will be happy here": Ibid.

CHAPTER 22 / THE WRONG VICTIM

114. My dear Friend . . . : Ibid., p. 1123.

114. "I tried my best to have it so you could come," Amy wrote: Ibid.

115. "So please try to come next Thursday . . .": Ibid.

115. "If you kindly mail me a check tomorrow . . .": Ibid.

115. "There were no signs of sickness . . .": Ibid., p. 30.

115. From "Franklin's roommate, Seth Ramsey . . ." until the final paragraph of this cluster detailing Franklin Andrews's quickly deteriorating health, "I will call on Mr. King," please see Seth T. Ramsey's

direct testimony, Ibid., pp. 322–330. Incidentally, Franklin Andrews's death (and life inside the Archer Home) was probably the most documented of all Amy's victims.

117. "Why, I didn't think he was so very sick," Ramsey said later: Ibid., p. 328.

117. "I just stepped up to the bed and looked at him": Ibid., p. 329.

117. He had lived in Windsor since 1899: Ibid., p. 238.

117. "Trivial things," King called them: Ibid., p. 241.

117. For the Howard King narrative of his visit to the Archer Home during Franklin Andrews's death, ending with the quote, "I need you back," please see Ibid., pp. 241–264.

118. "Your brother is sick and I am afraid he will not get well": Ibid., p. 279.

118. From "What's the matter with him?" to "Mrs. Archer, will you please call on a doctor?" please see Nellie Pierce's testimony, Ibid., pp. 279–280.

119. According to King, Franklin was practically dead": Ibid., p. 264.

119. Dr. Howard King signed off on Franklin's death certificate, citing the "primary cause" of death as "gastric ulcers": Ibid., p. 1177.

Chapter 23 / "Fit as a Fiddle"

120. "Neighbors felt that the presence of an old people's home . . . cheapened the neighborhood": "The Case of the Hearse at Midnight," by George Vedder Jones, *American Weekly*, January 8, 1950, p. 26.

121. "A black hearse comes at midnight to spirit away their bodies": Ibid.

121. From "When Nellie Pierce showed up near seven o'clock the next morning, she ran into Seth Ramsey" to "I recognized him all right," or the end of this narrative describing Nellie's second meeting with Amy, please see Trial Transcripts, pp. 274–283. Nellie gives a very detailed account of this conversation.

122. "I've come," Nellie said to Clifton Sherman: "The Case of the Hearse at Midnight," by George Vedder Jones, *American Weekly*, January 8, 1950, p. 26. (I need to commend Mr. Jones for this story he wrote in the *American Weekly*, a column that focused on true crime. Readers appreciated well-written true-crime stories. As a researcher and

author, I feel that Jones did a terrific job in interviewing those connected to the Amy Archer-Gilligan case who were still alive.) This entire section, I should note, in which a lightbulb finally goes on for Clifton Sherman, was made possible by Jones's excellent article.

123. "Well, I went to Windsor to visit [Franklin] just last [week]": "The Case of the Hearse at Midnight," by George Vedder Jones, *American Weekly*, January 8, 1950, p. 26.

124. Please let me know if you wish to take the room: Trial Transcripts, p. 1124.

124. "I am very sorry to have caused the delay but I could not possibly avoid it": Trial Transcripts, p. 1125.

125. "Milton School, and in early 1890 attended New Britain Normal School [and later] became a bookkeeper for a New Haven firm": *Chronicles of Milton: Village Left Behind by Time*, by the Milton Woman's Club (Litchfield, CT: Milton Woman's Club, 1997), p. 40.

126. "Did he give you a loan?" (as well as this entire scene of the Andrews siblings talking to Amy): Trial Transcripts, pp. 274–283.

CHAPTER 24 / PUBLIC SERVICE

127. "A stomach complaint, sudden death, and a body carried out at midnight," Sherman told Thayer: "The Case of the Hearse at Midnight," by George Vedder Jones, *American Weekly*, January 8, 1950, p. 26.

128. "I think we owe it to the public and to Mrs. Pierce to find out": Ibid.

128. From "That's nice" to the end of this meeting between Amy and Robert Thayer ("Yes," Amy responded, "it's our usual procedure"), please see Ibid., pp. 26–27.

130. On June 11, 1914, Loren and Alice Gowdy signed a life contract with Amy for $1,000: Trial Transcripts, pp. 1103 and 1127.

130. "She was in good health, certainly," Clark said: Ibid., p. 628.

131. King opened the door and "seemed irritated" by Thayer's cold call: "The Case of the Hearse at Midnight," by George Vedder Jones, *American Weekly*, January 8, 1950, p. 26.

131. Thayer described King as a "gray-haired man with a brisk, professional manner": Ibid., p. 27.

131. "There was nothing unusual about Andrews's death!" (along with the concluding quotations in this section): Ibid., p. 27.

132. By mid-July, Loren Gowdy trusted Amy enough to "quit-claim": Trial Transcripts, p. 1127.

132. The scenes beginning with "I am inquiring about giving my friend room and board" and ending "I went the same as usually," please see: Ibid., pp. 655–657.

CHAPTER 25 / TOO LATE

134. For the scene "We are the Gowdys' people—we would like to visit with them" to "Well," Alice said, "she tried to have me take some medicine, but I told her I didn't need it," please see Porter and Minnie Bacon's testimony in Trial Transcripts, pp. 618–626.

135. "She vomited profusely": Ibid., p. 43.

136. For the scene beginning "I am Amy Archer, speaking for Alice Gowdy," to Alice said her "stools [were] like water" and her vomit was the same, see: Ibid., pp. 523, 588, 607, 615.

137. "I gave her a tablet for nausea": Ibid., pp. 610–615.

138. Dr. Thompson later described her diagnosis as "cholera morbus": Ibid.

138. For additional details regarding the scene beginning "Come at once, Doctor, to see Mrs. Gowdy," and ending, "Mrs. Gowdy has died, Doctor," in which Dr. Thompson returns to the Archer Home, please see Ibid. The extended quote I used from Dr. Thompson's testimony—[T]he patient [was] ashy, blue—her extremities, her hands . . .—can be found on p. 612.

CHAPTER 26 / DONE TO DEATH

140. Louis Robert Thayer found himself taking over . . . : "The Case of the Hearse at Midnight," by George Vedder Jones, *American Weekly*, January 8, 1950, p. 26–27.

140. ". . . [hard] news was more than canned corned beef, 'and it took a man to get it.'": "Ex-*Courant* Man Recalls Career Here," by T. H. Parker, *Hartford Courant*, July 21, 1941, p. 2.

140. After speaking to Nellie Pierce, a woman he didn't "think was pipe-dreaming . . .": Ibid.

141. Then, in 1903, officials decided . . . : *Connecticut State Police, 1903–2003: 100 Year History*, by Ky Paducah (Turner Pub, 2003), p. 22.

141. By the time Sherman and Thayer were on their way over to Egan's Hartford office . . . : *Connecticut State Police, 1903–2003: 100 Year History*, by Ky Paducah (Turner Pub, 2003), p. 21.

142. One of the first State Police officers to be appointed . . . : Ibid., p. 22; and "Robert Hurley, 69, Ex-Police Official," *New York Times* (obituary), August 15, 1938, p. 15.

143. The information Sherman and Thayer brought forth . . . : "The Case of the Hearse at Midnight," by George Vedder Jones, *American Weekly*, January 8, 1950, p. 27.

143. "But it's too fantastic to believe": Ibid.

CHAPTER 27 / MAY THE CURSE OF GOD COME DOWN ON YOU

145. "Was some mentally unbalanced neighbor trying to get rid of the Home by murdering its inmates?": Ibid.

146. Nellie had gone through more of Franklin's records and found that an additional $500 in cash . . . : "Vituperative Letters Written by Mrs. Gilligan—Extortion of Money," *Hartford Courant*, May 9, 1916, p. 3.

146. "My brother's death . . .": Ibid.

147. "Mrs. Archer-Gilligan returned . . .": Ibid.

147. "Mr. Andrews gave to our home . . .": Ibid.

147. I will pray . . . : Ibid.

148. "May God punish you all," she ended the blistering missive, "and make example of your work": Ibid., p. 4.

148. "I'm a wealthy, friendless widow," Zola Bennett explained: "The Case of the Hearse at Midnight," by George Vedder Jones, *American Weekly*, January 8, 1950, p. 27.

Chapter 28 / Poison Control

149. "Mrs. Gowdy's body," Hugh Alcorn later explained: Trial Transcripts, p. 44.

149. More important, the death certificate specifically stated that "permit for burial is FORBIDDEN, if 'heart failure' or . . . : Trial Transcripts, p. 1173.

150. "I trust you will forgive . . .": Ibid., p. 1119.

150. "You hurt my feelings very much," Amy wrote: Ibid., p. 1120.

151. You spoke of Mr. Andrews's death being . . . : Ibid.

152. "Mrs. Gowdy's attack on Thanksgiving seemed a severe one . . .": "The Case of the Hearse at Midnight," by George Vedder Jones, *American Weekly*, January 8, 1950, p. 27.

152. "Why, in a majority of the cases, I say, they were old people . . .": Trial Transcripts, p. 255.

152. "How unusual?" Hurley asked: "The Case of the Hearse at Midnight," by George Vedder Jones, *American Weekly*, January 8, 1950, p. 27.

152. "I'm certain Mrs. Gowdy was poisoned": Ibid.

Chapter 29 / The Facts

154. "Toxic doses of the strongly ionizable inorganic compounds of arsenic cause gastro-enteritis with vomiting . . .": *Journal of the American Medical Association* (Chicago: American Medical Association, 1883), pp. 2134–2136.

154. ". . . vomit was liquid, as I remember it, and contained mucus . . .": Trial Transcripts, p. 250.

155. In King's own observation, he said later that "the presence of blood in . . .": Ibid., p. 251.

155. Death results from "either circulatory or respiratory failure . . .": *Journal of the American Medical Association* (Chicago: American Medical Association, 1883), pp. 2134–2136.

155. Arsenic causes paralysis of the walls of the capillaries . . . : Ibid.

CHAPTER 30 / GRAVE ROBBERS

158. "We'll need to have that body taken up tomorrow night": Trial Transcripts, p. 370.
159. This information and dialogue contained in the scenes detailing Dr. Wolff's secret autopsy conducted in the middle of the night on May 2, 1916, is outlined in great detail beginning on p. 441, Trial Transcripts (Wolff's testimony). All of the quotes from this scene with Hurley and Wolff and Keeler were taken from Trial Transcripts, pp. 441–445, as well as Wolff's notations and Captain Hurley's testimony, pp. 369–372.

CHAPTER 31 / MOTIVE

166. Superintendent Thomas Egan asked Clifton Sherman and Robert Thayer to meet . . . : "The Case of the Hearse at Midnight," by George Vedder Jones, *American Weekly*, January 8, 1950, p. 27.
166. "We're sure of five murders so far," Egan said: Ibid.
166. "That leaves us with only two suspects," Egan explained: Ibid.
166. "The doctor [King] and Mrs. Archer," Sherman said: Ibid.
167. "I was making a preliminary examination," Wolff said later: Trial Transcripts, p. 452.
167. "It was found thickly covered with a metallic layer of purplish-blue color . . .": Ibid., p. 453.
167. "[t]he presence of a metallic poison in the tissues": Ibid.
168. "When I examined it under a microscope, it absolutely defined . . .": Ibid.
168. Alcorn and Egan decided that Amy's bedside presence with Alice Gowdy . . .: "The Case of the Hearse at Midnight," by George Vedder Jones, *American Weekly*, January 8, 1950, p. 27.
168. "I can tell you that Mrs. Archer seldom took guests on a monthly basis . . .": Ibid.

CHAPTER 32 / IN THE DEAD OF NIGHT

170. "Come over to my office right away," Alcorn said: "Carlan H. Goslee Took Dual Role in Murder Probe," by Bob Zaiman, *Hartford Courant*, January 4, 1953, p. A1.

170. "Hold up your right hand," Alcorn instructed Goslee: "Carlan H. Goslee Took Dual Role in Murder Probe," by Bob Zaiman, *Hartford Courant*, January 4, 1953, p. A1.

170. Carl Goslee was, apparently, the one and only . . . : "The Case of the Hearse at Midnight," by George Vedder Jones, *American Weekly*, January 8, 1950, p. 27.

171. Enough circumstantial evidence had been accumulated . . . : Goslee report, p. 98.

171. Carl later said that "two large, black autos . . .": Ibid.

172. So they piled into the two vehicles . . . : "Carlan H. Goslee Took Dual Role in Murder Probe," by Bob Zaiman, *Hartford Courant*, January 4, 1953, p. A1.

CHAPTER 33 / OH, WHAT A BEAUTIFUL "MOURNING"

173. "The motor of the car was kept running," Maddock wrote years later: "Vivid Story of His 'Four Eventful Years' as a Newspaperman," by Aubrey Maddock, *Hartford Courant*, May 2, 1937, p. D1.

173. "Follow that car," Maddock shouted: Ibid.

173. "Away we went at a rapid pace," added Maddock: Ibid.

174. Amy Archer was at home on the evening of May 8, 1916 . . . : Goslee report, p. 99.

174. "It took a long time for the two cars to reach the house at 37-39 Prospect Street": Ibid.

174. "When the State Police finally moved in to make an arrest . . .": "Carlan H. Goslee Took Dual Role in Murder Probe," by Bob Zaiman, *Hartford Courant*, January 4, 1953, p. A1.

174. "I am glad you have come," Amy said: "Police Believe Archer Home for Aged a Murder Factory: Mrs. Gilligan is Bound Over," *Hartford Courant*, May 9, 1916, p. 1.

174. Beginning with the quote "We have come here to have a talk with you and look over your place" to "Mrs. Archer-Gilligan, look, we have a warrant for your arrest charging you with causing the death of Franklin Andrews . . . ," this entire sequence of dialogue is derived from Robert Hurley's detailed testimony, Trial Transcripts, pp. 377–378.

176. "What's going on in there?" the local asked: "Vivid Story of His 'Four Eventful Years' as a Newspaperman," by Aubrey Maddock, *Hartford Courant*, May 2, 1937, p. D1.

176. "What did you do with Mr. Smith's money?": Trial Transcripts, pp. 377–378.

177. "Very well," she said, "I'll need to get my cape and hat": Trial Transcripts, pp. 377–378.

178. Mrs. Gilligan was arrested . . . after she had been closeted for about one hour: Goslee report, p. 99.

178. "Yes, darling," Amy said: "Police Believe Archer Home for Aged a Murder Factory: Mrs. Gilligan on the Grill," *Hartford Courant*, May 9, 1916, p. 2.

178. "I cannot advise you, Mrs. Gilligan, but there are three [options] for you to do: Trial Transcripts, p. 378.

179. "I think I'll waive examination": Ibid.; and "Police Believe Archer Home for Aged a Murder Factory," *Hartford Courant*, May 9, 1916, p. 1.

179. "Throughout the trial and the intervals which preceded and followed it . . .": "Police Believe Archer Home for Aged a Murder Factory: Mrs. Gilligan Is Bound Over," *Hartford Courant*, May 9, 1916, p. 2.

179. "What are you doing to my mother? You can't do this to her!": Ibid. (additional headline: "Mrs. Gilligan in Jail—Shows No Signs of Emotion").

180. ". . . [H]er eyes began to water," the *Courant* reported: Ibid.

180. "You have heard the reading of the complaint," Judge Grant said: Ibid.

180. "I understand that you have decided to waive examination": Ibid.

180. Amy answered at once, in a "clear voice and without a trace of worry," saying, "Yes! That's right": Ibid.

180. "I proclaim that the prisoner be bound over to the June term of the Superior Court [in Hartford]," Judge Grant said: Ibid.

181. "She was bound over," Hurley commented later: Trial Transcripts, p. 378.
181. "After our general investigation of affairs at the Archer Home . . .": (Sidebar quotation), *Hartford Courant*, May 9, 1916, p. 2.
182. "She was wringing her hands," said one cellmate: Trial Transcripts, p. 38.
182. " 'Why did I do it? What made me do it?' " said the witness: Ibid.
182. "So far as Franklin R. Andrews dying from arsenic," Amy said rather stoically . . . : Ibid.

Chapter 34 / "Murder Factory"

183. "I had telephoned Mr. Sherman": "Vivid Story of His 'Four Eventful Years' as a Newspaperman," by Aubrey Maddock, *Hartford Courant*, May 2, 1937, p. D1.
183. "The *Courant* was required by its contract with the Associated Press," Maddock said: Ibid.
183. "Newspapers throughout the East," wrote one reporter years later . . . : "The Case of the Hearse at Midnight," by George Vedder Jones, *American Weekly*, January 8, 1950, p. 27.
184. "Mr. Sherman's greatest coup," said his obituary in 1946 . . . : "C. L. Sherman Dies; Retired Local Editor," *Hartford Courant*, February 7, 1946, p. 1.
185. The Lucy Durand narrative was written with the help of "[Mrs. Archer] Had Mrs. Durand Taken to Asylum: Inmate Visited Neighbors, Told Stories, Caused Investigation; WENT OUT FOR A RIDE, NEVER RETURNED," *Hartford Courant*, May 9, 1916, p. 3.
186. "Happiness and contentment were evident in her face," the *Courant* article reported: Ibid.
186. "I am a Hartford newspaperman," he said, to the end of this scene, ". . . I couldn't ask for anything more. And I had rather go to hell than go back to Mrs. Archer's home," please see Ibid.
187. "The exclusive story which developed . . .": "Vivid Story of His 'Four Eventful Years' as a Newspaperman," by Aubrey Maddock, *Hartford Courant*, May 2, 1937, p. D1.

188. I, Mrs. Amy E. Archer-Gilligan, do hereby state . . . : Trial Transcripts, p. 1127.

189. Being a smart-aleck, and citing the "Show-Me" state's famous motto . . . : "King Indicates Possible Line of Defense in Archer Home Poisoning Case," *Hartford Courant*, May 9, 1916, p. 10.

190. "Maybe I ought to have analyzed the contents of the stomach," he said: Ibid.

190. "There [was] nothing suspicious to me about the death . . .": Ibid.

191. "They [those five deaths] were not queer in any way": " 'We'll Fight for Mother,'" *Hartford Courant*, May 10, 1916, p. 1.

191. "You had better ask my mother's attorney": Ibid.

PART THREE

TRIALS & TRIBULATIONS

CHAPTER 35 / A CHANGING WORLD

194. Biographical information about Benedict Holden was derived from *Encyclopedia of Connecticut Biography*, Genealogical-memorial; Representative Citizens, by Samuel Hart (Boston: The American Historical Society, Inc., 1917), pp. 326–329. Direct quote can be found on p. 329.

194. . . . the "greatest naval battle of the First World War . . .": *GI Ingenuity: Improvisation, Technology, and Winning World War II*, by James Jay Carafano (Westport, CT: Praeger Security International, 2006), p. 102.

196. "He is still a hard worker," writer Samuel Hart said in 1917 . . . : *Encyclopedia of Connecticut Biography*, Genealogical-memorial; Representative Citizens, p. 329.

196. . . . Colin Evans called Schultze "a fussy, self-important man with a knack for insinuating himself into high-profile cases . . .": *Blood on the Table: The Greatest Cases of New York City's Office of the Chief Medical Examiner*, by Colin Evans (New York: Berkeley Books, 2008), p. 25.

CHAPTER 36 / THE GREATEST SUCCESS

198. "Shortly after Mr. Andrews's death," Amy said: "Mrs. Gilligan Says She Is Persecuted," *New York Times*, May 11, 1916, p. 4.
198. "When I was arrested, I asked the police officers ...": Ibid.
199. "Thank God I did not follow his advice": Ibid.
200. "This has developed in evidence in my possession into one of the biggest ...": "Dig Up More Bodies in Hunt for More Poison," *New York Times*, May 12, 1916, p. 8.
200. "He is suffering from a peculiar form of insanity," said one report: "Woman's Brother in Insane Asylum," *Hartford Courant*, May 11, 1916, p. 1.
200. One of John Francis's more bizarre ...: "Whatever Went Wrong with Amy?" by Bill Ryan, *New York Times*, March 2, 1997.
201. "There will be no insanity plea," he said: "Dig Up More Bodies in Hunt for More Poison," *New York Times*, May 12, 1916, p. 8.
201. "The grave had been opened and the box and casket taken out ...": Trial Transcripts, pp. 755–756.

CHAPTER 37 / WITCH OF WINDSOR

203. "Legislation intended to make impossible a repetition of events": "Bill to License Old Folks' Homes Is in Legislature," *Hartford Courant*, January 26, 1917, p. 5 (including excerpted passage).
204. "Woman Held in Poisoning Case May Never Be Tried": "Mrs. Gilligan Insane," *New York Times*, June 7, 1916, p. 13.
205. "Mrs. Amy Archer-Gilligan," the *New York Times* detailed ...: Ibid.
206. Vaughan later explained the particulars of the Miller case, noting that it "was a question of ...": Trial Transcripts, p. 836.
206. ... the court ordered that "the expenses of Dr. Otto Schultze," Amy's expert ...": "Fights Murder Charges," *New York Times*, June 9, 1917, p. 6.

Chapter 38 / Victory for the Vanquished

208. "*Voir dire* is really the start of a criminal trial": "The Art of *Voir Dire*," *Time*, by H-P Time.com, April 7, 1967.
208. Beginning with "Edward Stevens," along with all of the *voir dire* testimony, please see: Trial Transcripts, pp. 142–152.
210. Moreover, the global harmony Wilson trumpeted needed to be "peace without victory . . .": *The Great War*, by George H. Allen, Henry C. Whitehead, French Ensor Chadwick, William Sowden Sims, James William McAndrew, and Edwin Wiley (Philadelphia: G. Barrie's Sons, 1915), p. 464.
211. By now Alcorn had agreed to "proceed on the first count . . .": "Mrs. Gilligan Will Go on Witness Stand in Effort to Save Her Life," *Hartford Courant*, June 30, 1917, p. 1.
211. Gardiner Greene is the judge on this case, and he ordered that Mrs. Gilligan be tried . . . : Goslee report, p. 99.
212. According to the Attorney General's Office, Alcorn "came to symbolize Connecticut's tough . . . : "History of Connecticut's Attorney General's Office," http://www.ct.gov/AG/cwp/view .asp?a=2132&q=295136.
213. "Now, Dr. King, do you remember being called to attend to Mr. Franklin R. Andrews": Trial Transcripts, pp. 237–241.
215. "I think I followed my own judgment in that matter," King said: Ibid., p. 253.
215. Beginning "That's a . . . damned lie!" and ending, "Well, I would ask that you be careful of your expressions, Mr. Holden," this entire exchange can be found in: "Holden Uses Big, Big 'D,' in Courtroom; Alcorn Calls Him to Account," *Hartford Courant*, June 23, 1917, p. 1.

Chapter 39 / The Experts

218. "She rarely moves a muscle," wrote one reporter: "Mrs. Gilligan Will Go on Witness Stand in Effort to Save Her Life," *Hartford Courant*, June 30, 1917, p. 1.
218. For the conversation between Benedict Holden and Lizzie Sullivan, beginning with "Lizzie, how many times [have] you been put in

that jail in the last five years?" and ending "Offer the truth from the mouth of a woman who lives in that jail . . . ," see Trial Transcripts, pp. 668–672.

CHAPTER 40 / "DARK MURDER HOLE"

223. "The most amazing statement . . .": "State's Attorney Concludes Argument in Gilligan Case; Judge to Charge Jury Today," *Hartford Courant*, July 13, 1917, p. 1.

224. "Talk about the defense in this case," he said: Ibid., p. 2.

224. After Alcorn finished with some sort of bizarre rant about God and "the Great Temple on High": Ibid.

224. "He followed close to the evidence," the *Courant* reported the following morning: "State's Attorney Concludes Argument in Gilligan Case; Judge to Charge Jury Today," *Hartford Courant*, July 13, 1917, p. 1.

225. "What will it be?": Goslee report, p. 100.

225. There is a hush in the courthouse and all rise: Ibid.

225. He asked the sheriff in the room to "make a proclamation of silence and to have order preserved": "Amy E. Archer Gilligan Found Guilty of First Degree Murder; Sentenced to be Hanged Nov. 6," *Hartford Courant*, July 14, 1917, p. 1.

226. Amy shook her head, saying, "No . . . no . . .": Ibid.

226. "Amy Archer-Gilligan is guilty of the crime of murder in the first degree . . .": Trial Transcripts, pp. 487–490.

226. "Never before in the history of this country," wrote one reporter: "Amy E. Archer Gilligan Found Guilty of First Degree Murder; Sentenced to be Hanged Nov. 6," *Hartford Courant*, July 14, 1917, p. 1.

CHAPTER 41 / DRUG ADDICT

227. There would be "no need" for that, he answered, "until after the October session of the Supreme Court of Errors": "Stay for Mrs. Gilligan," *New York Times*, July 18, 1917, p. 11.

228. The information re: Amy's new attorney and the hearing in this section was derived from: "Mrs. Gilligan Under Drug Influence When Accused, Says Sister," *Hartford Courant*, June 25, 1919, p. 12.

229. ... the "matron of the Hartford county jail." Louise Cowles was ...: "Gilligan Trial Alienists Go Into Secret Conference," *Hartford Courant*, June 20, 1919, p. 1.

230. "I want to go home! I want to go home!": Ibid.

231. "One [of Amy's] sisters was born an idiot, and died when she was ten.": Ibid.

231. "No," Barnes said, "he just took my poison records": Ibid.

232. "Amy went to bed and slept more soundly than is normal": Ibid.

233. "prominent citizen of the town ...": "Windsor" (section), *Hartford Courant*, February 22, 1914, p. 16.

234. "It's you—you—you!" Amy snapped: "Mrs. Gilligan Under Drug Influence When Accused, Says Sister," *Hartford Courant*, June 25, 1919, p. 12.

234. "When was it that you discussed your mother's use of morphine with Dr. King?": "Judge Keeler Questions Mrs. Gilligan's Daughter on Her Drug Testimony," *Hartford Courant*, June 26, 1919, p. 1.

235. "In the spring of 1914," Mary answered confidently (and the remainder of the Mary Archer conversation with the judge): Ibid.

235. Sec. 2 That it shall be unlawful for any person to sell ...: *The Federal Reporter*, by Peyton Boyle, James Wells Goodwin, and Robert Desty (St. Paul: West Pub. Co., 1900s), p. 196.

CHAPTER 42 / ONE LAST TRICK

238. "Her mental trouble is of a peculiar nature ...": "Mrs. Gilligan, Life Prisoner, Declared Insane by Doctors," *Hartford Courant*, July 12, 1924, p. 1.

238. "She was ... declared insane ... ," one report said: "A Page From History, We Were There," *Hartford Courant*, January 30, 2000, p. G12.

238. "The only controversy," Meade said in 1986 ...: "Windsor Murders Live on in History," *Hartford Courant*, September 21, 1986, p. H4.

CHAPTER 43 / ARSENIC AND OLD LACE

239. "For Joseph Kesselring has written one so funny": Review, *New York Times*, by Brooks Atkinson, January 11, 1941, p. 8.

241. "In his adroit mixture of comedy and mayhem . . .": "Arsenic and Old Lace," Notes on Drama. Answers Corporation, 2006. Answers .com, 10 Nov. 2008, http://www.answers.com/topic/arsenic-and-old-lace-play.

241. "Legend has it that the play . . .": "Arsenic and Old Lace," *The Oxford Companion to American Theatre* (Oxford University Press, Inc., 2004). Answers.com, 10 Nov. 2008, http://www.answers.com/topic/arsenic-and-old-lace-play.

241. *New York Sun* drama critic Richard Lockridge described the play as "noisy": Review, *New York Sun*, January 6, 1941.

242. "[He] came to Hartford," Carlan Goslee wrote . . . : Goslee report, p. 100.

242. "Hardly knowing that it is happening and certainly not knowing how it happens . . .": "Drama by the Thames," Wireless to the *New York Times*, by W. A. Arlington, January 10, 1943, p. xi.

242. "If the author had put so much as a foot in the wrong place . . .": Ibid.

EPILOGUE / WHATEVER HAPPENED TO AMY?

244. "When a man contemplates evil as expressive of power . . .": Lecture by William McKenzie, *The Christian Science Journal*, by Mary Baker Eddy (Boston, MA: Christian Science Publishing Society, 1905–1906), p. 540.

246. "Benedict M. Holden," the newspapers reported the following morning . . . : "B. M. Holden Dies Suddenly in New York," *Hartford Courant*, February 20, 1937, p. 1.

247. . . . she was "a quiet, cooperative patient," adding, "Mostly she sat in a chair . . .": "Mrs. Amy Gilligan Dies; Figured in Murder Case," *Hartford Courant*, April 24, 1962, p. 6.

Selected Bibliography

Allen, George H., Henry C. Whitehead, French Ensor Chadwick, William Sowden Sims, James William McAndrew, and Edwin Wiley. *The Great War*. Philadelphia: G. Barrie's Sons, 1915.

Boyle, Peyton, James Wells Goodwin, and Robert Desty. *The Federal Reporter*. St. Paul: West Publishing Co., 190(?).

Calhoun, Charles. *The Gilded Age: Essays on the Origins of Modern America*. SR Books, 1995.

Cannal, J.-N., and Richard Harlan. *History of Embalming, and Preparations in Anatomy, Pathology, and Natural History*. Philadelphia: J. Dobson, 1840.

Carafano, James Jay. *GI Ingenuity: Improvisation, Technology, and Winning World War II*. Westport, CT: Praeger Security International, 2006.

Cashman, Sean. *America in the Gilded Age: From the Death of Lincoln to the Rise of Theodore Roosevelt*, 3rd ed. New York: New York University Press, 1993.

Connecticut. Budget Report, by Connecticut Board of Finance and Control, 1921.

Delaney, Edmund. *The Connecticut River: New England's Historic Waterway*. Guilford, CT: Globe Pequot Press, 1983.

Eddy, Mary Baker. *The Christian Science Journal*. Boston: Christian Science Publishing Society, 1883.

Evans, Colin. *Blood on the Table: The Greatest Cases of New York City's Office of the Chief Medical Examiner*. New York: Berkeley Books, 2008.

Grant, Ellsworth S., and Marion H. Grant. *The City of Hartford, 1784–1984: An Illustrated History*. Hartford: Connecticut Historical Society, 1986.

Hart, Samuel. *Encyclopedia of Connecticut Biography*, Genealogical-Memorial; Representative Citizens. Boston: The American Historical Society, Inc., 1917.

Herodotus, and Henry Cary. *The Histories of Herodotus*. New York: D. Appleton & Co., 1904.

Hickey, Eric W. *Serial Murderers and Their Victims*. Belmont, CA: Wadsworth Publishing Co., 2003.

Hughes, Patrick. *A Century of Weather Service: A History of the Birth and Growth of the National Weather Service, 1870–1970*. New York: Gordon and Breach Science Publishers, Inc., 1970.

Kipling, Rudyard. *Captains Courageous*. Garden City, NY: Doubleday, 1964.

McKinney, William Mark, and Thomas H. Calvert. *Federal Statutes Annotated: Containing All the Laws of the United States of a General, Permanent and Public Nature in Force on the First Day of January, 1916*. Northport, Long Island, NY: Edward Thompson Co., 1916.

Milkie, Ronald, and Gary Null. *Windsor: An Early Portrait*. Tuckahoe, NY: Nebko Press, no date available.

Milton Woman's Club (Litchfield, Conn.). *Chronicles of Milton: Village Left Behind by Time*. Litchfield, CT: Milton Woman's Club, 1997.

Nenortas, Tomas J. *Victorian Hartford: Postcard History Series*. Charleston, SC: Arcadia, 2005.

Paducah, Ky. *Connecticut State Police, 1903–2003: 100 Year History*. Nashville, TN: Turner Publishing, 2003.

Rees, Nigel. *Brewer's Famous Quotations: 5,000 Quotations and the Stories Behind Them*. New York: Sterling Publishing Company, Inc., 2006.

Slack, Charles. *Hetty: The Genius and Madness of America's First Female Tycoon*. New York: Ecco, 2005.

Snyder, LeMoyne, Harold Mulbar, Charles Morrow Wilson, and Clarence Weinert Muehlberger. *Homicide Investigation: Practical Information for Coroners, Police Officers, and Other Investigators*. Springfield, IL: C. C. Thomas, 1944.

Stiles, H. R. *Ancient Windsor*, Revised Edition (2 vols.). New York: 1891.

Town Crier (Windsor, CT). Windsor, CT: Town Crier Publishing Co., 1916.

Twain, Mark. *The Gilded Age: A Tale of Today.* New York: Penguin, 2001.

Weber, Gustavus. *The Weather Bureau: Its History, Activities and Organization.* New York: D. Appleton and Co., 1922.

White, Joseph F. *High Frequency Techniques: An Introduction to RF and Microwave Engineering.* Wiley–IEEE Press, 2003.

Whitnah, Don. *A History of the United States Weather Bureau.* Champaign: University of Illinois Press, 1961.

Windsor Historical Society (Windsor, Conn.). *Windsor. Images of America.* Charleston, SC: Arcadia, 2007.

Zannus, Susan. *Guglielmo Marconi and Radio Waves (Uncharted, Unexplored, and Unexplained).* Hockessin, DE: Mitchell Lane Publishers, 2004.

Selected Essays & Documents

Abbe, Cleveland. "A Short Account of the Circumstances Attending the Inception of Weather Forecast Work by the United States," *Weather Bureau Topics and Personnel*, April 17, 1916.

American Medical Association. *Journal of the American Medical Association*. Chicago: American Medical Association, 1883.

Connecticut. Public documents of the State of Connecticut. Hartford: Printed by order of the General Assembly, 1886.

"Evolution to the Signal Service Years (1600–1891): The Colonial Years," papers, Publication of the National Oceanic & Atmospheric Administration (NOAA), NOAA Central Library, Office of CIO/High Performance Computing and Communications (HPCC).

Report of Willis L. Moore, Chief of the Weather Bureau, October 15, 1907.

State of Connecticut v. Amy E. Archer Gilligan, Trial Transcripts, including letters and evidence, No. 667, Supreme Court of Errors, Hartford County, First Judicial District, October Term, 1917, Hartford Public Library.

Index

About the Author

M. William Phelps, whom *Radio America* called "the nation's leading authority on the mind of the female murderer," is the author of many nonfiction books, nearly 600,000 of which are in print. They include *Perfect Poison: A Female Serial Killer's Deadly Medicine*. He has been a consultant for the Showtime TV drama *Dexter,* and his many national TV appearances include *The Discovery Channel* and *Good Morning America*. He lives in Vernon, Connecticut.